retail
management

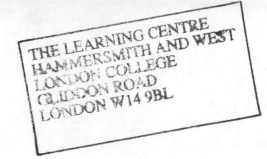

retail
management
functional principles & practices

Third Edition
Revised & Enlarged

Gibson G. Vedamani

JAICO PUBLISHING HOUSE
Ahmedabad Bangalore Bhopal Chennai
Delhi Hyderabad Kolkata Mumbai

Published by Jaico Publishing House
121 Mahatma Gandhi Road
Mumbai - 400 001
jaicopub@vsnl.com
www.jaicobooks.com

© Gibson G. Vedamani
© 'Paradigm of 1s' - B.S. Nagesh
Customer Care Associate & MD, Shoppers' Stop

RETAIL MANAGEMENT
ISBN 81-7992-151-4

First Jaico Impression: 2003
Third Edition (Revised & Enlarged): 2008
Twelfth Jaico Impression: 2009

Printed by Pashupati Printers (P) Ltd., Delhi-95

To

My Parents
Prof. Dr. VEDAMANI BALRAJ, Retired Professor of English, and
MERCY BALRAJ, Retired Teacher,
my first teachers of Management.

List of Tables

List of Figures

Foreword

When Gibson, as known to me, asked me to write the foreword for this book, the word spread around my office, and people commented that BSN had taken his first step towards retirement.

To be honest, after reading the book I felt much younger and started thinking about my days as a store manager, running a shop, interacting with the consumers, taking their compliments and their brickbats. What a wonderful time I have had as a retailer for the past 20 years in retailing directly in the 26 years I spent in the profession interacting with customers and retailers. Sometimes I feel professionals in sales and marketing who have not had stints in retailing or do not enjoy working in retail stores have missed 50% of the fun of Sales & Marketing. All CEOs should work at least once in retail stores of their product groups to understand their customers. To begin with they can start by reading a few chapters of Gibson's book on Retail Management.

Written as a text book for students of retailing, Retail Management gives definitive insights to students in business schools of all disciplines, and beginners. It makes very good reading for small retailers, entrepreneurs in retailing, the second generation of traditional retailers who can bring in science to the art of retailing. It would also be a good reference book for those already involved in retailing.

I call retailing the **"Paradigm of 1s"**© wherein **1** customer buys **1** SKU from **1** sq.ft. in **1** moment. "Paradigm of 1s"© is the research I am conducting to establish a theory on creating moments of magic for consumers. This theory supports the view that **"Retail is Detail"** and however small or big a retailer, they have to deal with only **1**s and multiple of **1**s. Managing the **1**s well can make a retailer a Shoppers' Stop, which manages 80,000 customers a day who buy 30,000 SKUs from 16,00,000 sq.ft. in 36,000 moments. Each customer has to be delivered a Moment of Magic, each SKU has to be part of the range plan, each sq.ft. has to deliver the GMROF for the retailer to deliver profitability and the HR department has to ensure that retail employees are trained to deliver those Moments of Magic.

A Wal-Mart manages billions of such **"Paradigm of 1s"**© to achieve a turnover of US$ 385 billion.

This book provides various insights into the retail business for the reader. I recommend that practitioners definitely go through the Buying & Merchandising and Visual Merchandising chapters wherein some principles can be used immediately.

Small retailers can learn from the strategic retailing and store planning chapters, as this will help them focus on the business and align the space and merchandise in their stores. I am sure readers will be able to apply these theories to deliver better results for themselves.

Students of management and retailing schools should definitely go through all the chapters and visit a store or meet a practitioner to get insights into the wonderful and exciting world of retailing.

I wish Gibson success and the readers of this new edition happy reading moments.

B.S. Nagesh
Customer Care Associate & MD, Shoppers' Stop

Preface

Although retailing in its various formats has been around in our country for many years, it was confined for a long time to family or 'mom-and-pop' stores. Now, various professional organizations are busy setting up shop and retailing in India; they have a passion to be closer to consumers. At this time, when the country's retailing business is going through a transformation, there is a compelling need for those involved in retailing — and those who want to be involved — to understand this phenomenon systematically so that they can practice it perfectly. I am sure this book will help you take the first step towards understanding organized retail management.

Secondly, in the course of my career as a retail practitioner and teacher for the past many years, I have strongly felt the need to use domestic examples and references. Many of my colleagues on the shop-floor and students in the classrooms have never gone abroad to see the kind of retail stores that the foreign textbooks they follow deal with. Hence this book on retail management, with references and examples from the growing retail organizations in India, is sure to help get the right associations in place for better learning.

The third reason why I decided to write this book was to disseminate retailing knowledge and skills to help students, professionals and entrepreneurs. This will help the industry to attract more people and persuade them to make a career out of retail management.

This may seem funny, but it is true. Often, on the retail floor, I have seen a few of my colleagues ducking under the counter to hide from their friends and dear ones; they felt it was almost ignominious to be on the retail floor in India! I have also come across situations where a girl's hand was not offered in marriage to a young man just because he was a mere salesman! To change these attitudes, it's necessary to create awareness about the industry and its prospects. Retail management will help create many retail professionals and upgrade the quality of the industry in India.

I am confident that this book will surely enable you to become a successful retail professional!

Gibson G. Vedamani

Acknowledgements

At the very outset, I thank my Lord and Saviour Jesus Christ who has been my prayer-answering God Almighty, enabling fulfillment of all my dreams. This book is a proof of one such fulfillment.

I would like to express my profound gratitude to B.S. Nagesh, Customer Care Associate & MD, Shoppers' Stop, for not just readily agreeing to write the foreword for this book but for shaking me out of my 'comfort zone' in the southern part of India to bring me to Mumbai to take up a responsible position in Shoppers' Stop in 1996. Since then my retail learning has been growing by leaps and bounds.

Prof. Dr. Uday Salunkhe, Director, Welingkar Institute of Management Development & Research, and my friend and former colleague Jaydeep Shetty, have been a great source of my pedagogical inspiration. My thanks to them.

It is with a deep sense of gratitude that I acknowledge the value added to a few chapters of this book by my friends and former colleagues, Brigitta George Abraham, former GM, Human Resources, Shoppers' Stop, Surender Gnanaolivu, VP, Store Development, Lifestyle Business, Reliance Retail, and Amitabh Basu of Idendesign. I am also indebted to my friends Malcolm Stephens, Director, Trident Communications & Management Services and Mahesh Rao, Managing Director, Carbon (Peakok Jewellery Pvt. Ltd.), Bangalore, for their timely inputs. My thanks are also due to Kumar Rajagopalan, Country Head-Retail of IBM and to Prasad Chandratre of Nike.

I would like to acknowledge with thanks the resourceful service and support rendered by Bharti Gunjikar, Librarian at Welingkar, my friends Zenobia Ferns, Naresh Bulchandani, Anirban Chatterjee, Indranil Nandi and those at 'Thinkwhynot': Sangram Surve, Rampratap Barai and Neha Tembey.

I want to thank my publisher friends at Jaico Publishing House, Akash Shah, Rayasam H. Sharma, and Theresa Chakravarty, for their unstinted encouragement and support throughout the writing of this book.

I am blessed with a few spiritual friends who constantly inspire me: my pastor Rev. Cecil Clements, Bro. Richard Samuel and Bro. Gene Robinette. I sincerely extend my gratitude to them for their inspiration and prayers.

This book would not be a reality without the loving influence of my wife Punitha, my son Wayne and my daughter Vinita. I thank them from the bottom of my heart.

Contents

CHAPTER 1

Introduction

CHAPTER OBJECTIVES

1. To define the concept of retailing
2. To underline the significance of retailing in the marketing mix
3. To elaborate on the role of the retailer in the marketing channel
4. To provide an overview of the global retailing scenario
5. To focus on the current status of retailing in India
6. To throw light on current growth opportunities and trends in India

DEFINITION AND SCOPE OF RETAILING

The word 'retail' is derived from the French word '*retaillier*', meaning 'to cut a piece off' or 'to break bulk'. In simple terms, it implies a first-hand transaction with the customer.

Retailing involves a direct interface with the customer and the coordination of business activities from end to end — right from the concept or design stage of a product or offering, to its delivery and post-delivery service to the customer. The industry has contributed to the economic growth of many countries and is undoubtedly one of the fastest changing and dynamic industries in the world today.

Retailing and the Marketing Mix

Retailing forms an integral part of the marketing mix and includes elements like product, place, price, people, presentation and promotion. *Place* relates to the distribution and availability of products in various locations.

Customers are first introduced to the product at the retail store. Organizations sell their products and services through these retail outlets and get feedback on the performance of their products and customers' expectations about them.

Retail stores serve as communication hubs for customers. Commonly known as the Point of Sale (POS) or the Point of Purchase (POP), retail stores transmit information to the customers through advertisements and displays. Hence, the role of retailing in the marketing mix is very significant.

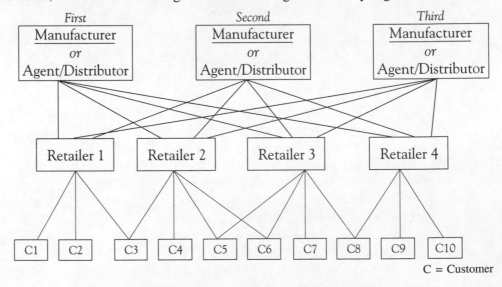

Fig. 1: *The Pivotal Role of Retailer in the Marketing Channel*

Channel Power

Channel power refers to the extent to which retailers influence marketers' decisions like pricing, promotion and product strategy. This emanates from the point of customer contact (the retailers), which is the one-point source of information feedback from customers to the marketer/manufacturer. Because of its communication capabilities, the channel is in a position to influence customers' decisions.

RETAILING SCENARIO — GLOBAL

Retailing is big business in more developed countries and it is better organized than what it is in India. According to recent reports, the US$ 9 trillion retail industry is one of the world's largest industries and the sector is still growing. 47 of the Global Fortune 500 companies and 25 of Asia's top 200 companies are retailers. In the developed parts of the world like the USA, most part of retailing is accounted for by the organized sector. The corresponding figure for Western Europe is 70% while it is 50% in Malaysia and Thailand, 40% in Brazil and Argentina, 35% in Philippines, 25% in Indonesia and 15% in South Korea. Organized retailing, however, has gained a great deal of momentum in China in the last few years especially after the opening up of the sector to 100% FDI in 2004, and it accounts for 20% of the total retail sales currently. Even as the developing countries are making rapid strides in this industry, organised retail is currently dominated by the developed countries with the USA, EU & Japan constituting 80% of the world's retailing. Retail is a significant contributor to the overall economic activity the world over: the total retail share in the World GDP is 27% while in the USA it accounts for 22% of the GDP.

The service sector accounts for a large share of GDP in most developed economies. And the retail sector forms a very strong component of the service sector. Hence, the employment opportunity offered by the industy is immense. According to the US Department of Labor, about 22 million Americans are employed in the retailing industry in more than 2 million retail stores — that is, one out of every five workers employed. In essence, as long as people need to buy, retail will generate employment.

Traditionally, local players tend to dominate in their home markets. Wal-Mart, the world's leading retailer, has about 8% of the market in the USA. Similarly, Tesco has a market share of about 13% in the UK market. The main value propositions that most large retailers use are a combination of low price, 'all-under-one-roof' convenience and 'neighborhood' availability. Globally, retailing is customer-centric with an emphasis on innovation in products, processes and services. In short, the customer is King!

Country	Organized Retailing	Traditional Retailing
USA	80%	20%
W. Europe	70%	30%
Malaysia	50%	50%
Thailand	50%	50%
Brazil	40%	60%
Argentina	40%	60%
Philippines	35%	65%
Indonesia	25%	75%
China	20%	80%
South Korea	15%	85%
India	6%	94%

Table 1: *Percentage of Organized and Traditional Retailing Globally*

RETAILING SCENARIO — INDIA

The retail scenario in India is unique. Much of it is in the unorganized sector, with over 12 million retail outlets of various sizes and formats. Almost 96% of these retail outlets are less than 500 sq.ft. in size, the per capita retail space in India being 2 sq.ft. compared to the US figure of 16 sq.ft. India's per capita retailing space is thus the lowest in the world. With more than 9 outlets per 1,000 people, India has the largest number in the world. Most of them are independent and contribute as much as 94% to total retail sales.

Because of the increasing number of nuclear families, growing size of the working women segment, greater work pressure and increased commuting time, convenience has become a priority for Indian consumers. They want everything under one roof for easy access and multiplicity of choice. This offers an excellent opportunity for organized retailers in the country who account for just 6% (and modern stores 2.5%) of the estimated US $385 billion worth of goods that are retailed in India every year. This figure is almost equivalent to the turnover of one single US-based retail chain, Wal-Mart.

The growth and development of organized retailing in India is driven by two main factors — lower prices and benefits the consumers can't resist. According to experts, economies of scale drive down the cost of the supply chain, allowing retailers to offer more benefits to the customer.

The retail business in India in the year 2007 was US$ 385 billion

(Rs. 1,540,000 crores) and a McKinsey study says it is estimated to go to US$ 1.52 trillion (Rs. 6,080,000 crores) by 2025. One expects that the share of organized retailing will be in the vicinity of 20% by then.

(Figures in Millions)

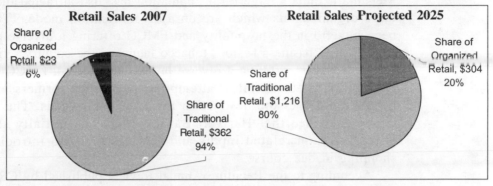

Retail Sales 2007	Retail Sales Projected 2025

There is a 9-fold increase expected by 2025 in organized retailing, although there is only a 4-fold increase projected in the total turnover.

Fig. 2: Retail Growth Potential

India is evolving rapidly into a competitive marketplace with potential target consumers in the niche and middle class segments. The market trends indicate tremendous growth opportunities. Global majors too are showing a keen interest in the Indian retail market. Over the years, international brands like Marks & Spencer, Samsonite, Lacoste, McDonald's, Swarovski, Domino's, Shoprite, LeMarche, among a host of others have come into India through the franchise route consequent to Foreign Direct Investment (FDI) restrictions in the retail sector in India. It was only in February 2006 FDI was allowed to the extent of 51% in single-brand retail. A few B2B retail operations like Metro Cash & Carry have been set up in India following the relaxation of FDI to the extent of 100% through the automatic route. Large Indian companies like Reliance Retail, A.V. Birla Retail, Essar Telecom Retail, Future Group, Shoppers' Stop Group, Tata, Goenka among many others like Wadhawan, DLF, etc. are investing heavily in this industry. The largest chain, Subhiksha, has some 760 outlets across India, while Big Apple aims to have 100 of its 7-Eleven-style convenience stores in Delhi alone by the end of the year 2008. Reliance Retail, a division of India's biggest conglomerate and arguably the most formidable player in the retail market, plans to invest $5.5 billion to open outlets in 784 cities across the country soon.

Organizations ready to take on this challenge can leverage the opportunities offered by a population of more than 1.2 billion. The prospects are very encouraging. Buying behaviour and lifestyles in India too are changing and the concept of "Value for Money" is fast catching on in Indian retailing. This is evident from the expansion of the Pantaloons chain earlier into a large value format, Big Bazaar, and the entry of new discount stores in food and grocery retailing, Subhiksha and in value apparel retailing, Vishal Megamart. India's large rural population has also attracted the attention of large organizations which are on a diversification mode. ITC, which has been hitherto in the hospitality and FMCG offering a diverse product range from FMCG business besides tobacco launched the country's first rural mall 'Chaupal Sagar', offering a diverse product range from FMCG to electronics appliances to automobiles, attempting to provide farmers and the rustic population a one-stop destination for all of their needs. The DCM Sriram Group launched the 'Hariyali Bazaar', that was initially started off by providing farm related inputs and services plans to introduce complete shopping in due course.

According to the Retailing Annual Review published by CRIS INFAC in September 2005, over the next five years, 73.78-million sq. ft. of floor space and Rs. 369,000 million worth of real estate investment will be required to sustain the growing organized retail market.

(Figures in Millions)

	1996	1997	1998	1999	2000	2001
Food Retailers	2.8	2.9	3.1	3.3	3.5	3.7
Non-Food Retailers	5.7	6.0	6.3	6.6	7.0	7.5
Total Retailers	8.5	8.9	9.4	9.9	10.5	11.2

Source: FICCI, Nov. 2003

Table 2: *Growth of Retail Outlets in India*

PROSPECTS OF RETAILING IN INDIA

Indian grocers were perhaps among the first in the world to acquire professional retailing skills. There is the old story of a good retail grocer and the bad retail grocer in India.

Once upon a time there were two grocers. One was perceived to be good and the other was considered bad. The good one always used to weigh his cereals, pulses, grams, etc. in such a way that if he had to weigh a kilogram he would initially place in the weighing balance produce less than a kilogram and then keep adding to it until it reached the required weight. The bad retailer, on the other hand, always rather unconsciously placed much more and then kept removing stuff from the scales until it weighed a kilogram. The good retailer had actually acquired such skills to create a positive image in the minds of the customers!

Long ago, the Father of the Nation, Mahatma Gandhi realized the importance of the customer for the retailer; he is in fact the first to emphasize on the importance of Customer Relationship Management practices in India. What he said about the importance of the customer is famous the world over. It goes like this:

"The customer is the most important person on our premises.
He is not dependent on us, we are dependent on him.
He is not an interruption of our work, he is the purpose of it.
He is not an outsider on our business, he is part of it.
We are not doing him a favour by serving him;
He is doing us a favour by giving us the opportunity to do so."

A survey conducted by FICCI (Federation of Indian Chambers of Commerce & Industry) and PricewaterhouseCoopers predicted that the Indian retail sector will undergo a sea change in size as well as format during this decade. Further, it indicated that by the year 2010 the country's top retailers will operate at least three to four formats, all scalable to size, location and providing value to their target customers with such diversity of formats that will allow the company to make use of its brand value across different segments and categories of customers.

Today many Indian organized retailers have launched many of their formats. Pantaloon Retail has ventured into home electronics, fashion, wellness and beauty, books and music, e-tailing, etc. in addition to their key formats of food and grocery and department store retailing. Similarly, Shoppers' Stop also has expanded their format base to hypermarket, airport retail, books and brand retail ventures such as Mothercare.

It is opined that in the next five years, India should have retail entities strong enough to compete with the best in the world. Formats such as department stores, hupermarkets, supermarkets and specialty stores are finding increasingly greater acceptance with the Indian consumers while the emergence of malls in India as a destination shopping concept has even broken through to the second-rung cities of the country.

India is more attactive than ever to global retailers. According to AT Kearney's Global Retail Development Index 2007 (GRDI), India is the most attractive retail destination for global retailers. India has topped the list for the third year in succession. The annual AT Kearney GRDI ranks thirty emerging countries on a 100-point scale – the higher the ranking, the more is the urgency to enter the market.

The growth in Indian retailing provides jobs to roughly 15% of employable Indian adults, and is the biggest contributor to India's GDP after agriculture. The growth potential of the industry is such that Retailers Association of India (RAI) estimates that the sector would require almost 2.2

million people to be employed in retail by the year 2010. Considering such opportunities, one needs to take a look at the organizations and institutes offering retail education and training in India. Some retail organizations like Pantaloon Retail have tied up with many Business Schools to jointly organize various educational programmes in Retail. There are currently a few B-Schools like Welingkar Institute of Management, Chetna's Institute of Management, K.J. Somaiya Institute of Management, Pearl Academy of Fashion, Mudra Institute of Communications Ahmedabad (MICA) among others that offer Post-graduate Program in Retail Management. Retailers Association of India has tied up with 15 B-Schools from the academic year 2008 to offer rai's PGPRM across India. The Indian Institute of Management, Ahmedabad (IIMA) and the Indian Institute of Management, Indore (in collaboration with rai) have established their Centers for Excellence in Retail Management focusing on research in Retail. While the first few steps towards sophisticated retailing are being taken, the biggest task for organized retail organizations is to locate and recruit knowledgeable, skilled and trained staff to handle their operations. So, to stay ahead of the pack in today's competitive and challenging retail world, one must be properly equipped and trained.

SUMMARY

- Retailing in India is becoming increasingly important, and organized retailing is poised to grow at an exponential rate. These growth opportunities have even attracted global majors who are setting up shop in India.
- With consumers now enjoying a wide variety of products and services to choose from, retailers who provide genuine value will be able to establish themselves in the long run. Consumers will emerge as the emperors of retailing in India with their discerning buying attitudes and their ever increasing purchasing power. Consumerism will empower them significantly.
- The growth of the retail sector will make retailers powerful intermediaries in the marketing channel, bridging the gap between manufacturers and consumers. Many manufacturers and marketers may hence take to retailing themselves to be closer to the consumers. Therefore it will be the power of the consumer as well as that of the retailer in the marketing channel that will spearhead the growth of retailing in India.

Questions:

1. What is your understanding of retailing?
2. What is the role of retailing in the marketing mix and in the marketing channel?

3. Compare the current status of organized retailing in India with the international scenario.
4. Show how organized retailing in India has grown, with suitable references to studies done recently.
5. What are the manpower challenges to be addressed by the retail sector in India at the moment?

The First Phase of Organized Retailing In India

It was Calcutta (now known as Kolkata) that saw the emergence of organized retailing in India way back in the 19th century itself. The Hogg Market, popularly and better known as New Market is one of Kolkata's earliest shopping centres. Designed by an East Indian Railway Company architect, R.R. Bayne, it was opened in 1874 and named after the then municipal commissioner of Calcutta, Sir Stuart Hogg. Earlier the Hogg Market even had a garden with a beautiful fountain adding to its ambience and benches too for tired shoppers. Today, the New Market continues to be a premier shopping area in Kolkata despite a part of it being incinerated in late 1985. Its red-brick Gothic clock-tower today bears testimony to the past grandeur of this first shopping centre of India. Today from linen to cakes and fruits to fishes everything is available at the New Market at a reasonable price and this has made the New Market sustain its popularity among the metro customers of Kolkata. The tenant mix of this first shopping centre is unique as it has a large number of 2000 stalls which are organized in an order of merchandize. There are rows of stalls dealing with one particular line of goods.

A retail researcher by name Christine Furedy in the 70s has observed in her article in the *Capital* on 24th December 1979 tracing the emergence of the New Market, thus: "Until the late 19th century New Market sold only produce. Its primary purpose was to supply wholesome food under clean conditions at reasonable prices. It is true, too, that it was designed for the Europeans but the municipality strove to have it accepted as a market for all Calcuttans. Changes began to occur: fancy goods dealers and cloth merchants could afford to pay higher rents for their shops than the food vendors and more and more they appeared in the market proper. Eventually the market was reorganized and food vendors were placed in the section they still occupy. Another difference in the 19th century was that no ads or encroachments were allowed. The facade of the market was unencumbered, showing its fine lines and good brickwork. Within the market stallholders had to keep their produce within their stalls and were not allowed to obstruct the corridors and paths. There was a garden and a fountain where shoppers gathered to chat. Begging and pestering were forbidden. On the other hand, it was strictly "caveat emptor". Two English women who were sold inferior cloth and complained to the Markets Committee in 1894 found they had no redress. The system of licensing coolies was introduced in 1885 after customers had complained of being disturbed by 'importunate coolies'. Only registered coolies were permitted inside: the registration fee was five annas and each coolie had to wear a simple uniform and a number badge, a requirement which is still in force today. Next time you go to New Market take a few minutes off from your shopping to look around. Compare the facade and clock tower today with its original unencumbered lines; look for the old original shops made of fine mahogany and teak. It is a great pity, in my opinion, that this historic building is under threat of revamping. At the very least its facade and some of the original shops should be preserved to remind us that the New Market became an example for the whole of Asia of an efficient and fascinating municipal market."

Furedy also mentions about the opposition that came up for building this municipal market. She says, "It is hard to imagine now how controversial the concept was. There was strong opposition from influential citizens, both European and Indian. Some Europeans were opposed to the idea of ''municipal trading" seeing this as the thin edge of a wedge which would dislodge the principles of private property and free enterprise. Others argued that the undertaking was not within the purposes of the Municipal Act and would be too great a burden upon the municipal coffers. This, indeed, was part of the objections of the Indian municipal commissioners who pointed out also that it was only the Europeans who were dissatisfied with the conditions of the markets and that they proposed to use municipal funds, derived largely from taxes upon Indian householders, to finance a market designed for the patronage of the European population only. Indian rate payers argued that already the better part of the municipal funds were put to improving the European sections of the town to the neglect of the areas inhabited by Indians. If once one municipal market was approved, there would be no end to the number of public markets which might be built at great municipal extravagance." Against all these odds the then Hogg Market evolved and it soon became a popular destination for shopping in Calcutta.

Furedy goes on to speak about the emergence of modern retailing in India. She mentions, "The most complex retail business of late nineteenth-century Calcutta, establishments which were to dominate the modern retail sector, were the department stores. Although every one has closed its doors, many Calcuttans still remember the names or recognize their converted, subdivided buildings: Francis, Harrison and Hathaway; Hall and Anderson; the Army and Navy Stores; Whiteaway, Laidlaw and Co. In their scope and outreach these shops rivalled those to be found in cities of the same size in Britain, Europe or the United States. The city's leading hotels, while they provided many services and housed a number of businesses, did not always own and run all of these. Their retail areas were perhaps more like arcades than department stores. The shops from which department stores rather literally evolved were the drapers' and mercers' shops. We know from trade directories that shops like Francis, Harrison, Hathaway and Co., which was described as "first class drapers" in 1864, had a large staff of 11 European assistants in 1880. (By the end of the century there were at least 40.). This was the first shop to adopt a 'departmental' organization, which was formalized in the 1890s and repeated at the branch shops in Simla, Lahore, Darjeeling and Allahabad. Incidentally, in 1880 one of the leading assistants in Hathaway's was Mr. E. Whiteaway who ten years later was the partner of Whiteaway, Laidlaw, occupying numbers 5 and 6 Chowringhee and employing 38 assistants. Two other employees of Hathaway's were to become equally famous in Calcutta's retail trade. In the early 1890s P.N. Hall and William Anderson set up together in a modest partnership selling suitings at bargain prices from a small shop on the Esplanade."

It is indeed amazing to know about the first phase of the evolution of modern retailing in India from Furedy's research. India is now witnessing its second phase of organized retailing!

Questions for Discussion

1. What are the lessons of retail evolution do we learn from the New Market in Calcutta?
2. Comment on researcher Christine Furedy's observations on the emergence of the New Market as an organized shopping centre in India.
3. Write a brief note on the 19th century Department Stores in India.

CHAPTER 2

Trends in Retailing

CHAPTER OBJECTIVES

1. To outline the significance of the share of the retail sector in the global business scenario
2. To enable a clear understanding of the phases of evolution of organized retailing globally and in India
3. To explain in detail the prospects of retail growth in India on a comparative platform of international performance
4. To provide insights into the global drivers that impact the way consumers shop
5. To enumerate the trends that will impact shopping in India in the near future
6. To list and elaborate the key drivers of retailing in India
7. To describe the projected retail trends and the growth path as studied by research agencies

Organized retailing in India has immense potential for both companies that venture into the field and consumers. This chapter focuses on the factors that fuel the exponential growth of organized retailing in India while looking at global scenarios and experts' opinions.

GLOBAL OVERVIEW OF RETAILING

The worldwide total retail sales stands at US$ 9 trillion and Retailing is the world's largest private industry, ahead of even Finance and Engineering. The top 200 largest retailers account for 30% of worldwide demand. As many as 10% of the world's billionaires are retailers. Retail sales globally are driven generally by the people's ability to buy (disposable income) and the willingness to buy (consumer confidence). The positive force at work in the retail consumer market in developed economies today include a high rate of personal expenditures, low interest rates, low unemployment and very low inflation. The negative factors which may hold retail sales back especially in developed economies include weakening consumer confidence, slowly increasing unemployment and decreasing levels of consumer household wealth. Volatility in global markets and significant continued layoffs at larger corporations may further require job migration to other developing economies like India and China who may offer better labour arbitrage and this may lead to large numbers of consumers in developed economies employed as temporary workers.

Goldman Sachs argues in its BRIC report in 2004 that the economic potential of Brazil, Russia, India and China is such that they may become among the four most dominant economies by the year 2050. The thesis was proposed by Jim O'Neill, a global economist at Goldman Sachs. These countries are forecast to encompass over 39% of the world's population and hold a combined GDP [PPP] of 15.435 trillion dollars. According to the report, on almost every scale, these countries would be the largest entity on the global stage. The report states that in BRIC nations, the number of people with an annual income over a threshold of $3,000, will double in number within three years and reach 800 million people within a decade. This predicts a massive rise in the size of the middle class in these nations. In 2025, it is calculated that the number of people in BRIC nations earning over $15,000 may reach over 200 million. This indicates that a huge pickup in demand will not be restricted to basic goods but impact higher-priced goods as well. According to the report, first China and then a decade later India will begin to dominate the world economy. Yet, despite the balance of growth swinging so decisively towards the BRIC economies, the average wealth level of individuals in the more advanced economies will continue to

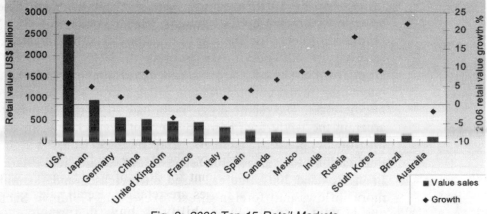

Fig. 3: *2006 Top 15 Retail Markets*

US$ Million

Rank	Retailer	Company name	Country	2006 Sales Excluding Sales Tax (Retail Value RSP)
1	Wal-Mart	Wal-Mart Stores Inc.	USA	235,322.7
2	Tesco	Tesco Plc	UK	63,985.4
3	Carrefour	Carrefour SA	France	58,326.9
4	Home Depot	The Home Depot Inc.	USA	54,963.2
5	Kroger	Kroger Co	USA	54,882.4
6	Walgreens	Walgreen Co	USA	52,205.9
7	Aldi	Aldi Group	Germany	50,794.5
8	Target	Target Corp	USA	47,687.9
9	CVS	CVS Corp	USA	42,528.7
10	Safeway	Safeway Inc.	USA	39,754.0
11	7-Eleven	Seven & I Holdings Co. Ltd.	Japan	38,627.8
12	Lowe's	Lowe's Companies Inc	USA	34,506.2
13	Lidl	Schwarz Beteiligungs GmbH	Germany	33,833.3
14	Best Buy	Best Buy Co. Inc	North America	28,737.6
15	Sainsbury's	J. Sainsbury Plc	UK	27,415.4
	Total Top 15			**863,571.9**

Source: Euromonitor International

Table 3: *Top 15 Retailers Worldwide (Brand Shares)*

far outstrip the BRIC economy average. Goldman Sachs assert in a follow-up report compiled by lead authors Tushar Poddar and Eva Yi in 2007 that "India's influence on the world economy will be bigger and quicker than implied in our previously published BRIC's research". They noted significant areas of research and development, and expansion that are happening in the country, which will lead to the prosperity of the growing middle class. The report says, "India had 10 of the 30 fastest-growing urban areas in the world and, based on current trends, we estimate a massive 700 million people will move to cities by 2050. This will have significant implications for demand for urban infrastructure, real estate, and services." In the revised 2007 figures, based on increased and sustaining growth and more inflows into foreign direct investment, Goldman Sachs predicts that "from 2007 to 2020, India's GDP per capita in US$ terms will quadruple", and that the Indian economy will surpass the United States (in US$) by 2043.

According to the UK based research firm *Euromonitor International*, in the global scenario, the emerging retail markets of India and China are witnessing strong growth and India especially is among the biggest and the fastest growing retail markets globally.

As many as 8 of the top 15 retailers worldwide are based in the USA. Wal-Mart holds the No.1 retailer's position by a huge margin, followed by the retailers based in the EU region, Tesco, UK and Carrefour, France.

Over the past few decades, retail formats have changed radically worldwide. The basic department stores and cooperatives of the early 20th century have given way to mass merchandisers (Wal-Mart), hypermarkets (Carrefour), warehouse clubs (Sam's Club, Makro), category killers (Toys 'R' Us, Sports Authority), discounters (Aldi) and convenience stores (7-Eleven). Organized retail formats worldwide have evolved in three phases:

I.   Retailers decide on the category and quality of products and services, differentiating them from other retailers. Retail formats in this phase are typically supermarkets, department stores and specialty stores.

II. During the second phase, retailers carve a niche for themselves based on a product category and price. Competition intensifies because the products and services on offer become virtually standardized and price becomes the main selling point. This phase normally gives way to discount stores.

III. The third phase arrives when competition peaks. This is when hypermarkets begin to evolve. Hypermarkets usually compete on price and a wider product range, but they normally lack product depth and service components.

Globally, three factors influence how consumers shop and will be shopping in the near future. These are:

1. Cross-border Movement.
2. Consolidation.
3. Migration of Formats.

1. Cross-border Movement: Retailers expand their businesses outside their traditional home markets, leading to the emergence of truly global retailers. Geopolitical developments, including trade pacts within regions, facilitate movement of goods and businesses across borders. The North American Free Trade Agreement (NAFTA) — and its likely extension to include some additional Central and South American nations in the next five-seven years, — the European Union (EU) and future alliances will gradually but steadily eliminate traditional geographical and political boundaries. Expansions will increasingly be a function of logistics and management across regions. Wal-Mart, the world's largest retailer, now has a strong presence in South America and Europe, and a more visible presence in Asia. Other global retailers include Carrefour of France, Marks & Spencer of the UK, Ikea of Sweden etc.

2. Consolidation: Another trend that is visible is the rapid pace of mergers and acquisitions. In recent times Wal-Mart's acquisition of Asda in the UK, the merger of Carrefour and Promodes in France, and that of Quelle and Karstadt in Germany have had a major impact on retailing and the supply chain. Each of these mergers has created huge retail organizations ranging in size from about US$ 26 billion in sales (Quelle and Karstadt) to US$ 345 billion (Wal-Mart — 2007 sales).

3. Migration of Formats: A large number of retailers are gradually adopting the classical formats of department stores, supermarkets, hypermarkets, mail order as they customize their offerings to different consumer segments. Britain's Tesco operates supermarkets, hypermarkets, neighbourhood stores, convenience stores, mail order, department stores and, like most others recently, e-stores. The most important theme for various old and new retailing formats is convenience in terms of a one-stop location, and ease of shopping or time saved.

Globally, organized retailing has brought tremendous benefits for the consumer and has actually helped the consumer to be King.

KEY DRIVERS OF RETAILING IN INDIA

Consumer Pull

In the pre-liberalization supply-led market, the power rested clearly with the manufacturers. In today's demand-led market, it's the consumer who calls the shots. Over the last decade, there has been a significant evolution in the Indian consumer, mainly due to the liberalization of the consumer goods industry that was initiated in the mid-eighties and accelerated through the nineties, combined with a growing consumerism driven by the media, new opportunities and increasing wealth. Although this change is most noticeable in the metros, it has affected consumers in smaller towns as well.

Consumers can be divided into two broad segments:

1. **High-income segment:** This comprises consumers who do not shop themselves, have a very low level of involvement and whose monthly grocery bill forms a very small part of the salary.

2. **Middle and lower income group:** This includes consumers who are highly involved in grocery shopping, as this expenditure constitutes 50% or more of the monthly salary. This segment is highly value-conscious, constantly looking for bargains and is made up of active shoppers. Modern retailing, characterized by value, variety, convenience and service for the consumer, appeals to this second segment. Supermarkets allow consumers to interact more directly with the products, read labels, compare prices, avail of promotions and offers, and so on.

Rising Incomes

Over the past decade, India's middle- and high-income population has grown at a rapid pace of over 10% per annum. Though this growth is most evident in urban areas, it has also taken place in rural markets. Further, the

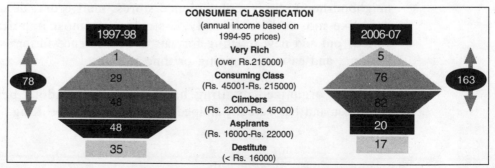

Growing Affluence of Indian Population

number of households earning above Rs.150,000 per annum is about 80 million today and is expected to grow to 200 million by 2015. This growing high-income population is triggering the demand for consumer goods, leading to the proliferation of higher quality/higher priced products.

Explosion of Media

There has been an explosion in media as well during the past decade. Kick-started by the cable explosion during the Gulf War, television has accelerated to a point where there are more cable connections than telephones in Indian homes (225 million vs 23 million), and about 70 channels are being aired at all times. This media bombardment has exposed the Indian consumer to the lifestyles of more affluent countries and raised their aspirations and expectations from the shopping experience — they want more choice, value, service, experience and convenience.

Change in Consumer Behaviour

The urban woman today is literate and, in many cases, employed. There is greater work pressure and increased commuting time. And with a shift in the family structure, nuclear families have become a significant component of urban markets. According to recent market research conducted in Bangalore, the share of nuclear families is estimated to be as high as 70%. Besides all these factors, the increase in the variety, quality and availability of products, and higher spending power has led to the growing popularity of supermarkets.

There has been a change in shopping behaviour in urban India over the past few years with consumers looking for convenience. That is, they want everything under one roof and a bigger choice of products. With an increase in double-income households, people do not have much leisure time and seek the convenience of one-stop shopping in order to make the best use of their time. They also look for speed and efficiency. Increased awareness has also meant that consumers now seek more information, variety, product availability, better quality and hygiene as well as increased customer service. The concept of "Value for Money" is picking up.

Traditionally, children seldom accompanied their parents while shopping for groceries. Shopping for children was confined to festivals when dresses were bought for them. But now, because they are pressed for time, working parents prefer to spend as much time as possible with their children; this includes their shopping hours also. As malls and supermarkets offer the option of entertainment along with shopping, younger couples prefer to shop there. Also driving the retail industry is impulse buying spurred on by higher brand awareness.

Consumer niches have begun propelling the market and are becoming more important, with positive and negative sub-segments of consumers gaining significance. The growth accelerator in 2002, for example, has definitely been the working woman, with the money spent by her averaging 1.3 times that of a housewife.

Consumerism Cycle

The consumer cycle starts with the industry dictating the market. Eventually over time the distributor gains control over the market; at this stage the distributor becomes an important link between manufacturer and customer. When the market starts developing and expanding its horizons, retailers turn into the vital link in this supply chain. India is entering this third stage where retailers control the market. Being the closest link to the consumer in the supply chain, retailers benefit accordingly. Manufacturers spend a lot of money promoting a product, but if it's not on the shop-shelf, consumers won't be able to buy it. Manufacturers have also realized that retailer recommendations matter, particularly in smaller towns where retailers are figures of authority or opinion leaders. With shopping attitudes changing, the Indian market today desires value-added products and services with good ambience and brands, which only a retailer can provide. Hence good retailer relations are a must. Manufacturers are ready to pay listing fees to get retailers to stock a product, or display charges to place it prominently.

The Rural Market: Waking Up

The rural market is beginning to emerge as an important consumption area, accounting for over one-third of the demand for most key consumer durables and non-durable products. In response, manufacturers of consumer goods — both FMCGs and durables — have begun developing new products (LG television, shampoo sachets, Ruf 'n Tuf jeans) and marketing strategies (using a village "haat" for brand promotions) with the rural consumer in mind.

Establishment of the Supply Chain

Over the past few years, the consumer goods sector has been transformed by increased liberalization, continuous reduction in customs duty, a shift from quota to tariff-based systems for imports and sophistication in manufacturing. Entry restrictions for multinationals have been removed in nearly all sectors. All this has enabled chain retailers to enjoy better range depth and sourcing options as well as improved average margins. There has been a proliferation in the range across all categories, with a simultaneous increase in the supply of products and quality retail space. According to a study, there are over 18,000 stock-keeping units (SKUs are products and their variants, of type and size, counted individually), while most retailers have the space for at most 5,000-7,000 units. This has tempted a number of real estate companies and other corporates into investing in malls and other retail formats.

Emergence of South India as a Hub of Retail Activity

The total retail market in terms of consumption off-take in the four southern states of India — viz. Tamil Nadu, Andhra Pradesh, Karnataka and Kerala constitute US$ 94 billion per annum, and out of that organised retail is expected to be in the region of US$ 8.9 billion. Tus the share of organised retail is around 9% of total retailing in South India. The growth of modern retailing happened in the Southern part of India much faster than in any other region. It is now estimated that organised retailing in South India is growing at around 35% per annum.

Chennai especially is a pioneer in the adoption of modern retail in India. 12% of Tamil Nadu's retail market is estimated to be organised. Chennai came to be known as the hub of specialty retailing in India as organised 'saree' and jewellery retailing evolved from there more than three decades ago. The emergence of organised formats in home electronics and household appliances retailing gained momentum in Tamil Nadu long ago with the establishment of Viveks, Vasanth, Rathna, VGP, etc. There are around 200 consumer durable outlets in Chennai and Viveks is the pioneer to introduce the concept of the New Year's sale which has become commonplace in consumer durables and home electronics retailing in South India. Stores like Saravanas, Nalli's, Spencer's, Landmark, Kumarans, G R Thanga Maligai, Kirtilals, etc. are renowned ones in Chennai. In fact the first large format in food and healthcare retail Spencer's was established in Chennai, followed by Nilgiris' expansion into Chennai from Bangalore in the early 80s. In addition, RPG established its supermarkets Foodworld, (earlier in collaboration with Dairy Farm International), a few years ago. Reliance Retail Ltd. launched 12 Reliance Fresh stores in Chennai in January 2007. With two anchor stores, Lifestyle and Landmark, the City Center is the new mall scientifically planned and developed in Dr. Radhakrishnan Road in Chennai. Univercell is a chain of cell phone retail and allied services retail outlets launched from Chennai recently in addition to The Mobile Store of the Essar group.

The state of Karnataka boasts of a good share of organised retailing and the state has around 9.5% of its total retail market organised. Currently, Bangalore has state-of-the-art malls like Forum, Garuda, Sigma and Eva which contribute largely to experiential retailing. Age old organised players include Nilgiris Supermarket, specialty retailers like Deepam Silks, Sankar's (the book people), etc. Organised retailing emerged in Bangalore with the development of two major high streets, viz. Brigade Road and Commercial Street over the last three decades, which house almost all the brand stores of India. Modern retail companies like Cafe Coffee Day, Monday to Sunday, Weekender, Ganjam Jewellery, Levi's, Lifestyle, etc. are headquartered in Bangalore. In March 2007 Reliance Fresh, the retail division of the Reliance group, has entered Karnataka by opening 11 stores in Bangalore, offering products ranging from fresh fruits and vegetables, staples, grocery to dairy items at competitive prices.

The state of Andhra Pradesh Hyderabad follows closely with 8.5% of its retail market organised. The famous supermarket chain of Andhra Pradesh Trinethra debuted in AP followed by the new hypermarket Magna in Vijaywada. RPG opened their first hypermarket format Spencers in Hyderabad a few years ago. The Future Group's Hyderabad Central mall is a great attraction for shoppers. Abid Road is a famous brand high street which known for all its brand outlets. Jewellery, sarees, books, food and grocery and apparel have more organised formats of retailing in the state of Andhra Pradesh. From November 2006 with the opening of the first 12 retail stores, Reliance Fresh has been opening many retail stores in the state of Hyderabad.

Kerala holds a share of 5.5% of organised retailing. Trivandrum and Cochin are estimated to have organised retailing at 4% and 8.5% respectively. Specialty saree retailing is famous in Cochin with renowned retail stores like Seemati. Varkeys Department Stores is one of the oldest organised players in Kerala. The most important commercial centre in Cochin is the M.G. Road (Mahatma Gandhi Road), a retail destination for all Kerala consumers. Here, one can buy stuff ranging from clothes to cosmetics to knick-knacks. Some of the most popular brands that you will find here are Allen Solly, Louise Philippe, Bennetton, Arrow, etc. The world's largest silk saree showroom, Kalyan Silks, has pitched tent. Alukkas Wedding Centre is arraying lifestyle products, gold ornaments and textiles under one roof. Big Bazaar of the Future Group has set shop and it has introduced to the Cochin housewife the concept of value and discount retailing. Malls like the Baypride mall and the GDCA (Greater Cochin Development Authority) shopping complex adorn the newly developed marine drive in Cochin.

South India yet maintains its pace of growth in organised retailing and this growth is expected to continue its momentum in the tier two cities of Coimbatore, Trichy, Pondicherry and Madurai in Tamil Nadu, Vijayawada, Vishakapatnam, Guntur and Rajamundhry in Andhra Pradesh, Mysore, Mangalore, Belgaum and Hubli in Karnataka and Kozhikode, Kollam and Kottayam in Kerala.

US$ Billion

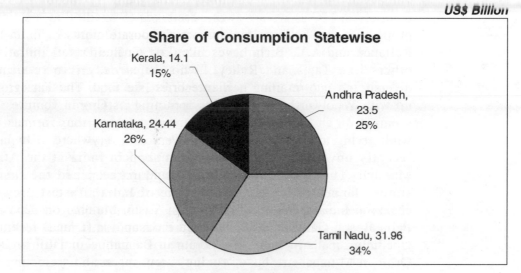

Share of Consumption Statewise

Kerala, 14.1
15%

Andhra Pradesh,
23.5
25%

Karnataka, 24.44
26%

Tamil Nadu, 31.96
34%

Fig. 4: *Total Retail in South India*

States	Statewise Share of Organized Retail		
	Total Retail in US$ BN	Organized Retail Value	% Organized
Tamil Nadu	31.96	3.84	12
Kerala	14.1	0.78	5.5
Karnataka	24.44	2.32	9.5
Andhra Pradesh	23.5	2.00	8.5
Total	**94**	**8.9**	**9**

Entry of the Corporate Sector

In contrast to the situation only about a decade ago, the level of interest in retailing as a growth opportunity has increased visibly now. Many organisations in India that have been for so long dealing directly with the primary distribution channel to reach customers have today embarked on reaching customers first hand by means of retailing by themselves. ITC as we are aware, has taken to retailing as a serious business proposition and as a strategic move. Corporate giants in India like Bharti, Reliance and A.V. Birla have embarked on their retail initiatives. A few others like Tatas and Rahejas who are already into retailing are fast diversifying into retailing embarked on reaching customers first hand by means of retailing by themselves. ITC as we are aware, has taken to retailing as a serious business proposition and as a strategic move. Corporate giants in India like Bharti, Reliance and A.V. Birla have embarked on their retail initiatives. A few others like Tatas and Rahejas who are already into retailing are fast diversifying into retailing new categories like food. The Tata group has tied up with Woolworth recently for supporting its Croma venture. The Future group is on an expansion spree, yet innovating various formats of retailing while trying to offer everything for everyone everywhere in India! Raymond recently unveiled its 350th Raymond shop in India at the Atria Mall in Mumbai. The French hypermarket Le Marche opened the first of the 25 stores planned in India. Odyssey, one of India's fastest growing leisure chains in India opened its first store in Vashi, Mumbai on 22nd April at the Palm Beach Galleria, a six hundred thousand sq.ft. mall recently opened. Upcoming malls in India like Forum in Bangalore or DLF in Delhi, or In-Orbit in Mumbai are busy 'zoning' their space and 'selecting' their mall partners to arrive at the right mall mix for their new malls! Many new players too are exploring this retail domain to get into! The latest good news is that the Nuance — Shoppers' Stop consortium has won the airport retail contract for setting up retail outlets both at the domestic and international airports of Hyderabad. The retail advancement is amazing as corporate giants are currently spearheading the retail growth in India.

Expansion of Family-Owned Businesses

The most successful of these are the Rs.450-crore Viveks, the 40-year-old Chennai consumer durables chain, the Rs. 3,558 crore Pantaloons apparel retail business, and Bangalore's food retailer Nilgiris. With the new-age demanding consumer preferring to shop in these big retail chains, traditional 'bania' shops will face a difficult time trying to meet consumer expectations. This will make retailing an unattractive proposition for them. The process is likely to be kick-started by grocery stores transforming into supermarkets since the margins in the grocery trade are the lowest in the business. Further, the 'bania' is no longer considered a trusted friend. "He is always trying to shortchange us by not passing on the promos or cheating on quality or weight," is a common complaint. Managing inventory is a challenge in the small spaces that they operate from and it is a tough balancing act between stocks-out and keeping low-turnover SKUs. The younger generation, however, is far more aware of the cost of real estate or indeed of higher-margin retailing opportunities. Moving up to newer business opportunities and creating the space for a new model will take top priority.

New Entrepreneurs

The growing attractiveness of the retail trade has begun to attract new entrepreneurs with ideas, and venture capitalists with funds. Subhiksha, an innovative discount grocery chain in Chennai, has expanded to a total of 50 stores in less than three years in 2003, and is one of the most successful retail start-ups of the recent past with over 700 stores in 2007. Venture capitalists like ICICI and IL&FS are also increasingly willing to invest in retail businesses.

Building Chains around Brands

Apparel, footwear and consumer durable brands have driven the growth of specialty chains and upgraded existing multi-brand outlets. Some like Reebok claim to have entered retailing because of the paucity of suitable multi-brand retailing options. However, many of these are emerging as large retailers (Titan, Madura Garments, Raymonds) today, and appear to be committed to developing their retail businesses. Thus there is an extension of consumer brand-seeking (promise, trust, comfort, image) from products to stores.

Foreign Retailers Looking for Entry Options

The increasing attractiveness of the sector has drawn the interest of a number of global retailers. With the opening up of the economy, more and more MNCs have entered the Indian business arena through joint ventures, franchisees or even self-owned stores. The very first MNC to get into the business was Spencer's, a tie-up between the RPG Group and Dairy Farm International, a $10 billion Hong Kong-based company, and a part of the Jardine Matheson group.

While foreign retailers cannot start operations on their own mainly because of FDI restrictions on the sector, a number of companies, including Tesco, Kingfisher, Metro, Carrefour and Ahold, are exploring entry options. In apparel, Benetton, Lifestyle and Zegna are already in business, and Dairy

Farm has a number of retailing joint ventures in India.

Technological Impact

Technology is probably the most dynamic change agent in the retailing industry. The computerization of the various operations in a retail store — including inventory management, billing and payments as well as database (of customers) management — widespread use of bar coding, point-of-sale terminals and Management Information Systems (MIS) has changed the face of retailing drastically. Apart from providing the retailers with better and timely information about their operations, the technology also performs such tasks as preventing theft (through the hi-tech Electronic Article Surveillance System), promoting the store's goods and creating a better shopping atmosphere. This is done with the help of closed-circuit televisions, video walls, in-store video networks, and other forms of interactive applications — ranging from CD-ROMs to virtual reality — to let customers select and buy products.

They make the customer's life a lot easier by facilitating the use of credit cards, debit cards and smart cards. Toll-free numbers have brought about a revolution in consumer ordering and feedback mechanisms. These also pave the way for tele-shopping and net-shopping. Emerging technologies also facilitate just-in-time management of certain products within the store.

PROJECTED TRENDS IN RETAILING

Retail outlets exist in all shapes and sizes — from a "panwala" to a Shoppers' Stop in India. However, most of these outlets are basic mom-and-pop stores — the traditional "kirana" shops in the locality, which are smaller than 500 sq. ft. in area with very basic offerings, fixed prices, zero use of technology, and little or no ambience. The number of outlets in India have increased from 0.25 million in 1950 to approximately 12 million today. This translates to a growth of 48 times over a certain period when the population has trebled.

The well-known consultancy firm, Technopak has listed ten retail trends in their recent report entitled Retail Outlook 2007. Technopak says that the trends, many of which are already apparent, will be propelled by an unprecedented investment of $35 billion over five years into Indian retail.

10 Top Retail Trends	
Trend 1	Modern retail will grow but traditional retail will survive – there's place for both
Trend 2	Consumption will shift to lifestyle categories – consumers shifting evaluation from MRP to EMI
Trend 3	New retail formats will emerge and grow – small format cash & carry; investment surge in forecourt retailing: growth of super-specialty format
Trend 4	Modern retail will witness enhanced private equity infusion
Trend 5	There will be creation of large retailer brands (private labels) – 'own label' branding trend on the rise, more in groceries, home care and clothing; provides profit margin advantage to retailers
Trend 6	There will be an interplay between retailers & suppliers – branded firms will collaborate with top retailers
Trend 7	Modern retail will face a few key bottlenecks – talent, retail space and supplier base shortages; India will witness a shortfall of almost one million people in the retail sector by 2012
Trend 8	New investments will happen in the back-end – enhanced focus on improving the supply chain; process of storing and displaying food will be in focus
Trend 9	Modern retail will benefit consumers and rural sector – rural retailing formats will ensure quality goods, easy accessibility and low rates: typical monthly shopping bill will reduce by at least 10%
Trend 10	Consolidation will increase in the retail sector – consolidation, through M&As, will increase and become the norm

GROWTH OF ORGANIZED RETAILING IN INDIA

Organized retailing in India intially began in the South. The availability of land at prime locations coupled with lower real estate prices (compared to Mumbai and Delhi) made multi-storeyed shopping complexes possible. And now south India — notably Chennai and, to a lesser extent Bangalore and Hyderabad — has emerged as a centre of organized retailing. In fact, in Chennai, nearly 20% of food sales now is accounted for by supermarkets and an equal share of consumer durables is sold through specialty chains such as Vivek's.

It took two years of recession for this concept of shopping to take root in major cities like Mumbai and Delhi. Recession brought down property prices in these cities, and it was during this slump that big business houses took notice of the potential in retailing.

India is rapidly evolving into an exciting and competitive marketplace with potential target consumers in both the niche and middle class segments. Manufacturer-owned and retail chain stores are springing up in urban areas to market consumer goods in a style similar to that of malls in more affluent countries. Even though big retail chains like Crossroads, Saga and Shoppers' Stop are concentrating on the upper segment and selling products at higher prices, some like A.V. Birla Retail's More, RPG's Spencers, Food World and Big Bazaar are tapping the huge middle class population. During the past two years, there has been a tremendous amount of interest in the Indian retail trade from global majors as well. Over the years, international brands like McDonalds, Swarovski, Lacoste, Domino's, Pepsi, Benetton among a host of others have come in and thrived in India.

Retailing is one of the fastest growing industries in India, catering to the world's second-largest consumer market. A sunrise industry, it offers tremendous potential for growth and contributes 8-10% to overall employment. However, this is still low compared to 20% in the USA. As India moves towards being a service-oriented economy, a rise in this percentage is expected. The number of the retail outlets is growing at about 8.5% annually in the urban areas, and in towns with a population between 100,000 to 1 million the growth rate is about 4.5%. With the increasing assertiveness of the Indian consumer, and a growing supply base — both from within India as well as from other countries (with imports becoming easier) — the retail sector in India is poised for a significant change in the coming decade.

However, the boom in retailing has been confined primarily to the urban markets. There are two main reasons for this. Firstly, the modern retailer is yet to exhaust the opportunities in the urban market and has therefore probably not looked at other markets seriously. Secondly, the modern retailing trend, despite its cost-effectiveness, has come to be identified with lifestyles. In order to appeal to all classes of the society, retail stores need to identify with different lifestyles. In a sense, this trend is already visible with the emergence of stores with an essentially 'value for money' image. The attractiveness of the other stores actually appeals to the existing affluent class as well as those who aspire to be a part of it. Hence, one can assume that the retailing revolution is emerging along the lines of the economic evolution of society.

A **four-gear path** for the organized retail trade suggested by KSA

Technopak places India in the second gear and predicts that it will match global standards by 2010.

Gear one is the **stage of infancy**. The Super Bazaar, as a concept focusing on price control, started during the inflationary period of the 1960s. The development of the modern retail industry began when Indian shoppers upgraded from local shops to Super Bazaars. The open layout and self-service concepts were new to the Indian consumer, who was used to being served while shopping. Gear I was driven by entrepreneurs like Subhiksha and Vivek's in the South, real estate owners like the Rahejas (who started Shoppers' Stop) and marketers who integrated forward from manufacturing to retailing (for instance, lifestyle brands like Zodiac, Park Avenue and Bombay Dyeing which opened exclusive stores).

This gave the new breed of retailers an opportunity to differentiate on the basis of good quality products, services and ambience. These retail formats raised the bar for consumers as far as retail interface was concerned. The first level also looks at retailers driving customer awareness. The model primarily applies to apparel more than any other form of retailing. For instance, manufacturers in the food and grocery business hardly get into retailing. It is completely driven from the demand side and not on the supply side.

The second gear is about **meeting customer expectations**. It is consumer-driven, where buyers are exposed to new retail formats. This leads to first-generation retailers expanding to multiple locations (Shoppers' Stop, Food World and Subhiksha expand their networks as well as their locations). Convenient timings, dial-n-order, free parking, provision for trial and taste, prices below MRP (maximum retail price), free home delivery and 'no-questions-asked' return policies are some of the features offered by these new forms of stores. Moreover, some offer facilities like taking care of the kids while the mothers shop, vending machines and entertainment for those accompanying serious shoppers, convenient floor levels for the physically handicapped and so on.

Pure retailers like Westside and Lifestyle provide a unique selling proposition of choice and width. They capture a higher share of the organized retail formats and cut across all categories. For example, Barista in coffee, Pizza Hut and McDonalds in quick-service formats, Swarovski in crystal, Swatch in watches, THS in home, Agrani Switch in technology products, Apollo pharmacy and The Medicine Shoppe in pharmaceuticals and Ceat Shoppe in tyres. Global retailers like Marks & Spencer and Mango are evincing interest in India with their pilot projects.

Gear II is a period of growth. India is currently in this stage.

The apparel retail market in India is a little more evolved than the rest. While apparel retailing can be said to be in the second gear, other sectors like electronics, food, etc. are still in the first gear.

Compared to the first two stages, the main differentiator in the next two is the **shift in the power equation between manufacturers and retailers**. In the third and fourth stage retailers exert more influence than manufacturers and therefore have stronger bargaining power. Furthermore, the third gear involves efficient back-end management. Retailers exploit economies of scale and offer the best prices to their customers. The focus is on customer acquisition and category management. Cost savings in terms of initiating vendor partnerships and increasing stock turns take priority. Retailers expand into non-metros and look at various customer loyalty programmes. Many retailers in China and South Asia are in this phase.

A distinctive mark of this phase is efficiency: profitability through heavy investment in the back-end. Aldi, a grocery chain in Europe and the US, is a good example of retail efficiency and can be roughly placed in the third gear.

The fourth and last gear is a **period of consolidation**. The organized sector acquires a significant share of the retail pie. It is the start of a cross-border movement, with mergers and acquisitions gaining in importance. Retailers in North America and Europe like Wal-Mart, Tesco, M&S and Carrefour are in gear four, where they are looking for cross-border movement. Furthermore, companies start adding more stores and newer markets to their portfolio. There is a fair degree of domestic consolidation as well. Sourcing gets done globally.

Thus retailing in India has a very long haul ahead. The process of getting into newer forms of purchasing has been gradual because of traditional buying habits and the manner in which traditional retailers manage relationships. There is no specific international format or an existing role model that can be easily adapted and applied in the Indian context. India is going through that phase in retailing which the US experienced in the eighties and early nineties. In order to develop the right proposition one needs to go through the learning curve. The growth and development of organized retailing in India will be driven mainly by two factors — low price and benefits the consumers can't resist. Economies of scale will drive down the cost of the supply chain and increase the benefits offered to the customer. From product-based shopping, the emphasis will shift to experience-based shopping.

SUMMARY

- Organized retailing in India will soon be catapulted through the different stages of its growth to its culmination in maturity.
- The key drivers of the growth of organized retailing in India are going to be:

— A growing consumerism that will pave the way for greater consumer orientation and consumer enlightenment.

— Establishing a robust and cost-effective supply chain backed by fast-developing technology.

— Creating a liberalized economic platform that will enable global retailers to look at setting up shop in India through various methods that are permitted now such as joint ventures, licensing, franchising, etc.

- The growth of retailing will continue to be fuelled by the consumer, his expectations and demands for more value.

- Retail organizations are scaling up operations rapidly to minimize costs and increase margins (particularly in the Indian scenario where retail margins are being squeezed) so that they can sustain/expand their business. This would help in the consolidation of retail growth.

Questions:

1. Discuss the key drivers of retailing in India.

2. What are the projected trends in retailing in India? Explain with reference to the various studies done on retailing in India.

3. Discuss the four-gear path suggested by KSA Technopak for the growth of organized retailing in India.

Reliance Retail: Setting New Retail Trends in India

With its foray into organised retail, Reliance aims to forge strong and enduring bonds with millions of farmers in India and take its relationship with end-consumers to a new level. Reliance Retail is undoubtedly creating a virtuous circle of prosperity by creating win-win partnership for farmers, small shopkeepers and consumers. This idea has been evolved based on the new paradigm in the area of the consumption of products and services in India. Reliance will expend over Rs.25,000 crores (US$ 5.6 billion) over the next few years in building a state-of-the-art retail infrastructure in India. It will follow a multi-format strategy by opening up hypermarkets, supermarkets, seamless malls/department stores, convenience stores and other specialty stores across India in over 1500 towns and cities. Through this effort, Reliance Retail will create over 500,000 jobs through direct employment and over a million through indirect employment. We are poised to unfold a new and expansive chapter in India's growth story. Reliance Retail entered the organised retail market in India with the launch of its convenience store format under the brand name of 'Reliance Fresh'. Since the launch of the first Reliance Fresh store in November 2006 in Hyderabad, the network has expanded to 96 stores at the end of the FY 2006-07 covering locations like Jaipur, Chennai, NCR, Guntur, Vijayawada and Visakhapatnam. During the year 2007, Reliance launched their B2B operations called Ranger Farms to cater to small retailers in Hyderabad. They also introduced their private label in the staples category under the 'Reliance Select' brand name. Reliance Retail also started its loyalty programme for customers by introducing the 'RelianceOne' membership card from the first day of operations in Hyderabad. Within five months of operations, the loyalty programme has over one million members enrolled and is growing at a rapid rate.

Reliance launched recently their first consumer durables and IT pilot specialty store branded as 'Reliance Digital' at the Shipra Mall in Faridabad. Reliance Digital aspires to be a one-stop solution provider for all technology requirements with a wide array of brands and products covering consumer electronics, home appliances, information technology and telecommunication. Reliance Retail also launched its much awaited and India's largest hypermarket under the brand name of 'RelianceMart' at Iskon Mall in Ahmedabad in August 2007. Spread over 165,000 sq.ft. of shopping area, RelianceMart carries a range of over 95,000 products across categories ranging from fresh produce, food & grocery, home care products, apparel and accessories, non-food FMCG products, consumer durables and IT, automotive accessories, lifestyle products, footwear and more. The store also ofers some unique services to the shoppers like tailoring, shoe repair, watch repair, a photo shop, gifting services and laundry services all within the store. The store network continues to expand at a rapid pace. Currently, there are over 300 Reliance Fresh Stores covering more than 30 towns and cities in 12 states. The organisation's focus in 2008 will be on the rapid roll-out of Reliance Fresh and hypermarkets in various parts of the country. Apart from these formats, Reliance is expected to open newer formats in select cities and towns.

Questions for Discussion

1. 'Reliance Retail is creating a virtuous circle of prosperity in India'. Discuss.
2. Discuss the multi format strategy that Reliance Retail has adopted to quickly attain growth.

CHAPTER 3

Retail Economics

CHAPTER OBJECTIVES

1. To provide a detailed insight into the factors and functions in retailing that can enhance economic value
2. To enlighten the reader on the economic implications of the growth of the retail sector in India
3. To offer a glimpse into government policies that can promote retail growth

THE RETAIL ENVIRONMENT

The retail environment can be used to offer benefits to customers. *Bulk breaking* is when retailers buy goods in large quantities and break them into smaller sizes for individual customers. As a result, purchases become convenient for customers — both in terms of quantity bought as well as expenses incurred.

The *assorting function* evaluates all the different products available, and offers to the target the optimum array of products to choose from.

The *storing function* involves stocking goods until customers are willing to buy and use them. This relieves customers of the task of anticipating their needs too far in advance. Retailers create *economic utility* for consumers by providing the products in the form and at the place and time they desire. Further, retailers help manufacturers smoothen the *production cycle* by placing orders for peak demands well in advance and by managing inventory even on behalf of the manufacturer.

Retailing is hugely labour-intensive, and studies indicate that given the level of investment expected, it has the potential to generate an additional 8 million jobs, both direct and indirect. The retail industry, in a way, is creating employment for a group of people for whom there are few opportunities. For instance, it has a high number of female employees compared to other sectors.

A direct fallout of retail consolidation in India would be employment generation. Most of the frontline employees in the retail trade normally have only about 12 years of formal education. For these youngsters, retailing not only provides employment, it gives them enormous self-worth and confidence and teaches them some very essential skills of managing their careers and work lives. A good indicator of this is the employment profile of Food World operations. As many as 70% of its employees are high school graduates, most of them children of daily wage earners. Today, they are on the threshold of a viable career, and many of the earlier recruits will probably be income-tax payers in a couple of years. The effects on the economy when hundreds and even thousands of the virtually unemployed today are made productive corporate citizens of tomorrow can only be imagined.

Retailers' Association of India (RAI) has estimated that up to 2.2 million jobs will be created in the modern retail sector in the next two years (2007-09). Modern retail's growth is expected to offer local employment opportunities. Besides, the growth of modern retail will see a large proportion of 'first-time' employment and 20% of organized retail employees will be first time tax payers in the country. More than 50% of the total employees in modern retail will be women.

Retailing not only provides employment, it also creates a service culture in society, which in turn has an important effect on the development of the country. For example, Singapore retailers insist on certification for prospective employees, who have to pass a weekly/monthly exam administered by the Singapore Retail Association before they join the firm. This leads to standardization, builds confidence in the employee of his/her abilities and helps the retailer get people who have chosen retail as a career.

Retail Consolidation

The road that all products in India take, from the original producer to the customer, is long and tortuous. According to estimates, supply chain costs in India across product categories are between 12% and 50%. This is largely 'cost' and not 'value-added'. In the case of basic products, a significant portion of these costs is sheer wastage.

A pioneering study done by McKinsey for its 'FAIDA' report on food and grocery retailing estimates that wastage in the Indian food chain accounts for over Rs.50,000 crore annually, almost all of it attributable to the archaic intermediary chain food has to go through to reach the final consumer. While the consumer ends up paying more, the original producer — in many cases the Indian farmer — gets paid much less than what he would have got in a modern retail environment.

Retail consolidation or organized retailing will aggregate demand at the retail end, bypass the intermediary system, invest in the supply chain to ensure zero wastage, ensure lower prices to the end customer and higher prices to the farmer/original producer. Over time, savings in the Indian economy on this count alone could be a whopping Rs.50,000 crore plus.

Value added Tax (VAT) enables increase in government revenue: VAT was introduced in the year 2005 in India. The economy of India is growing so rapidly competing with developed nations due to globalization and it has transformed into a market economy. The emphasis on new reforms is to broaden the tax net and make it simple so that a layman can understand it. VAT has replaced sales tax in India. Since VAT is charged only on value addition in each stage of business transaction it has eliminated the cascading effect in the old sales tax system and consequently customers benefit in terms of lower end-prices. VAT could change the nature of trade in the coming years, but it is opined by experts that the intermediaries of trade, that is clearing & forwarding (C&F) agents, distributors, stockists, etc. would face problems as the companies would reduce the tiers of such marketing intermediaries. Similarly small retailers would be required to maintain accounts and pay composition money to the Government. VAT will also in the long term, enable the reduction of administrative costs. The implementation of VAT has come as a boon to organized retailing as consumer awareness results in demanding a cash memo for every transaction. Many traditional retailing categories like jewellery outlets have resorted to perfect book keeping in addition to recording every transaction with a bill to the purchaser after VAT implementation. Changes have been taking place at a rapid pace in Indian retailing with respect to compliance to regulations so much that customers are moving towards buying without restrictions! And this has been increasing government revenues considerably too.

Market access: The hugely fragmented retail structure has given rise to a distribution network that is unique to India. The cost and complexity of such a structure acts as a huge barrier for new entrants or products. It also severely restricts the ability of India's small-scale manufacturers to reach customers. Given the large number of small-scale industries in India, retailing will provide a fillip to their ability to access the market. Also, the choice and range available to the end customer will go up significantly.

Rural India has (according to a recent study by NCAER) around 720 million customers across 627,000 villages and 17% of these villages account for nearly 50% of the total rural population as well as 60% of rural wealth. As retailers would soon penetrate these markets with specific retail formats and products, they will be able to cater to the needs of this rural segment which is known for its consumption capabilities.

CONTRIBUTION OF RETAILING TO THE INDIAN ECONOMIC SCENARIO

(a) **Real estate:** The retail industry's real-estate requirement will be in millions of square feet. This will release for productive use large tracts of land lying with various government agencies such as the ports, railways, the armed forces, mill land and so on. As we know already, 100% FDI is allowed in real estate development and this will make a large chunk of quality infrastructure available for modern retailing in India. Retailers' Association of India (RAI) has recently estimated that about 40 million square feet of retail space will be created over the next 5 years by existing retailers. Close to 3.2 billion dollars is being invested in infrastructure development which shall have the cascading developmental effect. In warehousing and distribution a large industry growth opportunity aligned with the current infrastructure development programme of the government exists where companies will invest in businesses related to supply chain thus optimizing efficiencies which will reduce wastage considerably. Currently supply chain development is happening even in the secondary cities, outskirts, supporting the National Highway Programme (NHP) and the Golden Quadrilateral connecting the metros of India.

(b) **Tourism/outbound shopping:** One of the best features of any city that attracts a large number of tourists every year — London, Singapore, Dubai, New York and so on — is a well-developed shopping environment. Organized retailing will help significantly in developing our cities as tourist destinations. And, if well-marketed and managed, it can significantly enhance government revenues, apart from spreading the word about ethnic Indian brands across the world.

(c) **Higher GDP:** The value that retailing can add to the economy should not be underestimated. Organized retailing has huge potential, which could lead to *higher GDP* growth and result in increased consumption. Organized retailing could also bring about the transformation of the agricultural supply chain, remove inefficiencies in the distribution of consumer goods and improve productivity while providing consumers with a better range of products at better prices in a better ambience at the same time.

(d) **Outsourcing opportunities:** If organized retailing is a billion dollar industry, how big can its *outsourcing opportunities* be? Pretty big, including everything from supply chain management to pilferage control to loyalty management. Take Solutions, a Chennai-based firm. It has set up a nation-wide network of transporters and warehouse owners. Companies like Polaris in India have developed specific IT products for retail. IBM in India has already set up a solutions and consulting arm for Retail. Many ERP solutions companies like JDA and SAP have already set up their Indian offices. Checkpoint Systems has just launched its pilferage prevention system, and Venture Infotek has come in with transaction management for loyalty programmes. Expenses on advertising and promotions have also gone up three-fold. The benefits are difficult to quantify, but clearly they will be huge. In countries where retailing and modernization has progressed, it has favourably affected the value-capturing capacity and modernization of the farming industry. It has also restructured the supply chain for all FMCG products, driven end-customer prices down on a sustained basis, created significant employment opportunities, been a source of considerable revenue for governments both local and national, and in general been a catalyst for creating considerable national wealth. There is no reason why it should not do the same in India.

FOREIGN DIRECT INVESTMENT (FDI) IN RETAIL IN INDIA

The small trader lobby has been vocal in opposing FDI into retail, and has ensured that government policy on this front remained unchanged. The lobbying is based on the premise that modern retailing will impact the livelihood of millions of small family-run businesses.

There are fears that the organized sector will put the small mom-and-pop shops out of business, as it did in the US. However, analysts say that this is not likely to happen in India; in fact, small stores in Europe as well as other Asian countries have survived and are doing well in the modern retail environment. In many south Asian countries, even after 10-15 years of allowing FDI in retailing, unorganized retailers still control a sizeable chunk of the industry. The Indian scene is expected to be no different. Some feel that small retailers in India should form cooperatives to purchase stock as is done in France, Italy and Spain. In India a small beginning towards this has been made in Mumbai, Tamil Nadu and Delhi.

The Government of India has already opened up 51% FDI in single brand retail outlets since 2006. And as the government is in a process to initiate a second phase of reforms, it is cautiously exploring the avenues for opening up various other luxury categories and sports goods before opening the multi-brand segment. The Communist Party of India (Marxist) has recently criticized the UPA Government that it should 'abandon the moves to permit FDI in retail trade through the back door', as in the case of the joint venture between Wal-Mart and Bharti whereby the former proposes to operate in the cash-and-carry segment while the latter in the front-end. The CPM has further said that it is obvious that this proposed joint venture is nothing but a subterfuge, to circumvent the existing policy regime, which does not allow FDI in retail. The CPM has opined that the entry of giant MNCs besides accelerating the already rapid growth of organized retail, would also sabotage any attempt by the Government to regulare the sector in order to protect the interests of the small retailers and farmers. It says that not allowing MNCs to operate in the retail sector should be the starting point of the national policy on retail. The CPM has proposed that the Government should prevent huge monopolies and hence there should be a licensing policy for allowing single large organized retailers to set up business. CPM has suggested that retail stores having floor space over an appropriate minimum floor area should obtain prior license from local authorities (city corporations or municipalities) and that corporate entities should not be allowed to operate retail outlets below the specified minimum floor area.

In India the retail sector is going to be location-driven. Most Indian shoppers cannot hop into a car or bus and go to an outlet that is located across town to buy groceries merely because it's a brand-name store. They will pick up their goods closer to home, and small retailers will co-exist with large retailers.

In the Indian scenario it makes sense for large chains to leverage their brand names and set up shop extensions in more places than one. The implementation of such a retail marketing strategy would not only yield benefits for consumers, manufacturers and wholesalers but also create economic utility.

Further, the study currently being done by ICRIER (Indian Council for Research on International Economic Relations) is expected to provide certain directions to the Government on FDI in retail in India.

SUMMARY

- The retail environment offers a great deal of customer convenience insofar as it tries to provide for consumer needs precisely and on time throughout the country. It is a vital element in triggering consumer spends.
- The growth in retailing will generate employment opportunities at different levels. More opportunities will be available in frontline retailing where the maximum number of people with the barest minimum qualifications can be employed.
- The cost of logistics and operations needs to be controlled. VAT has been designed to maximize government revenue.
- One major benefit of the growth of retailing in India is the development of (hitherto unproductive) real estate.
- Outsourcing opportunities for alliances in retail processes and information technology relating to retailing will grow rapidly.
- On the issue of FDI in retailing, we can learn a few lessons from the many south-east Asian countries where allowing FDI has not affected unorganized retailers but has in fact generated newer opportunities.

Questions:

1. Discuss the benefits of retail consolidation and the contribution of organized retailing to the Indian economic scenario.

2. Discuss how VAT has an impact on generating maximum government revenue.

3. Comment on the impact of Foreign Direct Investment (FDI) on retailing if allowed in India.

The MRP regime in India

India is in the cusp of moving on to the next level of economic development. Magnificent things are happening in India with the economic development largely dependent on internal consumption. The differentiating aspect of the economic liberation of our country as compared with that of China's is India's growing internal consumption. India's consumption has been growing from a low base which contributes to the rapid economic growth. In our country consumption currently accounts for more than 65% of GDP that is in fact higher than the consumption in China, Japan and even Europe. The burgeoning middle class of India and improving lifestyles change consumption patterns too. All these developments are amazing and the one question that keeps coming to one's mind often is that in a developing economy like India, should we yet have an MRP (Maximum Retail Price) regime!

India is fast becoming an informed country and so, will assessment of the value of merchandise and the justification of the prices be difficult any longer? Can competition among retailers not help bring prices down for consumers largely? MRP is the selling price at which a firm wants to sell its goods. This price which includes all taxes is printed on the packaging to actually stop the consumer from being cheated by the retailer. Does MRP benefit customers or manufacturers? On the one hand, it does benefit customers because it specifies the maximum value of the product beyond which the customer need not pay. Customers especially from the rural areas will know in an instance, the right price of products. MRP has been extended to pharmaceutical products too recently in India. Earlier when 'recommended retail price plus taxes as applicable' was printed following labeling requirements, unprofessional retailers used to profiteer by charging the customer an approximation of the taxes which were usually more than actual or a tax figure above the recommended retail price, that was not paid to the government at all. In order to let the customers know the right price the Department of Consumer Affairs Weights and Measures took the MRP stance and mandated the printing of MRP on all packaged products. This is of course right in a scenario where nearly a third of India's population can't read or write. Further, in a market where within one city, different products had different rates of taxes until the recent implementation of VAT, it was difficult for consumers to check whether the retailers were actually charging the right amount of local taxes on the products they sold. The MRP serves as an eye-opener for at least those who can understand that the retailer cannot sell a particular product at more than the printed price. But it has its flip side too when the mandated printing of MRP is done by manufacturers.

As retailing is booming in modern India, one wonders how far it would benefit the customers in the matter of charging the right MRP by manufacturers. If the manufacturers charge a higher MRP, there is no mechanism today available to find out the right prices. If MRP is printed on the package it lends an assumption that it is the right price! As retailers now demand more margins, errant manufacturers and suppliers of merchandise are likely to increase the MRP of products, thus acceding to the bargains of retailers in a positive way. This would amount to duping the consumers at large. Currently there is no method to regulate the margins of manufacturers on a cost plus basis. Now the manufacturers are free to decide their profit margins and this violates the principles of free trade in a liberated economy. A senior official in the Ministry of Consumer Affairs recently mentioned that the saving grace is that the excise levies are done on MRP and this would not allow manufacturers to inflate their profit margins. N.B. Grant, a retired brigadier in the Indian army while analyzing the issue way back in 1999 observed, "The moment you let manufacturers print a price to consumers, it tantamounts to authorizing manufacturers to dictate the profit and profitability which retailers and other members of the trade can get. This itself is violation of the very principles of free trade and in fact, is also violation of the RTP parts of our MRTP Act." He also argued that the law must be changed in favour of prices being put on products only by the retailers and not the manufacturers so that the consumer will know exactly what price they should pay for the goods. He is right when he says that the MRP should be printed by the retailer so that ultimately customers will be benefited.

As modern retailing expands rapidly in its frenetic pace in India especially in the food and grocery sector, such revised decisions on MRP will matter a great deal to our consumers. After all it is our responsibility to enlighten them. Or they may get duped by the lure of products being sold at less than MRP claimed as bargain prices, which in truth may be an offer less on inflated margins! Margins inflated unduly by manufacturers will affect consumers in the long run whereas competitive pressures in the marketplace will drive prices down if retailers print the MRP. And our consumers at the end of it all will emerge as winners!

Questions for Discussion

1. Does MRP benefit customers in India?
2. Explain the risk associated with the end price of a product to consumers when the mandated printing of MRP is done by the manufacturers.
3. What is the observation of Mr. N.B. Grant on the MRP issue way back in 1999?

CHAPTER 4

Retail Formats

CHAPTER OBJECTIVES

1. To explain the evolution of retailing in India
2. To provide insights into how retail formats enable the store or the organization act as differentiators, creating a unique identity
3. To take the reader through the different kinds of mediating retail formats
4. To provide a clear understanding of the key physical store format definitions
5. To help the reader understand store format scalability and its resultant factors
6. To provide insights into the retail format strategies of a few Indian retailing organizations
7. To compare the characteristics of different retail store formats in India

What is retailing all about? It's about reaching out to consumers first-hand through formats that differentiate offerings to suit their needs, to fulfill them every time and provide true shopping value. It's about efficiently providing a vehicle for mediation with the customers, with the right merchandise at the right place in the right quantities/assortment/sizes at the right price and at the right time.

RETAIL FORMATS AND THEIR EVOLUTION

Many researchers and retail analysts describe the growth of retailing in India as evolution, especially when they discuss retail formats. But, has the industry evolved? The Indian retailing scenario cannot be said to have evolved, as in the process of evolution one graduates and shifts gear from one stage to the next. It's more of a revolution than evolution.

It's a unique scenario. There is a retail revolution happening with more and more formats being defined by the day, not only by the marketplace but by the method of retail mediation with customers, by physical store characteristics, by merchandise characteristics, etc. At the same time, these newly defined formats co-exist with the most primitive ones. In fact, it is the store format that creates a unique identity for retailers, enabling recall in the minds of customers.

Conventional Retail Formats Defined by the Marketplace

Retail formats in India first emerged when the barter system was in vogue with the primitive format of the "shanty", where the produce were brought to the market for convenient access by consumers. Keeping the consumers in mind, small mobile retailers brought these products to villages on carts, bicycles, etc. Later retailers opened small shops, stocking them with such produce. As towns and cities grew, these retail stores began stocking a mix of convenience merchandise, enabling the formation of high-street bazaars that became the hub of retail activity in every city. Thus, to cite an instance, Ranganathan Street in Chennai came into existence initially, followed later by Pondy Bazaar, which had largely mom and pop outlets, as a high-street destination. Thus the gradual development of the marketplace led to the emergence of new formats.

Organized retailers are coming up with new retail formats that range from marketplace-based ones to newer forms which are now becoming commonplace. Modern retailing is thus about getting the customer's heart-share more than his mind-share by offering a differentiating value-proposition through various formats.

Contemporary Retail Formats by Customer Mediation

When we think of retail formats, the first thing that comes to mind is the various kinds of physical retail stores. We seldom realize that they are the means to reach customers with a configuration of products and services to ultimately gain a significant position in the customer's mind.

Most Indian organizations choose to reach the consumer through brick and mortar retail store formats. However, there are other methods too, including non-store formats such as catalogue, cable TV and the World Wide Web (WWW). While the method of mediation in a physical store format is human interaction, a non-store format like catalogue relies on paper and print. Television uses telecast/broadcast and the Internet the web-site. The most interesting aspect of a non-store format is that the entire store is brought to the customer. In a physical store format, on the other hand, an attempt is made to bring the customer to the store.

Where the mediation is by human beings, face-to-face sales and service interaction and actual presentation of products is important to achieve customer service objectives. In non-personal mediation customer relations are established through remote communication. At times this communication is coupled with voice and photographs, text, images or demonstrations while presenting the merchandise.

Each medium used to reach customers has both advantages and

Media Activity Elements	In Store	Catalogue	Cable TV	WWW	Telephone
Means of Mediation	Humans in Brick and Mortar Environment	Paper & Telephonic	Broadcast & Telephonic	Computer & Voice over Internet Protocol	Telephonic
Customer Interface	Face to Face Sales and Service	Remote, Print, Response Voice only	Remote, Voice only, Recreate Social aspect	Remote, Voice often Electronic	Remote, Voice only
Product Presentation	3-Dimensional Displays	Photograph & Text	Television image & demonstration	Computer image, Photograph, Text	Telephonic product & service description

Table 4: *Comparison of Retail Media Formats*

disadvantages. Retail organizations at times use a combination of these formats to fulfill their target customers' needs.

Physical store formats, which form a critical part of contemporary Indian retailing, are discussed here in detail.

WHAT ARE STORE FORMATS IN RETAIL PARLANCE?

Store formats — their positioning and differentiation — create a distinct image of the store among its customers. These formats are defined in terms of location, layout, size, design, merchandise, service experience offerings, etc. As there are many formats at present, it makes sense to have a clear understanding of the key store format definitions.

Store Formats by Location

If retail stores are multi-locational — linked by a common store presentation created by its signature store design, a synergistic merchandising plan, a cohesive promotional and service strategy, and owned and operated by a single organization — the format is known as the **chain store format.**

Store formats are defined by their location too. If a retail chain consciously seeks to locate its stores in busy shopping areas, it is known as the **high-street format** (generally less than 2,000 sft, with no parking facilities, and focused merchandise categories).

Independent retail stores that are located in a particular area with alluring propositions for the customers to visit the store with the primary intention of shopping only there, rely on the **destination format** (usually large in size, with ample concessions, huge parking space, wide merchandise categories).

If a retail store is located in a catchment area of its target customers who can quickly access it and choose from a wide array of consumable products and services, it is known as the **convenience store format** (typically less than 5,000 sft, extended hours of operation if not 24 hours, parking for a few vehicles, convenience merchandise such as beverages, ready-to-eat snacks, grocery type items, confectionery etc.).

Store Formats by Ownership

Retail stores owned and operated by individuals on behalf of (and licensed by) a large supporting organization adopt the **franchise format**.

When a retail store is owned by a single person or a partnership, and not operated as part of a larger retail institution, it comes under the **independent store format** classification.

Store Formats by Merchandise Categories

Retail stores can be classified according to the merchandise categories they deal in. In apparel retailing, if the store deals with all categories of merchandise to suit the wardrobe of a family, the format is known as the **family store**.

A **specialty store** retails merchandise narrow in product lines but with a good depth within that area. Specializing in a given type of merchandise, the specialty store offers attentive customer service. For instance, Park Avenue by Raymond's is a men's specialty store.

A store with several departments — apparel, cosmetics and fragrances, accessories, home-ware, electronics, etc. — under one roof with each section within the store functioning as a strategic business unit (SBU) is known as a **department store** (large in size, usually more than 10,000 sft, often owned by national chains, good concessions, with usually more than 100,000 SKUs). Shoppers' Stop is a department store.

A store that is departmentalized, specializing in foodstuff, grocery and rations and limited non-food categories with free access displays for customers so that they can pick products from the shelves is known as the **supermarket** (large, usually more than 3,000 sft, and more than 30,000 SKUs).

A retail store selling a variety of a particular group of merchandise is known as an **emporium** (sari emporium, art emporium, etc.). Example: CIE-Bangalore, Chennai.

Store Formats by Size

A single-level large store (usually more than 5,000 sft) selling food and non-food goods is known as a **superstore**. A superstore is generally twice the size of a supermarket and offers non-traditional goods and services like a pharmacy, flower shop, bookstore, salad bar, bakery etc. under one roof. (Nilgiris, Bangalore).

A **shopping mall** is an arrangement of retail stores and places for leisure activities such as dining, entertainment, etc., selected according to their contribution to an overall merchandising plan. A mall is spread over a large area of more than 200,000 sft and run as an integrated business by an individual or an organization, to which independent retailers pay for opportunities to participate.

A **shopping centre** or a plaza is a configuration of five or more tenant spaces of approximately 1,000 sft each used for retailing, and developed under one building plan such that it has a unified character (Kannaiya shopping centre in Linking Road, Mumbai; Fountain Plaza in Egmore, Chennai; Basant Lok in Vasant Vihar, New Delhi).

A **hypermarket** is spread over 200,000 sft and more, retailing groceries and general merchandise goods, with a pharmacy, flower shop, photo shop, other concessions, etc. It has a wide variety of merchandise offerings in large quantities in each category selling huge volumes at low margins (Giant, Hyderabad).

Store Formats by Price

The store configuration can be defined by its pricing strategy as well. The **discount format** retails merchandise at 25% or more below MRP. They purchase stock lots from manufacturers' overruns, irregulars like cut-sizes in apparel, unsold end-of-season merchandise etc., and retail them at discounted prices. This is also known as a bazaar format.

There are discount specialty formats that specialize in a given type of merchandise line. There are discount stores (found in the West in large numbers) that adopt an everyday low pricing strategy, through the **every-day-low-price (EDLP) format**.

A **category killer format** is a large specialty store featuring an enormous selection of its product category at relatively low prices.

The **factory outlet format** is owned and operated by the manufacturer selling discontinued merchandise, factory seconds, cancelled orders, etc. at very low prices and located in the vicinity of the factory itself. Some textile mills in Mumbai like Bombay Dyeing and Morarjee Mills have their factory outlets in their factory premises.

The **warehouse format** is a large sale of discounted merchandise by an individual or an organization in the free-access ambience of a warehouse. This format has a large width and depth in the many categories it retails.

A **single-price denomination format** store retails scrambled merchandise lines at just one price point, generally a low one. Such retail outlets are famous in the United States. The best example of this format is the Dollar stores, which are spread across the USA.

Store Formats by Concessions

The **stopover store format** is one that rides piggyback on another retail outlet, say a petrol pump. This stopover format is a concession that offers instant use or ready-to-eat categories of merchandise.

A **kiosk** is one such concessionaire format, placed in a mall, a shopping centre, a bus station, airport, etc. A kiosk is a small freestanding pavilion often open on one or more sides and used for information, sales and promotion.

Partnerships and alliances for concessions offer a lot of opportunities for increasing customer contact, "share of mind" and "share of heart", especially in large formats such as department stores, malls and hypermarkets. By striking alliances with brands that consumers trust, or with complementary marketers who are concessionaires, a retailer can add value and convenience, and broaden his relationship with customers.

Apart from alliances such as McDonald's with Crossroads, Qwikys with Lifestyle, Ritazza with Shoppers' Stop, retail ventures are trying to link with such concessions as travel, information, entertainment, communication, etc. in order to hit upon that winning signature configuration.

THE IMPACT OF SCALABILITY OF STORE FORMATS

Scalability is the most critical factor in retail formats, helping an organization to have the ideal format or the right format mix. Such efficient scalability facilitates:

- Achieving the highest long-term profitability.
- Ensuring an efficient rollout.
- Providing shoppers the greatest shopping opportunity and the highest customer satisfaction.
- Hitting upon a strategic mix of formats to mediate with the customers first-hand and cater to the needs of all target customer segments. For instance, a few organized retailers have an online format too, selling merchandise through their own Internet sites or through an URL alliance. Stores like JC Penney in the West effectively use formats such as online, catalogue and TV in addition to their brick-and-mortar operations.
- Enjoying the benefits of each format (if there happens to be a mix of formats), attempting to improve shopping experience while competing healthily within themselves to overcome the weaknesses of each.
- Helping the organization acquire the signature configuration for a common understanding of the store and achieve its 'positioning' in various locations with diverse customer demographic characteristics.
- Establishing a core differentiated value proposition for customers.

If the organization is to achieve all the above, it is necessary for all these store format requirements to be packed into scalable models.

Scalability of the chosen format enables the organization reach critical mass through efficient geographic dispersion or rollout. It can then achieve volumes (as margins are low in India) and increase profits so that it can grow. Food World's scalability is the highest as its supermarket format can be scaled up or down to fit any size or location — whether one with a high catchment density or a high street. The adaptability of the supermarket is such that even in markets with high real estate costs, it can shrink its physical format while expanding the DTH (direct-to-home) delivery base.

Characteristics / Retail Formats	Location	Space / Layout	Merchandise	Customer Profile	Example
Supermarket	Marketplace in metros, towns, cities	Large	Multiple, cohesive food and household categories	Family profile, mostly loyal	A Supermarket, "Apna Bazaar", "Foodworld"
Speciality Store	Strategic	Medium sized	Focussed single category	Individuals, groups and clusters of same class, mediocre to high loyalty	A footwear store, "Bata", A music store, "Planet M"
Department Store	Destination towns, metros and mega metros	Large	Cohesive category clusters/brands, skewed toward garments	Familly, high loyalty and involved	A store with deparment as SBU, "Shoppers' Stop"
The Plaza	Marketplace in metros, large towns	Large	Independent categories	Family and individuals, young at heart and seeking to spend time in hang-outs	Many points of purchase in the same complex, "GFountain Plaza"in Chennai, "Heera Panna" in Mumbai
The Mall	Destinations, mega metros	Huge	Independent but profiled and defined category mix like shopping, dining, entertainment, etc.	Family and individuals, young at heart, fun-loving entertainment seekers and diners of mediocre to high loyalty	Shopping, dining and entertainment facilities under one roof- "Crossroads" in Mumbai, "City Center" in Dubai
The Emporium	Marketplace	Medium sized / small	Single group category	Family and individuals, need based spenders	The cloth store, "The Bombay Dyeing" store
The Bazaar	Strategic	Large	Multiple, cohesive categories in reduced price bands	Price conscious individuals and family, less loyalty	The discount store, "Megamart", "Big Bazaar"
Stop-over	Piggy back location	Small to medium	Multiple, cohesive categories	Impulsive buyers	The store inside the petrol pump, "In&Out" of BPCL
Single Price Denomination	Busy marketplace	Medium sized, small	Multiple, non-cohesive categories - scrambled	Bargain seekers	The "Dollar Store", in USA
Kiosk	Busy marketplace	Very small	Fast moving consumables	Impulsive individuals satisfying nick-of-the-time needs	The bunk shop, dispensing formats like Pepsi fountain

Table 5: *Various Retail Formats & their Characteristics*

This combination of a supermarket and a 'Tele-Deli' format renders the operation profitable even in a city like Mumbai where real estate costs are high. Today, Carrefour is present throughout the world with its hypermarkets, a concept that it invented and has continuously nurtured and developed. Carrefour is known for its adaptable formats and products.

Pantaloons is yet another good example of format scalability. After realizing that its current formats were not so big and were even being intimidated by competition from other big-box formats, the company decided to try the large store format and shifted gears from its 'men's-store' positioning to family wear. These stores have more free access for pleasurable shopping under one roof and value-oriented products and services, offering target customers a new world of experience.

Pantaloons provides a good case study in the scalability of formats to fit towns, cities or metros of every size. The company has the advantage of being able to spread its operations all over India with this scalability and flexibility, shrinking or enlarging formats wherever required. The latest addition to the format bandwagon is a huge one by price bargains, Big Bazaar in Kolkata and Mumbai.

Retailers like Shoppers' Stop have stuck to the 'big box' format, which has a strong positioning platform but can be expanded only in 'affordable' cities and metros.

Even the most successful formats need to be reviewed and revisited periodically since customer needs keep changing and competitive offerings go on increasing. Adapting the format of the core business and its value-added services to suit the requirements of different customer segments can rejuvenate a slow-growth or plateauing business and even help compete effectively in the marketplace. It is the store format that provides the winning edge for the organization in the rat race to capture the customer's 'heart-share' while ensuring long-term profitability.

SUMMARY

- It is more of a retail revolution than an evolution that is taking place in the growth phase of retailing in India. Primitive retail formats still co-exist with developed retail formats. This is unique to India.
- Store positioning and differentiating identities are created in the consumers' minds through a robust store format strategy. Consolidating and maintaining consistent format element deliveries will help build the organization's exclusive format image.
- Though there are many kinds of retail store formats, it is the innovative combination of format elements that helps a retail store gain a competitive edge.

- The factor of format scalability has to be borne in mind. This gives the retail organization flexibility to reach out to the critical mass in different geographical areas through an adaptable mix.

Questions:

1. Write a brief note on the evolution of retail formats in India.

2. What are the different media formats in retailing? Compare the aspects of each media format.

3. Define the characteristics according to which store formats are defined. Briefly explain any three key store formats with examples.

4. What impact does scalability have in retail formats?

SPECIALTY RETAILING — FASHION JEWELLERY BRANDS

The Branded Jewellery Market in India: An Overview

Brands are built over decades, more so in high-value markets like gold jewellery. Of the Rs.70,000 crore Indian jewellery market, the diamond market accounts for around Rs.10,000 crore. Only 3 per cent of this market is branded jewellery, with around eight to ten brands. The Rs.2100 crore branded jewellery market in India is growing at the rate of 40% per annum. Gold jewellery dominates the market with a share of 98%. Despite a 20% jump in prices last year, gold consumption in India grew by 4%. Only 5% of the total production gets exported.

The industry till recenly has been characterized by traditional retailers catering mainly to the local population. However, Titan Industries Ltd., with its 'Tanishq' brand, launched in 1996 gave birth to the branded segment and its success led many other players like Gili, Oyzterbay (now Laabh), Carbon, Nakshatra, Nirvana and Intergold (now Orra), etc. to step up their efforts in this vastly untapped market.

There has been a perceptible shift towards diamonds with the entrance of players like DeBeers, Rio Tinto, etc. With growth in the number of independent females with higher income and lifestyles and creating occasions for jewellery, these players have been able to position diamonds as affordable to middle class as well.

Any national brand needs to acquire a good reputation for styling and reliability and must become an aspirational brand.

Though branded jewellery as a fashion accessory commands only a small share, it is growing at a healthy rate of 30-40 per cent annually. Urban consumers are shifting preferences from heavy gold jewellery to ligher, trendier ornaments, and they often choose to replace a single, expensive, chunky set with several lighweight ones fit for a variety of occasions.

Shop-in-shop format is being used to increase reach and simultaneously lower the costs. Though people prefer to buy higher value merchandise from destination stores, small format stores are more suitable for impulse purchase (smaller value).

Many retailers are now choosing malls to expand their business. A very recent phenomenon is the launch of the jewellery mall Gold Souk in Gurgaon and another one promoted by Fort Knox group coming up in Kolkata.

Branded jewellery retailers in India face stiff competition from traditional jewellers who have been serving families for generations. However, the new generation of consumers has taken to branded jewellery, thanks to effective promotions.

For a brand to become firmly established it must deal with several tangible and intangible factors. It requires focused advertising, customer confidence, name-recognition, display and astute salesmanship to compete with traditional jewellers. Success hinges upon how a particular brand can differentiate itself from the clutter. Most important, affordability and quality are the key elements in sustaining a brand.

The growth of a jewellery brand depends on the confidence it can instil in buyers about the purity of the gold, be it 14, 18, or 22-carat. It also depends on the mark-up in price. The cost includes making (labour) charges on top of value of the material, gold content and stones including diamonds and precious stones, if used. Besides, a system of hallmarking for the purity of metal and identification of the manufacturer and jewellery items is a need if not an imperative.

At present the branded jewellery business is in its infancy in India, constituting hardly 14% of the market. With the market growing annually at the rate of 25-30%, its share will expand. While domestic jewellery-makers have the advantage of skills which still form a sizeable component of value, the confidence factor (in traditional craftsmen) is, however, on the decline. This gives branded jewellery an edge over the traditional variety.

One handicap branded jewellers face is the differing tastes of consumers. Thus, inventories will be high as also the carrying cost. On the other hand, the convenience of readymade jewellery is an ace in the brand marketer's hand. The consumer has no time to waste on the whims of craftsmen. Earlier, there was not much of a choice available.

Consumer Perception of Gold Jewellery

India is the world's largest consumer of gold. The precious metal is traditionally purchased either as an investment or to make intricate ornamental heirloom jewellery.

The liberal economic dispensation ushered in at the beginning of the 1990s and the emergence of an affluent professional class led to the creation of a burgeoning designer wear/cosmetics/fashion accessory market in India. This encouraged some domestic jewellery manufacturers to carve out a niche in this market. The abolition of the Gold Control Order and the subsequent easing of restrictions on the import of the precious metal, including a substantial reduction in import duties, have encouraged the development of this new market.

In the mid-1990s the Indian consumer's attitude towards gold jewellery changed. Gold jewellery, from being just an investment avenue, was now seen as a way to make a lifestyle and personality statement.

Globally, 90% of the jewellery is sold as dress-wear — a part of the wardrobe and not the vault. Branded jewellery as a fashion accessory constitutes around one per cent of the Rs.70,000 crore per annum jewellery market in India. However, it is growing fast and has become a part of every girl's treasure trove. One can easily spot branded jewellery counters at Shoppers' Stop and Lifestyle. With exclusive designs, standardized pricing and superior finish, branded jewellery is aptly termed as *fashion accessories*, suitable for both western as well as traditional wear.

It must be mentioned that purchasing gold is not necessarily an urban phenomenon and market share gains are likely to be more rapid in smaller towns.

Though designer jewellery arrived in India in the late nineties, it was only in this millennium that the scenario changed. With aggressive advertising campaigns, the big brands — Tanishq, Carbon, Gili, Sparkles, Ishis, Orra and Laabh, to name a few — arrived, teaching the customer at the paying end to shop like his or her counterpart in the West. The message read loud and clear: "Your wardrobe includes jewels too!" Stiff competition from traditional jewellers forced the newcomers to introduce a series of exchange offers and guarantee certificates to woo the adventurous consumer. Nevertheless, this gold-loving nation has been very cautious in its appreciation of branded jewellery.

Much of the gold jewellery in India is 22-carat unlike in western countries where it is basically 14 carats or even 12 carats. Fine jewellery by international standards goes up to 18 carats. For stone setting alloys up to 18 carats are preferred.

Educated middle-income women, particularly working women, tend to wear less gold jewellery these days However, growing incomes — especially among NRIs — have increased demand.

Most jewellery consumers are women between 25-45 years and men in the 40-55 year bracket. Men largely buy lower-value items, such as rings, chains or tie-pins, frequently as gifts. While women are seen more often in jewellery showrooms, it is the men who are still the effective decision-makers as far as buying goes in a majority of cases. The phenomenon, however, is changing. People are now looking beyond traditional 22-carat jewellery. Changing lifestyles have made buyers more product and quality-conscious. And branded jewellery as an off-the-counter product is gaining greater acceptance.

In the past five years or so since branded jewellery entered the market, it has threatened the very survival of traditional jewellers and craftsmen in the same way as traditional tailors, who are being replaced by makers of branded readymades. Inroads are being made by branded jewellery both in the domestic and international markets. This indicates that Indian women are definitely showing signs of accepting branded jewellery.

The Forward Path

The future of the branded category of jewellery seems to be bright in India with the consumer becoming more conscious of fashion trends and also ready to bring gold 'from the vault to the wardrobe!' Fashion jewellery has come to stay. With people willing to spend lavishly on their clothes, it won't be long before they start looking for matching ornaments.

Country-wise Gold usage in Carat Jewellery (1990 to 2000)

(In tonnes)

Country	1990	1991	1992	1993	1994	1995	1996	1997	1998	1999	2000
Italy	381	415	461	441	435	446	439	500	535	511	509
India	238.6	227	293.8	259	346	400.6	427.8	594	682.6	644	655
USA	126.6	121.2	132.1	140	146.7	148.3	152.4	159	170.2	178.2	181.8
Japan	109.5	106.7	104	88	85	78	74	55	39	37	37
Turkey	130.9	102.6	116.3	126.6	80.7	110.4	140.7	168.1	159	115	177
Germany	49.8	51	45.4	44.5	41.8	38.9	37.2	35.9	34.3	32.6	30.3
Other Countries	1070.8	1163.7	1377.1	1250.1	1253.8	1345.6	1366	1580.4	1331.4	1416.2	1403.2
China	0	134.7	203	179	208	204	189	224	173	166	155
Soviet Union/CIS	0	36.9	29.2	26	21.9	20.2	25.3	29	27	28	33.7
Total	2107.2	2358.8	2761.9	2554.2	2618.9	2792	2851.4	3345.4	3151.5	3128	3182

Source : *The Gems & Jewellery Export Promotion Council.*

Major Diamond Jewellery Brands:

Carbon

Carbon, a pioneer in the branded jewellery segment, has a range of 18-carat fashion accessories that includes rings, necklaces, pendants, ear tops and bracelets. Established in October 1996, Carbon is a distinctive lifestyle jewellery brand for the sophisticated and contemporary woman.

The Carbon range is currently available in 48 outlets in a shop-in-shop format only and 8 stores as Exclusive Brand Outlets (EBO) across 16 cities, and will be in 23 cities by 2010. The company is also planning to have 4 more of its own outlets, before the end of 2009. It also plans to expand its market by going in for products for specific occasions such as festivals, birthdays and anniversaries. In addition, it's looking at cross-promoting Carbon jewellery with other branded lifestyle products such as perfumes, clothing and cosmetics.

The price range of Carbon products is modest (Rs.3,750 to Rs.20,000 per piece), and unlike traditional jewellery whose prices can be brought down through bargaining, its items have a nationally uniform MRP. Through its marketing and advertising campaigns, Carbon aims at creating a contemporary feel with more value for the wearer. More than ten years since its inception, Carbon's annual sales have reached a considerable Rs.17 crore (approx) in the domestic market, with an average piece value of Rs.5,000.

Carbon's products cover the entire spectrum of contemporary designs. Design is the sole factor that led to the birth of Carbon, the brand. It has contributed to Carbon's growth by elevating jewellery from the vault to the wardrobe and rewarding it the identity of a fashion accessory. In 2001, Carbon's *Persona* collection was chosen to be exhibited at the National Institute of Design – India Trade Promotion Organization (NID-ITPO) Design Showcase exhibition in New Delhi. The *Persona* collection comprises five pendants depicting five facets of a woman. Besides women's earrings and pendants, Carbon has something for men too: cufflinks, tie-pins and bracelets. Carbon's product strength lies in its collections like *Venus* and *Sunsign*.

Carbon is one of the organized and more successful ventures in branded jewellery retailing from the house of Peakok Jewellery Private Limited. It was incorporated in Bangalore in early 1991 and spearheaded by Mahesh Rao, a young entrepreneur with extensive experience in the fashion accessories market. Mr. Rao felt in the mid-1990s that the Indian consumer's attitude towards gold jewellery would change from being an investment avenue to one that made a lifestyle and personality statement. Seizing the opportunity, he initiated within the Peakok fold, besides their exports, a new brand of 18-carat gold jewellery called Carbon for the domestic market. Peakok has a state-of-the-art manufacturing facility in Koramangala, Bangalore.

Tanishq

Titan Industries Limited is a joint venture of the Tata Group and The Tamil Nadu Industrial Development Corporation (TIDCO). Its product range includes watches, clocks and jewellery. In a short span of time, the company has built an enviable reputation for its corporate practices, products and services.

After entering the watch segment in 1987, Titan ventured into the precious jewellery segment in 1995 under the brand name *Tanishq*. It is India's only fine jewellery brand with a national presence and is an acknowledged business leader in the country's jewellery market.

In early 2000, Titan organised itself into two business units: watches and clocks, and jewellery and this has helped the company redefine its business purpose and focus. Tanishq has invested Rs.60 crore in its manufacturing unit in Hosur, Tamil Nadu.

Tanishq worked tirelessly on a two-pronged brand-building strategy: (i) cultivate trust by educating customers on the unethical practices in the business, and (ii) use innovative methods to change the perception of jewellery as a high-priced purchase. Tanishq has leveraged the design skills that are part of the Titan heritage to refine its products, and has invested a lot in R&D and consumer research on what the Indian woman is looking for and how she is evolving.

Tanishq jewellery is sold exclusively through a company-controlled retail chain which now has 108 outlets — ten per cent of these are owned by the company and the rest run by franchisees — spread over 61 cities and is still expanding.

The locations are chosen on the basis of geographical spread and the shopping dynamics of a particular metro. The primary promotional medium for Tanishq is its boutiques, which explains the emphasis on store design and layout. Its stores demonstrate design leadership and differentiation and provide excitement around the collections in the outlets.

Tanishq made its foray into 18-carat jewellery in the early 1990s; switched to 22-carat and again turned to 18-carat jewellery. To meet the increasing demand, it plans to nearly double the number of its outlets and offer a range of 'wearable' products. The brand caters to customers looking for items in between costume jewellery and real gold ornaments.

Major collections of Tanishq include:

Aria: Tanishq *Aria* is a spectacular collection of diamond jewellery. With over 80 exquisite designs of earrings, finger-rings, bangles and neckwear, the prices in this collection begin at as low as Rs.3,200.

The collection targets the contemporary woman, with designs representing a seamless blend of the traditional and the modern. *Aria* has been crafted by experts with a thorough understanding of the Indian woman's jewellery needs. The *Aria* collection is available at all Tanishq showrooms.

Collection G: The World Gold Council recently launched a range of 22-carat lightweight gold jewellery called *Collection G*. This range is promoted by Tanishq and is an exclusive concept/brand of WGC. It includes pendants, earrings, finger-rings and bracelets, and targets urban women in the age group of 18-30 years. In 22-carat gold, the designs are stylish and modern and go with all forms of attire — casual and formal,

Indian and Western. It has multiple finishes on a single piece to convey a modern look. The jewellery is priced from Rs.595 to Rs.4,995.

Gili

Gili, a distinctive brand established by the Gitanjali Group, is one of India's largest exporters of fine diamonds and a De Beers sight holder. It came into existence soon after the abolition of the Gold Control Order by the Indian government. Gili offers a wide range of 18-carat plain gold and diamond-studded jewellery, designed to appeal to the contemporary Indian woman. Indian and western styles and motifs combine to produce truly unique ornaments that are finely crafted and extremely attractive.

Gili's products are available through a mail-order catalogue and shop-in-shop counters in fine stores all over the country. In addition, it has special promotional offers during special events like Valentine's Day, Raksha Bandhan and Diwali, and beauty contests and shows.

Gili jewellery comes with a guarantee on the quality and weight of the diamond and gold. Gili's Millennium Series diamonds are triple certified and come in a special box, ideal to give as a gift or keep as a souvenir of a one-in-a-lifetime occasion.

In 1997, Gili launched a collection of 18-carat gold ethnic Indian ornaments with traditional forms and motifs, created with the most modern technology available today. These pieces are well finished, beautifully polished and available at extremely affordable prices.

The Gili Gold range caters to the modern individual, with locally manufactured designs in 24-carat gold that are elegant, simple, timeless and very attractive. The range is guaranteed .995 fineness and includes rings, pendants, earrings, necklaces and bangles.

Gili has captured the 18-carat diamond-studded jewellery segment in the price range of Rs. 2,500 to 15,000.

Orra

Rosy Blue is among the largest sightholders for Diamond Trading Company. Rosy Blue group, the parent company of Intergold and Orra Diamonds, has repositioned the Intergold outlets across the country as Orra Diamond stores. The new stores have been the vehicle for launching the $1.8 billion global diamonds brand Orra in India. Although the compnay has converted Intergold stores into Orra outlets, it continues to market the Intergold brand of jewellery in India. Selected Orra stores continue to stock the Intergold brand along with Nakshatra, the DeBeers brand.

Intergold is the biggest exporter of diamond-studded jewellery in India. It started off more than a decade ago as a diamond exporting company in Mumbai and has achieved unprecedented success in the diamond industry in a short span. The export division has a 6,000 sft factory, which churns out 3,000 high-quality pieces for export daily.

The Orra store has a strong identity of its own: the place looks inviting and is aesthetically appealing. The décor and design of the stores have been conceptualised to harmonise with the actual product design. Thematic window displays attract customers and see-through glass windows virtually compel them to walk in without being overawed, as they usually are at diamond jewellery showrooms.

The products in the store are divided into categories like pendants, necklaces and earrings for the convenience of buyers. They are further divided according to price so a customer doesn't need to worry about affordability for each product. Showroom personnel are knowledgeable about the products and sales techniques, apart from being trained to use audio-visual aids for the benefit of consumers.

Orra specializes in diamond, platinum and Italian jewellery and white gold. There's something here for buyers from all age groups with varying tastes. In the women's range, Intergold offers pendants, rings, earrings, small sets and necklaces, whereas men can go in for classy tie tacks, tie pins, button covers, sherwani buttons, belt buckles, cuff links, pendants and rings.

Orra sells only through exclusive retail outlets and has branches in more than fifteen cities in India. All Orra stores are equipped with ultrasonic cleaners for cleaning jewellery and diamond testers to check whether the gems are genuine.

Laabh

In July 2000, six professionals from Tanishq left the organization to float a new start-up — Oyzterbay.com — for branded jewellery. Oyzterbay had a chain of brick-and-mortar retail stores. They had 28 exclusive outlets (both its own and franchisees) across the country. Oyzterbay signature stores showcased and displayed precious metals, gemstones and crafted jewellery designs.

Oyzterbay, as a young company, was at the forefront of change in the jewellery industry. In February 2001, it launched its first internationally styled store at Bangalore, with a stunning range of precious jewellery in carat gold and silver at affordable prices. The Oyzterbay network covered all major Indian cities and an overwhelming response has induced the company to expand very fast.

Oyzterbay was taken over by Rajesh Exports, one of the world's largest jewellery makers and currently the jewellery brand has changed to Laabh. In the new set up, the management of Oyzterbay continue as stakeholders in the organization and manage the operations of the new Laabh stores.

Laabh now positions itself as well-styled, high-quality jewellery for young women. Delicate and bold, traditional and modern, the designs reflect the change in the attitude towards jewellery: from heavy overdressing to elegant daily wear, and from ostentatious display to understated panache. Prices start at a mere Rs.500 for sterling silver jewellery, and all products — including solid gold jewellery — are priced below Rs.10,000, a move that also positions Laabh as the only chain catering to the burgeoning gift market. The range is continually refreshed based on market feedback and emerging design trends.

Laabh stores lead the market in attitude, ambience and service. Laabh stores sport a contemporary and inviting glass-front store design in soft colours of wood with accents of steel, in stark contrast to the forbidding opulence of traditional jewellery stores. Complemented by modern in-store graphics and merchandising, the house colours pervade all elements of the corporate identity. The Laabh web store in the Rajesh Exports website replicates the store experience with state-of-the-art features that make buying and gifting Laabh jewellery quick, easy and secure. Several campaigns for Laabh have created awareness waves with its fresh approach to the jewellery market. Jewellery for the Living has rapidly become a byline for jewellery for the young woman of today — that is, jewellery for the joy of wearing, not destined for the safe-deposit locker.

Sparkles

Sparkles is carrying on a family tradition in producing 9-carat, 14-carat and 18-carat jewellery. The objective is not only to provide off-the-shelf diamond jewellery in a wide array of designs, but also to offer customers an affordable range of choices. A trend-setting initiative in the Indian market, Sparkles became a revolutionary success and grew to become one of the market leaders in the branded jewellery segment.

Sparkles sells through 68 outlets in more than twelve major Indian cities. With a wide range of designs and more coming out every month, it is only a matter of time before it covers more cities and outlets. Besides these regular outlets, its web-site sparklesindia.com has been a pioneering effort that has taken branded jewellery to the newest communication medium — the Internet. During the past few years Sparkles has been tracking what its customers want, and is striving with every new design and product to meet their expectations. Total satisfaction and loyalty vindicates their commitment to constantly strive for quality.

Sparkles — from Poddar Jewels, Mumbai — is the only company to have added an ethnic touch to the usual collection with nose studs.

D'damas

D'damas is the brand from Gemplus Jewellery, a joint venture of the Digico Group and Damas Group of the Middle East, and one of the largest exporters of diamond studded jewellery to the overseas markets. The brand brings in international quality with Indian values encompassing an entire spectrum of emotions in 10 pioneering collections, with jewellery for every occasion. Customers are offered the promise of luxury and trust thus creating the D'damas heritage and living up to its bye line of jewellery that is truly the art of beauty.

The D'damas stores stock diamonds and gold collections. The diamond range includes the Vivaaha (the diamond ring collection), DAMAS Solitaire collection, an exclusive line of signature diamond solitaires inspired by the "BIG B", the IIFA Glitterati range, a line of jewellery inspired by filmstars, D'damas Origin, a range of diamond jewellery inspired by nature, endorsed by Miss Universe — Jennifer Hawkins.

D'damas Bridal Wear range, D'damas Unique Setting range, D'damas Occasion Wear range which comprises diamond and gold jewellery and D'damas Victoria's Desire Collection which comprises complete diamond jewellery sets at very attractive prices. The gold range comprises D'damas Collection G, a collection of funky, playful jewellery pieces for the contemporary working woman of today. Gold Expressions range designed by renowned Indian goldsmiths in association with The World Gold Council.

D'damas range comprises ornaments like pendants, earrings, chains, necklaces, bangles, bracelets and sets. D'damas offer a certificate from International Gemmological Institute with every diamond jewellery product. D'damas has a whole host of Brand Ambassadors for their various products. These include Amitabh Bachchan, Suniel Shetty, Akshay Kumar, Mahima Chaudhary, Celina Jaitley, Simran, Lara Dutta and former Miss Universe Jennifer Hawkins.

D'damas operates through shop-in-shop format and also through their Exclusive Brand Outlets (EBO).

The brand first entered India through a 50:50 joint venture with Gitanjali Gems and Jewellery. This JV sells under the D'damas name and will continue to do so.

D'damas in India: Things changed in 2005 when D'damas felt confident enough to launch a 9,000 sq. ft. standalone store in Bangalore. The company is investing enough over a period of three years to open 108 stores. Of these, 11 are already up and running, and another 25 will come up by March 2008.

Ishi's

A sightholder of Diamond Trading Company (DTC) and owner of comprehensive operations for the cutting and polishing of rough diamonds and for the manufacture of diamond jewellery, Suashish Diamonds made its first foray into jewellery retail with the launch of its Ishi's brand, complementing its chain of production.

In terms of the marketing of the brand, Suashish Diamonds has embarked on a progressive route aimed at reaching out to a wide number of people. According to Ramesh Goenka, Chairman of Suashish Diamonds, Ishi's represents a new direction in the marketing and retail of diamond jewellery, as it seeks to reach out to a broader society than that which diamond jewellers presently address.

The styles featured at Ishi's represent both the classic and the contemporary, in keeping with an audience of national, Asian and Western customers. The majority of the styles available at Ishi's have been created by design houses in the US and India and hand-picked Lebanese designers.

Currently Ishi's diamond jewellery outlets are present across India and Dubai both in the shop-in-shop format and in the Exclusive Brand Outlet (EBO) format but the company hopes to enter Europe and the United States for future growth, both as a vendor and as a retailer.

The company has more than 40 outlets now and the opening of the store in Lamcy Plaza, Dubai recently was part of the first step of going global.

Adora

Adora was launched in July 2003 by Mumbai-based Concept Jewellery (India) Pvt. Ltd. Concept is part of M. Suresh Group, Diamantaires since 1968, and a sightholder with Diamond Trading Company (DTC).

Adora was conceived — and is now established — as an accessible brand, both affordable and high-end, that rises above the concept of jewellery and approaches the bigger concept of lifestyle expression. In other words, Adora was conceived and launched as a brand with a high aspirational value backed by the highest degree of customer trust.

Adora has been trusted by Lata Mangeshkar, a living legend in vocal music, to craft her diamond jewellery creation, Swaranjali, and reach it out to connoisseurs of jewellery and her millions of admirers.

Adora was launched with only seven retail outlets in Mumbai. Currently, the brand's retail network comprises about 65 outlets in 35 cities all over India — and the network is still expanding. This rate of growth has earned Adora the distinction of being the fastest growing jewellery brand in India.

Adora has also ventured into the international marketplace, starting with Dubai to be followed by Malaysia and Singapore. In Dubai, Adora is retailed through 'Crossover Bollywood Se (CBS)', the style lounge conceived by movie star Suniel Shetty. CBS retails designer clothing and fashion accessories created by top designers in 'Bollywood' (nickname for the Hindi film industry), and Adora is the exclusive jewellery outlet there. The CBS lounge in Dubai is the first of a chain of 10 such stores to be located in different cities in India and around the world.

Questions for Discussion

1. Do you think that an exclusive brand retail store would work in India? Or a mix of formats for a brand? Discuss.

2. Will the franchisee route to a faster roll-out of retail outlets work for these jewellery brands? What are the pros and cons?

3. Depending on large chains by having a shop-in-shop format may perhaps entail the following risks:

   (a) A shop-in-shop format can be risky as damage to the reputation of the chain may affect the brands marketed from their outlets.

   (b) Over a period of time the mega stores may hike the rentals or may dictate terms to change the layout to suit their internal policies.

(c) The location of the shop-in-shop may not be ideal for the brand. Or the cost parameters may not allow much choice for the company. Discuss.

4. What should be the strategy of the domestic branded jewellery players to increase branded jewellery consumption in India? What steps would you suggest to help consumers buy jewellery in the same way as they would buy garments?

5. Will you recommend the formation of a consortium by branded jewellers to promote the consumption of branded jewellery, focusing on the 'trust' factor?

6. Will road shows such as the 'gold souk' held at Dubai or the annual Basel show help in promoting branded jewellery and accessories in India?

CHAPTER 5

Mall Management

CHAPTER OBJECTIVES

1. To provide a detailed understanding of mall management in India
2. To offer insights into the development of malls in India's growing retail scenario
3. To explain the emerging new types of malls in India
4. To provide an understanding of customer perception of malls in India
5. To examine the key aspects of facilities management in malls

WHAT IS A MALL

With the emergence of the mall as a retail format in India, there are many who have asked the question: How is a mall different from an array of shops or a shopping centre? The mall must have a few signature characteristics for it to be known as a mall, as otherwise it will become a shopping centre. According to the norms, a mall needs to have three distinctive characteristics:

1. *In a mall, space should never be sold*
2. *The mall should have its anchor stores well defined and signed up in advance*
3. *A successful mall must have a strong mall management team which will professionally manage the mall*

1. Mall space is never sold. Even if one is compelled to, not more than 5% of the total space should be sold out. Instead, space needs to be given away on lease to the tenants. When the mall space is planned for occupancy by tenants, the mall developer will be tempted to sell space as the value proposition for the mall would appreciate in terms of both the enhanced value of the property and the returns on investment. A mall developer should not sell the property as he would lose control of the tenant mix if he does so as the ownership would change. A professional mall is where space is only leased to tenants may be for long periods of time, with relevant conditions governing the merchandise and services that would be extended from the premises. For example, if a women's garment store in a mall by virtue of its business proposition has gained tenancy on the women's floor, the store shall not change its product offerings to sell exclusive men's categories as this would become a deterrent to the profile mix on the floor of the mall. This will also disturb the business of other mall tenants. The major advantage of the tenancy arrangement of a good mall is that the profile of the tenant-mix can be kept intact following the mall management's plan of its tenants to cater to the targeted customer profiles. Adequate care needs to be taken while one deals with lease agreements with tenants.

2. The mall should have its anchor stores well defined and signed up in advance — even before the mall's execution work begins. The success of a mall would largely depend on the tenant mix and, more so, on the anchor tenants. The agglomeration of the stores in malls helps consumers to reduce their search costs. This means that customers don't have to walk from store to store in different locations.

Researchers and most retailers across the world claim that consumers are attracted to malls because of the presence of well-known anchor stores. Anchors in a mall undoubtedly create benefits by increasing sales, and also help in the reduction of promotional expenditures and other overhead costs of smaller stores coexisting in the mall along with the anchors happily. The mall anchors will attract a large number of footfalls that will result in abundant sales, while for consumers it is the holistic experience of shopping, dining and entertainment that the mall would offer. Having many stores in a mall along with anchors would enhance the prospects of the total area becoming vibrant with the expansion of the market. A well-planned mall with the desirable tenant mix and the right anchors can create 'agglomeration economies' for the non-anchor tenants. While some may argue that the disadvantage is that each mall store is subjected to more direct competition from competing stores within the mall, it is experienced by more tenants that such competition generally brings more footfalls which result in larger sales for every tenant. Besides, when a cluster of stores compete with each other in the same location, it is easier for the customers to shop in these stores as research has proved the enablement of price and value comparison by customers. The tenant mix is significant for the success of a mall in general and for the holistic success of the mall too, and the anchor stores play a larger role in fulfilling the expected footfalls and conversions. It is, finally, the anchors who enable a homogeneous agglomeration of stores that can appeal to distinctly differentiated target profiles of customers in India.

3. A successful mall will have a strong mall management team which will professionally manage the mall. A strong mall management team will differentiate a good mall from others. Robust professional mall management teams headed by a mall manager assisted by various functional heads such as a finance head, marketing head, HR head, facilities management or projects head and so on are required to manage a mall efficiently. The functional team heads will see that the mall operates efficiently trying to satisfy customer needs and wants. In a mall, the marketing team, for example, plays a very significant role. The marketing team would handle the customer relationship activities of the mall, trying to create customer stickiness to the mall. The marketing team could work on co-promotions along with the tenants in addition to a few cross promotions too across tenants. Another example of professional management can be the jobs executed by the facilities management team of the mall. Good housekeeping, providing the right security services to both the tenants and the customers and maintaining the services of the mall are key functions executed by the team.

THE EMERGENCE OF MALLS IN INDIA

The mall as a retail format has been emerging very rapidly in India. It began long ago, with the advent of 'shopping complexes', where the entire structure assumed a 'build and sell' real estate model. Since the late nineties the actual *Mall* format has been founded — a format which only leases out spaces and manages the mall mix with a professional mall management team. This has led to many retailing companies looking at malls as good retail destinations. Over the last few years malls in India have been very successful and can be compared to those in developed economies. They have contributed to the growth of modern retailing in India, giving global brands the promise of good '*retailable*' space in India.

The emergence of the mall culture in India is a sign of positive development. The availability of key real estate space in future will determine the faster growth of retailing companies that want to expand at a rapid pace. Rapid urbanization coupled with a plethora of infrastructural developments has put many Indian cities on the global market. And Central Business Districts (CBDs) and high-streets in many cities today are not capable of supporting the massive growth plans of retailers and hence retailers look up to the developing malls for fulfilling their expansion plans. By the year 2008, the top eight cities of India alone will have 210 professionally managed malls.

Number of Malls in 2008

City	No. of Malls
Delhi	96
Mumbai	55
Bangalore	14
Chennai	6
Kolkata	10
Hyderabad	12
Pune	19
Ahmedabad	7

Source: *Trent Ltd (Deutsche Bank Research, May 8, 2006)*

The demand for retail spaces has gone up currently in cities like Hyderabad, Mumbai and Delhi as organizations like Reliance, AV Birla Retail, Bharti, Pantaloons Retail and others are interested in booking spaces almost three to four years ahead from now. In doing such advance booking they can have the best rental costs for greater business viability.

NEW MALL CONCEPTS EMERGING IN INDIA

The new concept of seamless mall: The seamless mall as the name suggests is laid out seamlessly without boundaries within the floor plate, which offers direct walk-ins to brands. This is designed in such a way that it helps the brands to attract maximum footfalls and thus greater conversions into sales. The consumer gets to experience the brand in a seamlessly uniform ambience with no boundaries in between. The tenant-mix brands housed in the mall have the opportunity to co-promote and cross-promote themselves through the umbrella management team of the seamless mall. The greater advantage is that though these brands exist inside the seamless mall as different entities, for the customer it appears like a single large department store and not a mall. The customer gets the benefit of seeing and buying all the brands under one seamless store umbrella. Pantaloons Bangalore 'Central' is based on this concept of a seamless mall with the objective to provide a world-class retail experience to customers and brands. Pantaloons through the seamless mall Central is extending the experience beyond just shopping to "Shop, eat and celebrate", the spirit that currently symbolises affluent India. Pantaloons has always been the pioneer in the retail market and with Central they hope to create new benchmarks in mall management.

Specialty Mall: A specialty mall is one that focuses on the depth of a category of merchandise and services. The specialty mall trend started in the National Capital Region, Gurgaon when the Gold Souk opened in the year 2002. The specialty of this mall is that the tenants are jewellers conducting their family business, and also new and upcoming jewellers and reputed international jewellers. This mall is positioned as an exclusive gold mall and has since its opening become a destination for gold shopping. The Gold Souk has more than 100 jewellers having their retail outlets there. A specialty mall pulls customers from various locations, thus becoming a destination for wider catchments. This is one of the factors that have contributed to the success of the specialty mall. For instance, 40% of Gold Souk customers are said to come from even far away places like Simla, Jaipur, Muradabad, Ludhiana, Chandigarh, Jammu, Agra and Meerut and the others from Gurgaon and Delhi. Similarly, there are other upcoming malls focused on category depth like the automobile mall, soon to open in India.

Specialty can be focused on other aspects than that of category. For example, a specialty mall can focus on being a discount mall. The Huma mall in Mumbai houses all the discount stores as tenants. The customer expectations while visiting a mall like Huma mall are around obtaining huge bargains.

The concept of luxury malls is catching up with the times in India. Luxury malls would do well if the location is right in the first place. Second in the order of significance comes the retail brand mix and if this is not in tune with the luxury positioning of the mall, it may see its doom. Any one discordant note in the symphony, which is orchestrated by luxury-profiled services as well, will prove to be a deterrent to the success of luxury malls in India. The mall management team needs to understand the luxury elements of each proposed brand before space is committed to the tenants and this will ensure the success of luxury mall operations in India. Mall management teams should not be in a hurry to clinch deals without understanding the DNA of each retail brand as such hurry will lead malls into a state of despair. Luxury malls must do thorough research on both their tenant mix and the customer profiles at the mall planning stage itself in order to ensure grand success.

CUSTOMER PERCEPTION OF MALLS IN INDIA

The mall phenomenon is changing the way people shop and the way they look for entertainment for the family in India. Malls in India are becoming the single-point destinations for food, shopping and entertainment. Malls have been revolutionizing retailing that is leading to a significant increase in consumption spending. Customers in India are enjoying the environs of the malls as they provide opportunities for fun and entertainment besides shopping and dining. In India we have nuclear families and malls address all the needs of the family members irrespective of their demographic differences. More than 50% of India's population is less than 25 years of age currently and hence malls focus on teenage and youth segments largely with appropriate offerings in all categories. Malls are perceived to be great places to visit, do a good deal of walking around along with shopping and dining or visiting the multiplex in the mall. Many malls come with multiple screens in the multiplex format offering the movie entertainment which is very popular in India. So, malls are perceived to be a one-stop destination for family entertainment and for enjoying the fun of shopping and eating out. In the urban areas the frequency of visits to malls is increasing and in the case of many affluent families the frequency of visit to a mall is almost once a week. As mall development would happen in tier two and tier three towns, we can expect to see a similar trend there too. Earlier, many were of the opinion that malls have more footfalls and fewer conversions into business, but this is being addressed by mall management teams effectively ensuring the availability of merchandise and services at the right price points following the needs in specific locations.

FACILITIES MANAGEMENT IN MALLS

For malls, outsourcing facilities management (FM) of the premises seems to be the best possible way to ensure cleanliness, good maintenance and proper security both for customers and the tenants. The route that most of the malls in India are adopting these days is outsourcing. Many facilities management companies offer a comprehensive range of industrial and commercial housekeeping, security and maintenance services, which are designed to match the requirements of malls, and customized as per their client's specifications. In developed markets, facilities management is closely integrated with property management services that include rent collections, lease management as well as event management, in some cases. Maintaining the landscaping in malls or the parking spaces also would fall under the purview of facilities management in malls. However in India, for the industry as a whole, the concept of facilities management has not matured enough to provide complete property management solutions.

Parking Spaces in Malls

The ratio of parking to the area of the mall in developed economies is 6 car parking spaces for every 1000 square feet of space. For a mall of 200,000 square feet, there needs to be a provision for 1200 parking spaces. Inadequate parking spaces and insufficient requirement stipulations render a good deal of inconveniences to customers who come driving into the Indian malls. Walkways, crosswalks, decorative paving, stop signs for cars, and landscaping are needed to allow ease of walking through the parking spaces of malls. Needless to say that a mall has to provide for an adequate number of spaces exclusively reserved for handicapped drivers for their convenience of parking. Currently in India no local zoning rules stipulate such parking space norms for malls. Many in India for a long time did not own cars and they were using alternative modes of transport like the public transport system, either by road or rail. In addition to this, off site parking spaces were available for parking, such as private parking spaces and those maintained by the local governments for a paltry fee. Hence in India we did not have stringent requirements for parking regulations. But in the last few years the scenario has changed. With developments taking place largely, it's high time we in India had such regulations for the benefit of offering customer convenience.

THE REASONS RESPONSIBLE FOR THE FAILURE OF SOME MALLS IN INDIA

The reasons for the failure of some malls in India are specific to each mall, and one needs to study those in detail to address them. In general terms if the mall's retail tenant mix is not coordinated well to match the target customer profile, it is bound to meet with failure. As mentioned earlier, any successful mall needs to have a strong mall management team who can coordinate and synergistically leverage the strength of all the tenants to design strategic programmes to increase footfalls, conversion, up-selling and cross-selling! The credibility of the mall developer is very important, as there should never be an opportunity for any gap to exist between promises and delivery. In India mall spaces are booked a few years in advance and in this scenario, the reputation of the developer to deliver what was promised to the retailer at the time of booking is very important.

The mall culture has just begun to evolve in India and is here to stay. As customers are evolving in a growing economy like ours, malls will redefine the landscape of modern retailing in India. In future, as such consumer developments take place in India our traditional malls will give way to malls that become "lifestyle centres". As trends will change, fashions will change and consumer attitudes will change along with the availability of good retail spaces in malls in India, mall retailing has a good future.

Summary

- The mall is a very successfully emerging retail destination format in India. A few key characteristics determine the mall format and they have to be adhered to while developing a mall in India.

- The new concepts of seamless mall and specialty mall are evolving rapidly, carving their own niches, and these key innovative concepts will help draw the right footfalls while offering a delightful experience to the target customers.

- Malls are perceived to be great places to visit, do a good deal of walking around along with shopping and dining. The young customer population enjoys hanging around in a mall.

- Facilities like good housekeeping, security, maintenance, parking management, enabling a disabled-friendly environment are the key aspects of professional mall management.

- Malls have a good future in India provided they are managed professionally.

Questions:

1. Explain the key features of a professionally managed mall.

2. What are the key roles of anchor stores in a mall?

3. What are the new concepts of malls emerging in India?

4. What are the various customer perceptions of a mall in India?

5. Explain how facilities management is important to a professionally managed mall.

Indian Malls: Key Characteristics

Jones Lang LaSalle Meghraj, International Property Consultants recently conducted a study on the product mix and corresponding rental returns from a typical retail mall development in India. The percentage break-up and comparison between areas and their respective returns to the mall developers in all the categories of products can be understood from the table and graph, which have been averaged out by considering:

1. Inorbit and Phoenix malls in Mumbai,

2. Forum mall in Bangalore,

3. Forum mall in Kolkata and

4. Sahara mall in NCR (National Capital Region)

Tenant Mix	Lease Rentals	% Area Occupied
Hypermarket	7.25%	14.49%
Departmental Store	14.49%	21.43%
F&B (Including Food courts)	10.14%	8.57%
Multiplex	5.07%	8.57%
Entertainment	1.55%	2.29%
Apparel	26.09%	17.14%
Shoes	4.35%	2.86%
Books & Music	1.93%	2.29%
Furniture	4.35%	2.14%
Jewellery	4.83%	2.86%
Impulse	4.11%	2.86%
Miscellaneous	15.85%	11.71%
Total	100.00%	100.00%

Tenant Mix (% break-up of area occupied in a typical retail mall)

% Break-up of returns from lease rentals in a typical retail mall in India

It was observed that the anchor components, comprising hypermarket, departmental store and multiplex in the operational Indian malls occupy approximately 44% of the total mall area, whilst the balance is occupied by small format retail shops of various categories. While the anchors occupying 44% of mall space contribute 27% to mall rentals, the small format retailers occupying 66% contribute nearly 73%.

Therefore in principle, the contribution of the smaller retailers to mall rentals is relatively higher than the anchors' collective contribution.

However, the lease rentals paid by anchor tenants are much lower compared to that paid by small format retailers since the anchors occupy large space and hence, can command discount on the lease rental. It would hence not be entirely inappropriate to say that although the anchor tenants help in attracting footfalls, it is really the other tenant categories that are profitable for the mall developer. Having said this, it is because of having secured anchor tenants that the mall developer can command more lease rentals from these smaller format retail tenants.

Also the responsibility of the anchors is to bring with them a major brand creating a landmark for attraction of footfalls. Further, anchors in India, book the spaces before the other tenants during the pre-construction phase.

What would be the future for anchor tenants?

Globally, in malls such as at Blue Waters in the UK and Deira City Center in Dubai, anchors get discounted rent space and at times free for the first three years of their long lease tenure. Jones Lang LaSalle believes that the mall rentals for anchors in the future will continue to decline and in areas where there are a large number of malls, as is the case in Gurgaon, anchors will be invited to take positions in malls at nominal rentals. According to Jones Lang LaSalle, if the international experience is to be considered, mall developers, state authorities might end up even paying an anchor to entice to stay on in a mall. They say that in December 2004 Cincinnati city in the USA paid retailer Saks Fifth Avenue $6.6 million to stay in the 483.000-square-foot Tower Place.

Jones Lang LaSalle foresees that the same will happen in India eventually.

Major Malls in India

Select Citywalk, New Delhi: Opened in October 2007, Select Citywalk is a 1.3 million sq. ft. mixed use development comprising of a shopping mall, a multiplex, serviced apartments, offices and public spaces. The mall was developed by Select Infrastructure, a joint venture between the Select group and the Aarone group. The mall just opened to the public in October 2007. The mall is divided into three broad zones — staple traditional (family), celebration (centre-stage) and high voltage (youth). There are eight anchor tenants including Goodearth Verandah, Pantaloons, Crossword Bookstore, Mothercare, Arcelia, and Home Stop. The mall also has 125 stores representing many major international brands of clothes and apparels including Mango, Esprit, Tommy Hilfiger, French Connection, Replay, Guess, Levi's, United Colors of Benetton, Next, Aldo, La Senza, MAC, Clinique, and The Body Shop. The mall has a multi-cuisine food court, Food Talk, along with several restaurants including The Coffee Bean & Tea Leaf, Cocoa By Belgique, Geoffrey's, Spaghetti Kitchen, and Gelatto Vittorio. It is also home to a 6-screen PVR Cinemas multiplex, which will be opening soon. There is also a 100,000 sq ft outdoor open plaza, Sanskriti, for art festivals, fairs, exhibitions, performances, and al fresco dining.

Inorbit Mall, Mumbai: Inorbit Mall belongs to the K. Raheja Corp (the group that has majority stakes in Shoppers' Stop and owns Hypercity), and is situated in Malad, Mumbai. The mall is well planned and spread over a sprawling 0.5 million square feet of space. It houses over 300 of the best Indian and international brands. The spaces are well zoned. The gaming zone comprises more than 100 games. The huge car park that the mall has can accommodate 1500 cars. A large food-court serves a variety of cuisines. Inorbit mall is one of the country's large retail destinations offering exciting experiences to the customers in terms of shopping, dining and entertainment. Inorbit mall's footfalls on an average are 25000 per day during weekdays and 50000 per day during weekends. The mall provides world class infrastructure and services and ensures that every customer need is met. Inorbit has opened its new mall in Vashi, a suburb of Mumbai. Inorbit's expansion into Hyderabad is expected to happen soon. The Inorbit mall was chosen The Mall of The Year 2005 both by KSA-Technopak and by Images Retail Awards.

The Forum Mall, Bangalore: The Forum Mall is from the Prestige Group of Bangalore. The mall has revolutionized the concept of modern retailing in Bangalore perhaps leading to the new experiential concept of 'Retailment'! Located at Koramangala in Bangalore, a prosperous and high density catchment area and a mere 10 minutes' drive from Brigade Road, the mall is built on four and half acres of main road abutting land. The mall measures about 0.65 million sq.ft. of shopping space, offering a multi-brand bonanza with top global levels, wooing and attracting shoppers. The Forum is a place one can go to for almost anything one wants to buy. The mall has everything from shoes to exercise equipment, from home furnishings to electronic goods, from books to video games! The anchor stores are Landmark which houses everything from soft toys to office stationery to CDs and Westside, which is from the Tata Group. One can indulge one's taste buds at Transit, KFC, Pizza Hut or the forever crowded McDonald's, the first one in the South. With its huge food court and eclectic cuisines, it can cater to almost every taste bud in the world! Global brands like Soch, Ishis, Mustard, Weekender, Provogue and Benetton succeed in bringing contemporary world fashions to Bangalore and its beautiful people. The Forum mall deserves the credit for being the first one to bring the world renowned brand of Tommy Hilfiger to South India. The Forum houses a multiplex, PVR, with 11 screens showing the latest movies — all this with stadium seating, wall-to-wall screens and mind blowing sound. The mall's facilities management systems include close circuit security, computerized parking management systems, ATM machines, 100% generator backup and a state-of-the-art housekeeping plan. The Forum has become a landmark in the city and the Prestige Group has plans of opening up another Forum at a new township in Bangalore, the Prestige Shantiniketan. The group is also planning to build the Forum Value Mall in Whitefields, Bangalore, soon.

Questions for Discussion

1. Discuss the findings of the Jones Lang LaSalle Meghraj study on the space occupied by anchors and their revenue contribution in Indian malls.

2. Why are anchor tenants considered imporant to a mall's success?

3. Write short notes on three major malls in India.

CHAPTER 6

Retail Strategies

CHAPTER OBJECTIVES

1. To explain in detail the strategic areas that retailers need to focus on to emerge as winners
2. To explain the bases upon which a retailer can build a sustainable advantage
3. To detail the strategic approaches of various retailing organizations in India
4. To examine how strategic planning can help build the retail business

A retail organization must have a clear strategy and a competitive edge over other retailers in order to emerge as a winner. In retailing there are three generic strategies to get a competitive advantage. But first, it should:

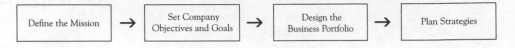

Develop a Mission Statement: It must set out what it hopes to accomplish in each market.

Set Company Objectives: It is essential for the organization to set objectives and goals so that it moves in a clear direction, both in the short term and in the long run.

Design the Business Portfolio: This comprises the collection of businesses and products that make up the company.

Plan Strategies: The retail firm needs to plan its strategies to achieve its mission.

In retailing, there are three generic strategies to acquire competitive advantage. They are based on getting an edge in the following three dimensions:

➢ Operational Excellence.
➢ Product Differentiation.
➢ Customer Intimacy.

Operational Excellence: This is achieved when all the operating processes of the retail organization are well-defined and it is able to satisfy customers in a progressive and a cost-effective manner. The organization can attain operational excellence if it sets for itself — and achieves — high standards in its area of operations. For instance, McDonalds in Mumbai claims that it can deliver the order before the hour glass runs out; the customer service associate keeps track of the process time, from when the order is taken to the time it is delivered. There needs to be high operational standards and quick delivery processes to achieve this operational excellence.

Product Differentiation: The product differentiation strategy comes into play when there is product innovation, or when the merchandise has unique characteristics exclusive to the retail organization. For instance, the ready-to-wear garment retailer Westside has merchandised its stores with its private label brands, unique to its stores. Sheetal Design Studio has a 'creator' for its designer merchandise, with Hemant Trevedi designing exclusively for the store.

Pricing Strategy: Differentiation by a distinctive offering of merchandise

PRICE

QUALITY		HIGH	MEDIUM	LOW
	HIGH	(1) Premium Strategy	(2) High-value Strategy	(3) Super-value Strategy (loss leader)
	MEDIUM	(4) Over charging Strategy	(5) Medium-value Strategy	(6) Good-value Strategy
	LOW	(7) Rip-Off Strategy	(8) False economy Strategy	(9) Economy Strategy

can also be done through an effective pricing strategy. Pricing does a great deal for the retailer. For instance, the retail store may be able to increase its footfalls with a leader pricing strategy or it may provide value for customers with a loss leader pricing strategy. Loss leader pricing means selling merchandise or some of the merchandise at cost or near cost for promotional purposes to attract customers and establish a 'low-price' reputation. Developing the pricing strategy, hence, is critical to a retail organization. It may have a high, medium or low pricing strategy as shown in the chart above.

Customer Intimacy: A progressive customer service strategy creates the 'stickiness' with the store so that customers visit it repeatedly. This is one area where every retailer yearns to achieve the highest standards.

Many retail organizations have customer relationship management (CRM) programmes that help them find out about their customers' purchase patterns. This also enables them to design a comprehensive benefit package for them. Retail organizations like Shoppers' Stop have used customer loyalty programmes with success, increasing their active base of consumers and delivering innovative benefit plans for them. They also focus on getting a larger share of sales from the loyal base of consumers.

Customer intimacy helps in achieving differentiation when the retail organization exceeds the expected levels of customer service. For example, in a Nordstrom retail store, the customer care associate needs to 'take

Fig. 5: *Strategies to achieve competitive advantage*

permission' from the higher-ups if he or she has to say 'no' to a customer.

Store Location Strategy: It is a popular saying in the retailing industry that the three success factors of a retail store are Location, Location and Location. The retail organization should plan its location strategy carefully. For instance, if it is located in high-streets, where the cost of real estate may be high, it will need to sell more. Destination locations on the other hand may be suitable for large formats or for formats that have an exclusively pulling product mix. Such destinations may be less expensive in terms of lease rentals but there may be more marketing costs involved for generating footfalls and conversions. Sometimes retailers may decide to relocate stores as new markets develop, or may move into malls as mall partners to avail of the ready footfalls available there.

Growth Strategies

Market Entry Strategy: Setting up a store will depend on the geographic markets the organization wishes to be in. An organization needs to plan its market entry strategy very carefully, testing the concept and studying the target market's response patterns and entry barriers if any.

There may be entry barriers while expanding to a particular town. One entry barrier for a woman's western wear store in a town away from the metros' influences, for instance, may be the strong conservative attitudes that is pervasive in India.

Retailers plan their entry or expansion strategy according to the Market Potential Value (MPV) readily available for all Indian cities and towns. Then a focused research is done on those specific markets where the organization plans to enter or expand its retail presence.

Market Expansion Strategy

Market Penetration: Market penetration refers to selling more in current customer markets without changing products. The strategy may be to add new stores in the current market areas, improve advertising, prices, service, store presentation, etc. An appropriate example is the expansion of Shoppers' Stop department stores in Mumbai; the company has just opened its fifth large format outlet in the suburb of Mulund.

Market Development: Market development refers to developing new markets for current products. Retailers like Pantaloons and Food World explore new markets to set up stores.

Product Range Development: This involves offering modified or new products to current markets. McDonalds, for instances, constantly changes its product offerings to suit the Indian palate — like 'tikki' burgers!

Diversification: This involves having new retail formats for new markets. Pantaloons has a diversified format in Big Bazaar, which is a separate business altogether. It has helped the organization foray into many new markets.

However, strategic retailing depends upon the specific nature of merchandise categories and services and the target profile of the organization's customers. Some organizations look at gaining a first-mover advantage by entering a city or a town with their organized retail format for the first time. Large format department stores like Shoppers' Stop or Westside cannot expand so fast into other cities and towns like a small chain format like Music World or Barista. Small formats achieve their scale of operations only when they have a large number of stores. Robust retail strategies with such dynamic plans have always helped retail organizations forge ahead.

SUMMARY

- A retail organization has to develop a clear strategy for its various functional areas of operations and create strategic plans based on its mission and objectives.
- Strategic planning helps in developing and maintaining a fit between the organization's goals and capabilities and changing opportunities.
- Robust retail strategic planning provides many benefits such as encouraging the firm to think ahead systematically and helping teams coordinate internally to achieve the desired performance standards. Besides it also helps the organization to respond quickly to environmental changes and sudden developments.
- Revisiting strategies after evaluating performance and opportunities is significant in a dynamic market scenario.

Questions:

1. Define the retail strategic planning process and its four steps.

2. Explain 'Operational Excellence' with a suitable example.

3. Product differentiation is a definite means of attaining leadership in

retailing. Discuss with a suitable illustration.

4. With an appropriate example, explain how customer intimacy can be a differentiating factor in retailing.

5. Discuss the factors that impact the location strategy of a retail organization.

6. Write notes on the growth strategies that can be applied for a retail store/organization.

CASELET: BOBCAT

Bobcat India Limited revolutionized footwear selling in India. The company hit upon the idea of reaching customers through exclusive retail stores way back in 1932 and set up its own outlets, which numbered around 1,200. It was no mean task setting up such a large network of retail outlets, especially when 90% of them were owned and operated by the company, the rest being dealer-owned and operated. This chain store format identity has been a strong differentiating factor in the Indian retail sector, being the first of its kind. Combined with the high quality of the footwear, the brand soon had top-of-the-mind recall and stayed there for many years. Until a few years ago, the name 'Bobcat' was synonymous with organized retailing in India, the only one of its kind.

The Chain Store Format

The Bobcat chain store format had its own credo — a signature store-design with exclusive signage and windows in order to facilitate easy association in the minds of the Indian consumers.

At present there are only two major categories of stores in the Bobcat Chain Store format:
(a) Bobcat Family Stores
(b) Bobcat Bazaar

(a) Bobcat Family Stores

These are sub-divided into two formats again, based on the size of the stores. They are:
  (i) Super Stores, generally more than 5,000 sq.ft. catering to customers in the footwear category.

(ii) High-street stores that are anywhere between 500 and 1,500 sq.ft., found in busy shopping areas.

(b) Bobcat Bazaar

Bobcat Bazaar stores sell the company's planned economy product lines and marked down merchandise round the year. Known as R-Pair stores, their performance depends heavily upon the availability of marked-down merchandise. Such markdowns are done on products that have suffered quality accidents, are shop-soiled, lines that are closed-out etc.

Recent Format Developments

New retail formats have begun to supersede conventional ones. Independent big-box multi-brand department stores have started selling footwear as a category, especially in metros and cities. Malls are another new shopping format that is growing rapidly in the metros. Many upcoming footwear retailers are obtaining space inside the malls as mall partners to take advantage of the ready footfalls available. For the existing independent Bobcat stores it is expensive now to run campaigns and promotions to attain the required footfalls and expected conversions.

Merchandising in Bobcat Family Stores

The exclusivity of the 'Bobcat' brand to the Bobcat retail stores was the differentiating factor for customers until recently. However, a few years ago the company decided to sell Bobcat branded goods through its channel sales wing called Bobcat Wholesale. Hitherto, the wholesale channel had a different brand for itself called BSC. This wholesale channel supplies merchandise to footwear retailers across India through its authorized distributors. The brand Bobcat has now been extended to this wholesale channel too, which means that Bobcat branded goods are available in every other local footwear store. The exclusivity of the brand to its own outlets has come to an end. And, even as the sales of the wholesale division remain stagnant, what compelling reasons can a customer have to visit a Bobcat Store now? A peculiar feature of the Bobcat store was its odd price points: Rs 149.95, 199.95, etc.

Merchandise Presentation and Visual Merchandising

Bobcat pioneered the concept of show window displays in India with a style that was unique to the company. It was professionally managed, with an exclusive team handling the motif and the design. Every month the direction to decorate the show windows were given by a mailer prepared by special decorators. Sales personnel in each store were trained to be window decorators too. Recently, these windows had to be done away with because the company thought that they should follow the contemporary practice of free-access retailing, where all merchandise pairs are displayed in open shelves to enable customers to help themselves. Remember, in India footwear is always tried on a footstool and bought after considerable service extended by the salesperson personally.

Free-access retailing may work when there is adequate space inside a store to move around. The effect of such 'pigeon-hole' free access is that they give an impression that they are Bobcat's R-Pair outlets. What can now entice the customer into entering a Bobcat store?

Customer Service

Though Bobcat faces tough manpower challenges (the store sales personnel and managers have separate labour unions), the sales personnel who are on its permanent rolls are trained in selling footwear. However, there is a large proportion of untrained temporary hands. Further, salespersons do not wear any uniform and hence customers can hardly identify them. There is as yet no loyalty programme to create customer stickiness to any store or the brand, and most of the stores are not connected by a central information system or ERP (enterprise-wide resource planning) as the organization has its limitations when it comes to investing in such initiatives. Organized retail companies need to have non-negotiable standards of customer service or they will lose customers to its competitors.

The company is now losing its market share despite its strong position in categories like men's footwear, children's uniform shoes, etc. However, the number of stores it has around the country is around the same, at 1,200. The company now needs to put together a plan for both its survival and growth on a war footing. The top management is revisiting its strategies in every functional area to turn the company around.

Questions for Discussion

1. What store format mix would you recommend for the company?

2. Did the company do the right thing by extending the in-store brand to the wholesale channel? What should it do now?

3. What course should the company take in the area of merchandise presentation and visual merchandising?

4. What would you recommend to improve customer service in the stores?

5. Should the organization plan a customer loyalty programme now?

6. Can Bobcat recover its leadership status in retailing in terms of its differentiating capabilities? Discuss.

CHAPTER 7

Store Planning, Design and Layout

· **CHAPTER OBJECTIVES**

1. To highlight the process of store planning, including identifying and selecting the right location
2. To list the elements of a few location and site assessment formats that can help as decision-making tools
3. To explain in detail the elements of store design and the retail image mix that help consumers relate to these stores
4. To provide an insight into effective retail space management
5. To take the reader through the store layout applications in retailing
6. To enable the reader to understand store circulation plans thoroughly
7. To provide an effective methodology to measure or audit retail space performance

STORE PLANNING

An important feature of store planning is location planning followed by site selection. It is the method of selecting the right location and an appropriate site for the store with the catchment definition for each store. The rollout plan defines the types of locations selected on the basis of the retail store format.

LOCATION PLANNING — TYPES OF LOCATIONS

(A) High-Street Location:
   a. Very busy with high customer traffic.
   b. Has an array of retail stores in small sizes.
   c. Has stores that are generally found in clusters based on product categories.
   d. High real-estate rentals.

Examples: Linking Road in Bandra, Mumbai, Brigade Road in Bangalore.

(B) Destination/Freestanding Location:
   a. Does not have high footfall rate (customer traffic needs to be pulled in through the store's marketing efforts or product/service/process differentiations).
   b. May not be a commercial retail area at all.
   c. Low real-estate rentals.
   d. May have large parking area.

Examples: Phoenix Mills Compound and Shoppers' Stop in Mumbai.

(C) Shopping Centre/Mall Location:
   a. Has existing mall traffic.
   b. Has a clean environment.
   c. Has a designated parking area.
   d. Medium to high rental cost.

Examples: DLF Mall in Delhi, Spencer Plaza in Chennai, Crossroads in Mumbai.

Location Mapping: While planning the location strategy for the retail organization is significant, it is also imperative to map the locations so that the extent of each store's reach to the customers is well defined.

Location Parameters: It is necessary to define the store location identification parameters in a format and see if the desired attributes are available.

Site Selection

Site selection in retailing refers to the type of building the retailer needs and its affordability. Retailers should decide whether they should own the property, lease the premises on rent or have a joint venture with the landlord. Site selection depends on the nature of the building, façade requirements, size requirements and costs. The site selection format is furnished below as a specimen.

Address of the property	
Details of adjacent occupants – north, east, west, south	
Can the site be used commercially?	
Name & address of the title holder	
Is the site free of encumbrance?	
Are all relevant taxes paid and currently up to date?	
Is the site free of any civil suit?	
When was the building constructed?	
Total number of floors	
Other prominent facilities nearby	
Details of facilities space / parking space	
Revenue details / rate per sq.ft. / details of built-up to carpet space ratio / terms of contract (if JV or lease)	

Fig. 6: *Detailed Site Selection Parameters*

LOCATION SELECTION FORM

Area: _____

Locality: _____

Nearby major landmark: _____

Detailed Description of the premises:

Commercial/residential/ high-street/mall/complex/ retail destination outlet (specify)	
Total number of offices/ buildings within a 50 to 100 metre radius	
Total number of offices/ buildings within a 100 to 200 metre radius	
Any general store/ kirana/supermarket etc. within a one-km radius	
Any general store/ kirana/supermarket etc. within a 2-km radius	
Any competitors in the premises or nearby Yes/No	

Detailed description of the building/location

Total number of floors	
Other prominent occupants	
Number of employees visiting companies/ offices in the catchment of 1 km	
Number of flats/residents in a catchment of 1 km.	

Fig. 7: *Location Selection Format (for a Supermarket)*

Customer Flow:

During Weekdays:			
	Residents/ People in transit	Students	Professionals	Others Please Specify
Lean Period				
Medium Period				
Peak Period				

During Weekends:			
	Residents/ People in transit	Students	Professionals	Others Please Specify
Lean Period				
Medium Period				
Peak Period				
Total no. of footfalls expected				
Total no. of conversion into purchase expected in terms of %age				
Total estimated sales per day in that area				
Average expected value of purchase per customer				
Terms & Conditions discussed				

Prepared by:-   Approved by:-

Fig. 8: *Customer Flow Chart*

STORE DESIGN AND THE RETAILING IMAGE MIX

The needs of customers who go to a local grocer differ from those who visit a specialty goods retail outlet or a department store. Each retailer strategically plans a mix of elements to match the needs of his customer. A mix of the following six elements meet the physical and emotional needs of the customer:

(1) *Employee Type and Density:* The retailer employs sales staff to match the selling and image needs of his store. A specialty store like one selling saris will have a higher density of staff at about one per 100 sft and the salesperson would be one who caters to the needs of the customer — speak the local language and look more homely (as the customers are mostly women). In contrast, in a large department store the density of staff would be one per 400 sft. They will be well educated and suitably dressed (in most cases in western clothes as these form a major chunk of the store offering).

(2) *Merchandise Type and Density:* The type of merchandise determines its density in the store. A supermarket is very dense and averages about 8,000 pieces per 100 sft whereas a large department store would have about 750 pieces per 100 sft. A designer-wear exclusive store, a boutique or a furniture retailer would have low density so as to make the merchandise appear exclusive.

The density of merchandise also determines the margins planned on the merchandise. The lower the density the higher the margins.

(3) *Fixture Type and Density:* The fixtures have to complement the value of the merchandise. A jeweller uses a lot of expensive woodwork and stones like marble and granite to add value to his merchandise, while a sportswear goods store uses more of metal and plastic.

The density of fixtures is measured as the number of fixtures per 100 sft of store space. This should complement the density of the merchandise as it has a big impact on the convenience of shopping.

(4) *Sound Type and Density:* Sound can be pleasant or unpleasant and can have a direct impact on the store atmosphere. A pleasant sound, like music in a department store or the sound of the balls rolling and pins falling in a bowling alley adds to the intensity of the experience. An unpleasant sound like motor traffic or the roar of jet planes, on the other hand, can have a negative effect. The category of the merchandise determines the type and density of sound. Soft

instrumental music is usually used in jewellery and cosmetics while the casuals and youth fashionwear segments are complemented by contemporary sound tracks from new bands. Department stores play music based on the category of merchandise.

(5) *Odour Type and Density:* Like sound, odour too has a positive or negative effect on the store atmosphere. Positive odours like that of fresh coffee beans or flowers add to the shopping experience in the men's wear and cosmetics departments in a store. Negative odours like those of a musty carpet, cigarette smoke, etc. can drive the customer away. The strength of the odour is also important and even the right odour if it's too strong can have a negative effect.

(6) *Visual Type and Factors:* These are a result of the overall store presentation — the interior design, display and visual merchandising. Elements like lighting and colour can be controlled to make customers buy more. Warm yellow shades of lights complement gold jewellery as they add richness. Natural shades (daylight colours) are good for garments as they bring out the true colour of the merchandise. Warm colours like bright red or yellow are said to increase the pulse rate in human beings and trigger impulse purchases (FMCG goods use this effectively). Softer colours like pastels keep the pulse rate comfortable

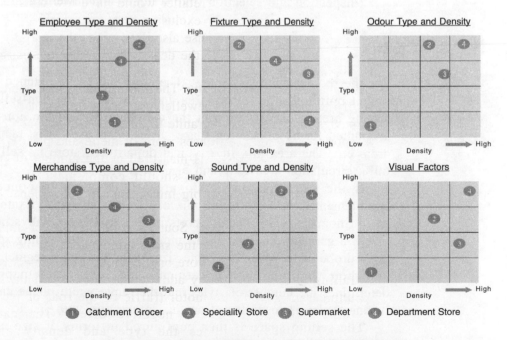

Fig. 9: *Store Image Attributes — Type & Density Model*

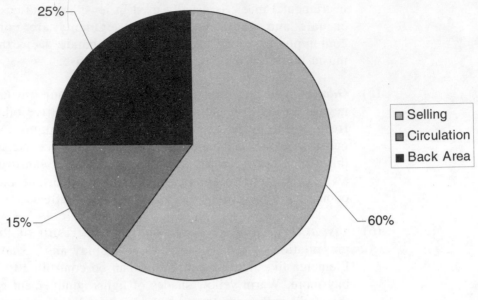

Fig. 10: *Area Mix*

and are used in merchandise backdrops that need a longer time for inspection and selection (like watches and jewellery).

THE SPACE MIX

For the retailer space is money. The store has to be planned in such a way that it optimizes the selling area and minimizes the non-selling parts. The selling area is used to present the merchandise and the non-selling part is accounted for by circulation space, aisles, staircases, lifts, facilities, the back area, etc. The area mix in a typical department store is: selling area about 60%, circulation area 15% and back area 25%.

If the store has any extra area, it is given to concessionaires to complement the store offering mix and to de-risk space. Examples are Planet M in Shoppers' Stop, Planet Sports in Piramyd and Qwikys in Lifestyle.

In a garment retail store, planning the size of the selling space starts with a wardrobe audit where a sample size of the customer segment is intercepted and their wardrobe mix of garments and accessories mapped. This then determines the number of styles and the range width of the category. Then a business plan is made based on this integration with space.

The selling space is then configured in terms of size and location of goods based on the mix of staple, convenience and impulse merchandise.

Staple goods are the core USP of the store. These constitute about 55% of the store offering and are kept at the central and deeper ends of the store. This enhances visibility, since the customer has to pass through the entire store to reach them. The shirts and trousers section in department stores form the staple merchandise. Similarly, grains and sugar are the staples in a supermarket.

Convenience goods are no-fuss basic merchandise that constitute about 30% of the store and are bought in multiple units. These need to be in convenient locations in the store to ensure conversions. Undergarments and white basic cotton T-shirts in a department store are convenience merchandise.

Impulse purchase merchandise — which usually constitutes about 15% of the store and has the highest rate of sale — is given maximum exposure in order to tempt the customer into buying them. Candies in a supermarket and socks and hair accessories in a fashion store are impulse purchase items and are kept near the cash counters and entrances/exits. The customer picks them up after shopping for convenience and staple merchandise. The locations of various goods are chosen carefully to ensure that the customer is exposed to the entire store, thus increasing the possibility of a purchase.

Talking about space management and optimization in a retail store, Ajay Mehra, CEO, Fun Cinemas, says: "Space management does not end with just optimization, but has a much larger opportunity for merchandise promotion and display which not only can bring profit for a retail organization but entertain and delight customers too."

EFFECTIVE RETAIL SPACE MANAGEMENT

The sight of a good retail store with attractive windows and an enticing entrance induce the customer into entering. The customer enters the store and often keeps walking inside following the walkway wherever it leads, or sometimes takes a while to look for directions within the store. Sometimes the customer's attention is drawn to certain displays and merchandise presentations before he moves on. To reach his destination inside the store, the customer tends to follow directions to reach there, especially in a big-box format. Seldom does he realize that subconsciously he is directed to 'walk' the entire store and thus exposing him to all that the store has to offer. This is achieved through a well thought-out and laid-out retail floor design.

A well-planned and properly designed retail floor achieves a great deal for the store:

(a) It enables a smooth and efficient customer flow into the store and within it. The design of the fixtures, the placement of merchandise and the fixtures on the floor too direct customers through the store.

(b) It helps the customer reach and access the merchandise he is looking for, without fail.

(c) It helps create a feeling of comfort in the minds of customers, enabling them to waltz their way through without facing any bottlenecks on the way. (It is said that generally the customer, while walking through the retail floor, thinks of the benefits he is going to get from his prospective purchase and feels happy about the right choice he is currently making).

(d) The aesthetics of a well-planned floor are a visual feast for the customer and trigger the 'come-back' feeling in him, as he feels a sense of belonging in the store.

(e) A well laid-out floor, in essence, helps the store to sell more effectively and retain customers.

Effective retail floor space management is critical to the successful operation of a retail store, as more and more sales from the same space would lead to increased margins for the organization. According to R. Sriram, former MD & CEO of Crossword: "Space planning is integral to the success of any retail store since the biggest investment in retail is in space."

Let us now look at the ground rules for effective floor space planning and management. At the same time, let us get an insight into the customers' physical and emotional needs that contribute to store design conceptualization and space planning.

STORE LAYOUT: THE CIRCULATION PLAN (THE "SILENT GUIDE")

Once inside the store, the customer needs to be guided silently to where he/she wants to go and also expose him/her to the entire store offering. This can be achieved by planning the circulation and the location of the merchandise.

While designing store layout, circulation planning is done to lead the customer from area to area with the help of aisles that weave through the merchandise area. Focal points highlighted with accent lighting and displays strategically placed along the aisles pull the customer from section to section in a 'Pinball Effect'. A series of these ensure that the customer is silently guided through the entire store.

The width of the aisles is planned according to the density and traffic pattern. The main aisle or 'highway' in a department store is six feet wide,

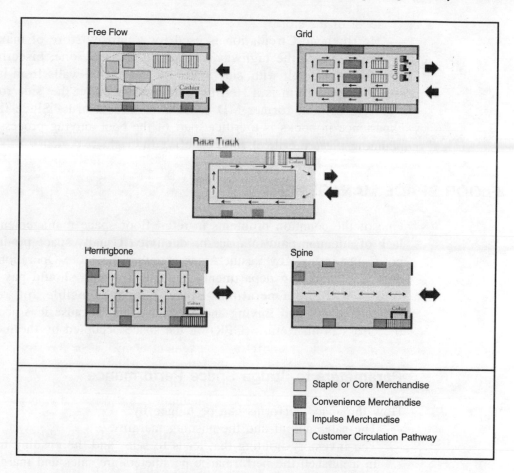

Fig. 11: *Store Layout & Circulation Plan*

which is the width of a double doorway, and facilitates easy passage in both directions. The side aisles or 'side roads' that branch out are three to four feet wide. In supermarkets, the aisles are three feet wide and form a denser grid around the fixtures.

The aisles form a circulation pattern that can be of different types depending on the store configuration. The area occupied by the aisles is normally 12-15% of the store carpet area. Some of the layout circulation types used are Free Flow, Grid, Race Track, Herringbone and Spine.

— Free Flow Circulation is used in stores where the merchandise and fixtures are grouped in clusters as in boutiques.

— Grid Circulation is used typically in a supermarket where the aisles and fixtures are at right angles to each other.

— Race Track Circulation is used in larger and wider stores where the customer is made to circle around the floor and get back to the beginning, usually the lift or the staircase lobby, to move to the next

level of the store.
— Herringbone Circulation is used for a narrow store of maximum 40 ft width where the highway is a single two-way one, bisecting the store along its length with 'side roads' leading to the walls from it.
— The Spine form is a Herringbone layout without the 'side roads'.
Says Sriram, former MD & CEO of Crossword: "Since the browsing experience in books is a critical part of the book-buying process, circulation planning plays a critical role, enabling the right experience."

FLOOR SPACE MANAGEMENT

One of the common problems in retail floor space management in India is lack of attention paid to space productivity. Usually space productivity does not figure in the Key Result Areas of either the Store Operations or Buying and Merchandising departments. But ideally both should pay attention to this area. Store Operations, since it is responsible for reorders and replenishments, and Buying and Merchandising because it is accountable for the Gross Profit Return (GPR) on the space occupied by the merchandise.

Parameters to Judge Space Performance

How the space performs can be judged by:
— The sales output and the ensuing margins.
— The inventory holding that leads to sales and the ensuing margins.
In a nutshell the performance parameters are sales and margins and their direct relationship to the stock holding on the retail floor.

- Sales per square foot, or top-line plan (sales): Here, space productivity is measured by sales volumes and value achieved per square foot per day.
- Margins per square foot, or bottom-line plan (gross margin returns on footage, or GMROF): Here, space productivity is determined by gross margins earned per square foot per day.
- Stock-holding per square foot, or bottom-line tool (gross margin returns on inventory, or GMROI): Here, space productivity is determined by the average inventory holding per square foot per day and how it measures against the ideal level of stock holding planned for a designated space in the store. Stock-turns in such designated space play a vital role in earning good revenue returns on the space occupied when they are optimized.

This space performance measurement can be done for any of the rungs in the SKU hierarchy: a department/division, a category/class, a sub-category/

sub-class, a brand and even for any style or size options.

Says G.S.M. Ghaznavi, former Senior Vice-President (Retail) at Bata India Ltd: "One must analyse statistics of the value of merchandise and margins broken down to the space occupied by micro-groups of merchandise in the store. This will help retailers develop a blueprint for profitable deployment of space especially in chain store operations. In addition, not only should merchandise categories be placed in the right locations that will maximize profitability but such placement should help attain uniformity for comfortable shopping by customers."

Space Audit: Non-treaded Space and Black Holes

Any successful retail store audits its space productivity from time to time. This audit looks at the various retail functions and activities for which space is employed and analyses returns in order to optimize them. It compares the performance of each function or activity with others in relation to space occupied.

Hot Spot Analysis: Hot spots are areas where the offtake of merchandise is the highest. Similarly, there are warm spots and cold spots, where merchandise sales are lower. An analysis of these hot spots, warm spots and cold spots is made periodically and steps taken to convert cold spots to warm spots and warm spots to hot spots while retaining the best sales and the stock-turns of the hot spots.

Such audits reveal non-treaded space, where there is no customer traffic, and less treaded space which has low traffic. The possible reasons for these are analysed and hurdles and bottlenecks identified and removed to ensure that there are no non-treaded and black hole areas.

Efficiency of Selling Space to Non-selling Space: The utilization of selling and non-selling spaces — back area, facilities area, etc. — are periodically monitored for their efficiency in deliveries. A good retailer always aims to optimize selling space to improve the bottom-line, while taking care not to compromise on the efficiency of deliveries of the non-selling space.

Ground Rules for Successful Space and Layout Management

➢ Remember the golden rule of the retail floor space planning and management game — the convenience of the customer comes first.
➢ Provide the greatest opportunity for the customer to walk around the store and browse through all the merchandise displayed, for it is the browsers who turn into buyers — buyers of a larger basket size.

➢ Optimize the trading space to achieve maximum sales, while not neglecting the non-trading area for customer convenience/concessions in order to ensure that they spend a longer time in the store and increase revenues.

➢ Make the right floor space management decisions after every space audit, effecting the necessary course-corrections on time as space costs a good deal of money.

➢ Appeal to all the five senses of the customer by creating an aesthetic and functionally effective ambience (which should eventually become the credo of a successful store) so that you can cling to the mind-space of the customer and bring him back to the store again and again. Remember, a retail floor designed, planned and managed well with the target customer in mind helps to make an emotional connection with the buyer.

SUMMARY

- As the saying in the industry goes, the three most important success factors in retailing are location, location and location. It is the location that determines the number of footfalls into the store. For a retail store in a high-street the location will determine the rate of eyeballs (i.e., the number of times the store catches the eye of people) and footfalls as well. The following formula works in retailing:

  If the number of customers entering the store in a day is 100, at a 80% conversion rate, 80 customers will buy an average of Rs.500 worth of goods, taking daily sales to Rs.40,000.

Daily Footfalls (Customer Entry) → No. of Customers who buy (Customer Conversion) → At what average value? = Daily Sales

- Location is so important because it controls the first sales trigger element of customer entry.

- The store design and the retail image mix, if appropriately planned and implemented, will create the right ambience for the customers to buy its products; this helps in the conversion factor. A proper customer circulation plan makes it more convenient for customers to move around the store. The more the time they spend inside the store comfortably, the higher is the sales. If any element of the store design, the image mix or the circulation plan is faulty, it will drive customers out of the stores.

- Space for a retail store is money and has to be used very carefully without any waste. As retailing is dynamic, it is essential to ensure space productivity by analysing the margins earned against the occupancy cost periodically. The success of the retail store will depend on effective retail floor management that results in both an increased conversion rate and augment the average purchase value per customer.

Questions:

1. What factors should a retailer consider while selecting the location for his store? Discuss with examples.

2. Define the key site selection parameters for a retail store.

3. Describe how the various elements of the retail image mix contribute to the store design with specific references.

4. What are the different types of store layout and circulation plans? Briefly narrate with examples the various situations when each plan is used.

5. Define the key parameters to measure efficient space management in a retail store.

THE STORE FAÇADE

When a customer goes shopping, it is the façade of the store that makes him or her decide whether to enter or not. It is the store façade that creates a lasting impression in the customer's mind. A combination of elements such as design and ambience, product and service offerings too help form an image of the store. This 'retail identity' impacts customers to a large extent.

For example, the façade of the Harrods store is instantly identifiable because of its distinctive architecture. The store is not a museum, but customers know a Harrods store from afar! It is hence important for the store to say something about itself.

In creating an identity for the façade, a retailer has to ask himself these questions:
— What does my façade tell my customers?
— Does it have a distinct identity?
— Does it have distinguishable features to set it apart from others in the category?
— Is the façade in tune with the understanding of the target profile of customers?

Let's now take a look at how strong identities are created. Nike is an ideal example. The Nike swoosh and its 'Just Do It' slogan have become so synonymous with the brand that its retail stores even in India can sport just the 'swoosh' in the signage for customers to identify the brand! The identity is so strong that it just 'swooshes' customers in. McDonalds is yet another example of a great façade identity that has taken deep root in customer's minds. The red running all through the frontage creates the characteristic façade of McDonalds and the significant yellow 'M' in its own style beckons the customer.

The façade identity helps a retail store in the following ways:

A great façade invites customers silently: When it comes to façades extending a silent invitation for the customer to enter the store, we find an excellent example in Bata stores, especially in India. The Bata façade stands distinct with its red-and-white logo and unique show windows. The Bata show windows are known for the unique way in which they display merchandise with a seasonal motif, punctuated with its 'odd' price-points.

A great façade makes the store memorable: The look and feel of the store is exemplified in the façade itself and one immediately knows whether the store matches the requirements of its target customer profile. The stronger elements of store design — which creates an impact on the greatest number of people, including passers-by — are embedded in the façade. Its design integrity makes a store memorable.

A great façade creates top-of-the-mind awareness of the store among customers: A lasting impression is created in the minds of the customers when the façade of the store has distinctive features. And consistency in façade design makes recall easier. The McDonalds storefront is one such example.

A great façade conveys what is in store: There's a saying that 'the face is the index of the mind'. A great façade conveys the promises the store holds for its customers; a Disney store means fun and frolic and this is writ large on its façade. The largest Disney store in Japan features a nighttime light show set to popular Disney songs on its façade!

The Scenario in India

The concept of retail identity (rather than just façade identity) is yet to take shape in India. What makes creating an identity difficult in India is the real estate oriented nature of the business. More often than not, retail stores are built by real estate developers, for whom retailing is just one among various activities.

As store planning and design concepts have not evolved in India in a professional way, it is the architect of the building who dictates the look of the store, or the advertising agency that designs the image elements. Managers change, and so do the advertising agencies hired by the retailers. Identities too undergo drastic changes whenever their custodians change. Customers are therefore confused as a result of this lack of consistency.

An important fixture in the store façade is the security guard in his own agency's uniform instead of a "greeter"! These security personnel scan customers' belongings at a counter adjacent to the entrance. This often drives away the happy frame of mind that customers have when they go shopping. It is important to detail every element of the façade identity to create a lasting impression and thus ensure that customers visit again and again.

Questions for Discussion

1. What factors should retail stores consider while designing the store façade?

2. Discuss importance of the store façade identity in the retail business.

3. What in your opinion should organized retail stores in India do to create the required store façade identity for themselves?

CHAPTER 8

Retail Merchandising

CHAPTER OBJECTIVES

1. To provide a basic understanding of the merchandising concept
2. To underline the relevance of merchandise planning in a retail organization
3. To provide information on merchandise grouping, defining the concept of merchandise hierarchy
4. To provide an insight into the concept of planogram in merchandise presentation
5. To explain what is meant by merchandise buying and replenishment planning
6. To introduce the reader to the use of the forward planning tool of 'Open To Buy' in the buying process
7. To define category management and focus on its advantages
8. To explain merchandise performance metrics, including the concept of Gross Margin Return on Inventory

The term 'merchandising' is unique and exclusive to the retail industry. It refers to the entire process of inventory planning and management in a retail organization. Merchandising, when done properly, leads to an increase in the return on investment (ROI). The greater the ROI, more the profitability.

Merchandise Planning

For a retailer, the objective of merchandise planning is clear: achieving the following seven 'RIGHTS':

The Right Product
The Right Place
The Right Quantity
The Right Quality
The Right Price
The Right Mix or Assortment
The Right Time

In order to satisfy every customer's needs, the retail store must have the right product in the right place, in the right quantity, with the right quality, at the right price, with the right mix of sizes or variants and at the right time. The function of merchandising is to achieve all these 'rights' so that sales are high with an ideal level of inventory holding and thus more profits.

Merchandise Hierarchy

While planning the merchandise mix, a retail organization has to start with a clear definition of its merchandise hierarchy. The merchandise hierarchy is a disciplined way of grouping the merchandise mix at different levels, starting from a high-level grouping to the lowest level of the stock-keeping unit (SKU). The grouping may at times have even more than four-five levels as shown in the following example (see Fig. 12).

The merchandise hierarchy forms the platform needed to create the store's merchandise mix. The merchandising vision for the store dictates the different divisions and the lower rungs that the store must have in the hierarchy.

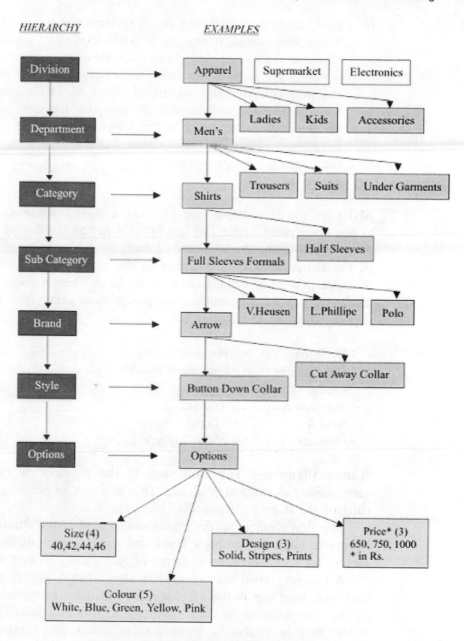

Fig. 12: *Merchandise Hierarchy*

Building the store's merchandise mix by following the concept of merchandise hierarchy has its advantages:

(a) One can define in terms of ratios the mix of elements at each level of the hierarchy.

(b) One can analyse and drill down through the rungs of the hierarchy to the problem areas, if any, up to SKU level.

(c) One can remove or add elements following security escalations. This means if the store's merchandise decisions have to be taken based on the performance, say, of the millions of SKUs contributing to the formation of the merchandise pyramid for the store — the peak being the divisions — decisions at the lower rungs can be taken by front-line personnel. Those at the higher levels, which would impact the merchandise proposition/image of the store, can be taken by the higher-ups.

SKU: To use an example (see Fig. 12), a 40-size white shirt of solid design at the price-point of Rs.750 (all options in the last level) having a button-down collar of the Arrow brand in the full sleeves sub-category or sub-class of the shirts category belonging to the men's department of the apparel division in a retail organization is an SKU. The levels in the merchandise hierarchy may be different for various product categories. For instance, in a supermarket, the levels may be:

Division	:	Food
Department	:	Packaged Food
Category	:	Sauces
Sub-category	:	Tomato
Brand	:	Maggi
Options	:	250g, 500g, 1kg.

Range Planning: The first step in the process of range planning is merchandise assortment planning. This is a mix in percentage terms at every rung of the store's merchandise hierarchy.

The first element in the merchandise plan is the Strategic Plan. This is normally taken at the high level and used to set out the critical success factors for merchandising in terms of sales, margins and stocks.

A category-level margin plan is also created to plan the gross margins that each level (up to the SKU level) contributes to the store. The definition of the merchandise and the assortment planning based on the hierarchy levels help in analysing weekly sales, stock and intake plan etc. at the category, sub-category, brand or SKU levels. With this, one can also identify any problems in sales or inventory holding at any level and take corrective action. It is here that Open To Buy (see 'The Buying Function' below) is planned in the process of buying. This is normally the first significant success factor in the implementation of the planning process.

Example of an assortment of shirt for 20 pieces in stock:
Small / 2, Medium / 6, Large / 7, X'tra Large / 4, X'tra X'tra Large / 1 = 20 pieces

Such an assortment plan helps replenish items to the store stock after they are sold by establishing minimum and maximum levels of stocking units. For instance, in the above example if the assortment ratio is planned as per the planned stock-turn for the store as 20 pieces, then the maximum stock that is available in the SKU can only be 20. The replenishment trigger can be planned so that it is set off when the stock reaches a minimum specified level after sales. Another way of planning replenishment — which is done generally in high-turnover categories — is to trigger off reorders as and when the merchandise is sold with a cap on the maximum stock holding.

Planogram: There is another type of assortment plan that is emerging now. It is a graphical range plan called the planogram. This sort of plan moves away from the purely numerical type of planning that has been used until now and allows the range to be put together in a visual way. Typically digitally stored images are manipulated into collage-type storyboards. Space planning software packages like that of AC Nielsen support such graphic base stock mapping, which helps in easy replenishment planning and effective store space utilization.

Thus merchandise assortment planning and base stock mapping — numerical and visual-numerical methods respectively — enable one to take account of the space utilization in a store by calculating the Return on Space Employed or Returns on Footage.

THE BUYING FUNCTION

Buying for a retail organization is a critical function of merchandising. The process begins with the preparation of the buying plan, called 'Open To Buy' or OTB. It helps retailers project and control future buying so that the flow of merchandise in the store matches anticipated sales at desired stock turn rates to give a positive cash flow.

For organized buying one needs to follow the OTB planning, since it prevents over-buying, eliminates confusion and enables the organization to make more profits.

So what exactly is OTB? OTB refers to merchandise budgeted for purchase during a certain period of time for which the stocks have not yet been ordered. It is also the process of forecasting sales and purchases. OTB is a planning tool that assists in setting budgets for sales and merchandise inventory levels and in monitoring the current status of the OTB amount, which is the amount remaining to be ordered to meet the budget.

Every retailer needs to use an OTB plan, as most tend to overstock when sales increase and understock when they are low. Often a small increase in sales leads to excessive buying that ultimately affects the retail organization's bottom line. OTB helps a retailer fix the ideal amount of stock that should be on hand at the beginning of any given month and the quantum of new merchandise to be received during the month.

An efficient OTB plan has the following elements:

(a) **Forward Sales Planning** (Sales Forecast): The sales plan ought to be prepared for the entire year with month-wise details of planned sales. A good OTB plan helps one to react to variations in sales plans (as the current month comes to an end), reschedule deliveries and cancel or alter purchase orders for future deliveries, as the case may be.

(b) **Forward Cover:** This is based on the planned stock turns for the retail outfit. For instance, if the planned stock turns for the store is four times in a year, then the ideal stock holding at any point in time should be equivalent to three months' stock cover.

(c) **Stock Required:** This is based on the forward cover planned for the store. If the forward cover is for three months and the current month is month 1, then the stock required will be the sum of the planned/forecast sales of months 2, 3 and 4.

(d) **Opening Stock:** The value of the opening stock is a flow calculation. In OTB planning, the first entry is an estimate. From the second month onwards, the opening stock is the closing stock figure of the previous month.

(e) **Intake Requirement:** This is the difference between the required stock and the opening stock.

(f) **On Order:** These are stocks that have been already ordered and due for delivery during the relevant period.

(g) **Open to Receive:** This figure is arrived at by deducting the stock on order, if any, from the intake requirement. This figure indicates the OTB quantity.

(h) **Closing Stock:** To arrive at this figure, one needs to take the opening stock, subtract the sales, and add the on-order and open-to-receive quantities.

Advantages of an Open To Buy Plan

(1) The OTB plan enables retailers to estimate in advance the amount

	Month 1	Month 2	Month 3	Month 4	Month 5	Month 6
Forecast Sales	1000	1500	2000	1500	1000	1000
Months Forward Cover	3	3	3	3	3	3
Stock Required	5000	4500	3500	3000	3000	3000
Opening Stock	2000	5000	4500	3500	3000	3000
Intake Requirement	4000	1000	1000	1000	1000	1000
On Order	2000	1000				
Open to Receive-OTB	2000	0	1000	1000	1000	1000
Closing Stock	5000	4500	3500	3000	3000	3000

Table 6: *A Model OTB Plan*

of working capital that needs to be employed in inventory from month to month.

(2) It helps ensure the right inventory level to support planned sales and to attain the best Gross Margin Return on Inventory (GMROI).

(3) The OTB plan places restraints on merchandise commitments so that the store receives the right merchandise at the right time and not before or after.

(4) It enables a continuous flow of fresh merchandise into the store month after month during the season.

(5) The OTB plan establishes goals so that the actual performance can be compared with the plan and corrective action taken in the required areas.

6) Above all, an efficient OTB plan provides the organization more opportunity for profit.

Retailers who follow a well-formulated OTB plan are successful in their merchandising and buying efforts. The merchandise management system employed in the organization generally supports such statistical techniques in the OTB plan, but it is the buyer's insight and decision-making capability that help deliver the best results.

Category Management

Category management in retailing is defined as the process of managing categories (explained in the merchandise hierarchy) as strategic business units (SBUs). This produces enhanced business results by achieving a robust bottom-line for each category.

A category is a merchandise group that addresses similar consumer needs and wants. Goods in a category are displayed and sold together in a retail environment so that customer choices are easier, thus enhancing the shopping experience.

It is felt that category management in retailing is similar to brand management in manufacturing, as product groups become the focal point in terms of development, merchandising and marketing. The category management process in retailing involves the following steps:

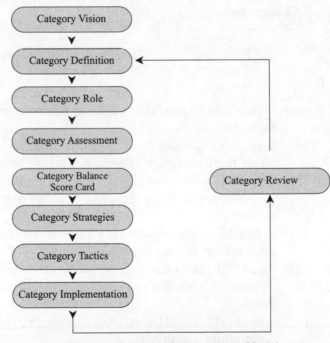

Fig. 13: *Category Management Model*

Category Vision: This refers to the top management's view of what each category ought to achieve in terms of customer satisfaction or value offering and the differentiation thus achieved for leadership.

Category Definition: This is made based on customer segmentation and the specific SKUs that belong to the category. For example, a broad category definition can be 'soft drinks', a narrower sub-category can be 'aerated soft drinks' and one of the SKUs within the same can be 'Pepsi 500 ml'.

Category Role: This defines the objective of the category in the entire merchandise mix and determines its relative importance. Some categories may play a 'destination' role in the product mix — as in the case of the grocery category in a supermarket — and some an 'impulse' role.

Category Assessment: The category assessment is done to identify gaps if any between the category vision and the existing contributing SKUs to the category. This assessment helps improve the category's business by identifying opportunity gaps in sales, stock turns and profits.

Category Balanced Score Card: This helps measure the performance of the retail business. It establishes specific business targets for the category while reflecting on its performance.

Category Strategies: These aim at achieving the best of customer off-take from the shelves, ringing in the maximum number of transactions, earning maximum margins and achieving certain subjective goals like excitement, sensationalism, etc. for customer satisfaction.

Category Tactics: Category tactics refer to the tactical requirements to achieve the score card targets. These tactics are compared with those of the competition to attain the best advantage and edge and may centre on the areas of assortment, pricing, space planning, promotions, etc.

Category Implementation and Review: This refers to the store-level execution of the category business plan and strategies and monitoring category performance against the plan to take action on an ongoing basis.

Successful category management in retailing is a customer-driven process. It enables the retailer to have the right category mix through the preparation and implementation of an efficient category plan.

MARKUPS AND MARKDOWNS IN MERCHANDISE MANAGEMENT

Markup is the percentage amount (calculated on cost) added to cost in order to arrive at the maximum retail price for a product. Hence,

Markup = percentage of margin calculated on cost added to arrive at the maximum retail price.

Cost = Maximum Retail Price – Margin

Margin = Maximum Retail Price – Cost

Maximum Retail Price = Cost + Markup

Markup is based on cost and is expressed in percentage terms.

Problem: What is the markup percentage for a dress that costs Rs.200 and retails for Rs.400?

Markup % = Difference between MRP and cost (Rs.400 – Rs.200) ÷ Cost (Rs.200) x 100

= Rs.200 ÷ Rs.200 x 100

= 100%

Sometimes the retailer needs to look at the cost of an item and determine what that item should retail for. It is fixed if the target customer is willing to pay that price.

Markdown is the amount reduced from the maximum retail price to arrive at the new retail price. Markdown is calculated as a percentage of MRP.

Problem: What is the markdown percentage for a dress whose original MRP is Rs.400 and the new retail price after markdown is Rs.200?

Markdown % = Difference between old MRP and new MRP after markdown (Rs.400 – Rs.200) ÷ old MRP (Rs.400) x 100

= Rs.200 ÷ Rs.400 x 100

= 50%

Markdowns are done when product sales are low or when the season draws to a close and the product line needs to be cleared from the shelves. Merchandise is also marked down when inventories are high, when saleable merchandise is shop-soiled or when certain price-off promotions are done. Markdowns are also effected when products that have manufacturing defects but are still saleable are found at the floor level. It is essential that the markdown percentage is kept at the lowest, as it directly affects the returns on gross margins in a retail store.

SHRINKAGE IN RETAIL MERCHANDISE MANAGEMENT

At periodical intervals, a difference between the actual stock quantity or value — found or established by an actual physical count of all inventories — and the book value figure can be found. The book value is what exists in the inventory accounting system or in the books of accounts of the retail store. The difference between the two — normally where the figure physically counted is less than the book value — is known as **'shrinkage'** and is expressed as a percentage of sales.

The annual shrinkage average ranges from as low as 0.1% to a high of even 2.5% of sales depending on the type of store and its merchandise. This shrinkage leads to a direct reduction in the store's net profits.

How does shrinkage occur? Globally, the three major reasons attributed to shrinkage are: incorrect paperwork, customer theft and employee theft. While incorrect paperwork like wrong recording of invoices, receipting of merchandise and issuing of credit notes are said to account for a tenth of the total shrinkage, customer theft and employee theft are presumed to share the balance in equal measure.

GROSS MARGIN RETURN ON INVENTORY

The critical performance measure for merchandising and buying in retailing is the Gross Margin Return on Inventory (GMROI). Every retail organization must strive to ensure profitability by achieving the best possible GMROI.

GMROI is calculated by dividing the total margin earned by the average inventory held during the period. The average inventory held may be considered either on cost or at MRP value, but consistency needs to be maintained while measuring growth in GMROI or comparing the same for different periods.

Problem: What is the GMROI for a retail store if its margin earned is Rs. 30 lakhs and the average inventory held during the month is Rs. 2 crores?

Margins = 30,00,000 (Turnover at MRP – Cost of Goods sold)
Average Inventory Holding = 200,00,000
Hence, GMROI = 30,00,000 ÷ 200,00,000 x 100
    = 15%

The significant means of achieving better GMROI is by:
(a)   Reducing the Cost of Goods Sold (COGS) by achieving better buying efficiencies.

(b) Increasing the stock turnover rate by reducing the average inventory held.

(c) Increasing sales constantly, retaining the same average value of inventory held.

SUMMARY

- Merchandising is a significant function of retailing. It deals with merchandise planning, presentation and management in a retail store with the objective of having the right product in the right place, in the right mix, in the right price and at the right time.
- The merchandise range and mix in a store has to be planned meticulously and grouped in a merchandise hierarchy for a better understanding and analysis of sales and stock.
- Merchandise presentation too is important for a retail store. Hence a planogram depicting the placement of merchandise in the right places and right quantities requires to be worked out.
- Following an OTB purchase plan for a retail store helps a retail organization plan purchases intelligently and efficiently.
- Category management with a strategic business unit approach helps manage merchandise profitably besides enabling a speedy response to customers' requirements.
- Careful planning of markdowns and prevention of shrinkage will yield better margins for a store.
- It pays to measure the merchandise performance of the store by understanding the concept of GMROI so that efforts can be taken to get the highest margins for the store.

Questions:

1. Define merchandise hierarchy and explain how it helps build the merchandise mix for a retail organization.

2. Write short notes on: i) range planning for a retail store and ii) planogram.

3. Describe the concept of open-to-buy as a buying tool for a retail organization.

4. What are the advantages of using the OTB plan for buying?

5. Describe the concept of category management in retailing.

6.   Write short notes on:
  –   Shrinkage
  –   Mark-up
  –   Mark-down
  –   GMROI

PRIVATE LABEL BRANDS

Every organized retailer in India — whether involved in food retailing or garments — has to ask himself these questions:

1.   How do I differentiate myself from other competing stores that sell various brands of merchandise available everywhere?
2.   How do I create a sustainable differentiation for my product offerings?
3.   How do I stay ahead of local competition, providing a good shopping experience and yet maintain profitability?
4.   How can my store remain profitable especially in an environment where margins are being squeezed?

The answer to all these questions seems to be to create a private label brand for the store.

Private Label Brands: Global Scenario in a Nutshell

Over the years supermarkets and garment retailers across the world have resorted to building their own private label brands, which are steadily increasing their share of sales at the cost of nationally advertised labels. In 2001, the market share of store brand products was higher than the strongest manufacturer-brands in nearly 30% of all categories in the supermarket. Store brands ranked No.1 in 79 out of 266 individual product categories (such as pasta, cheese, baby food, ice cream, etc.) Store brand products were either No.1 or No.2 in 131 product categories — nearly 50% of the categories in the store.

The private label brands' contribution to Wal-Mart's total sales is almost 40%. And the same is the case with Tesco. The aim of the global retailing industry is to attain category distinction through private label brands. Many supermarkets have explored non-food markets as an area where they can develop their own labels. Tesco's plans to extend its Finest range into home ware is part of that shift in direction. Own-label sales generate 38% of Sainsbury's total revenue, with its Taste The Difference premium range estimated to contribute between £200 million and £300 million. Sainsbury's has approached the own-label market through segmentation. Its brands include Free From, Way To Live and Blue Parrot Café as well as its value and premium ranges. Like Tesco, it is also moving deeper into non-food markets with sub-brands Perform+Protect and active: naturals. One of the most famous own-label brands to have emerged from the UK supermarket chains is Asda's 'George' clothing range. This is estimated to be worth around £1 billion in sales, making Asda one of the leading clothing retailers in the UK.

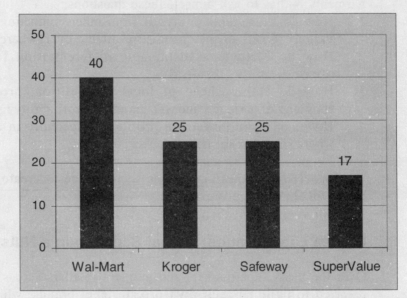

Private Labels as percentage of sales for top 4 US Grocery Retailers, 2006

The Current Scenario in India

Retailing in India is plagued by weak gross margins compared to those in global retailing. While apparel retailers manage to get gross margins of 30-33% after struggling a great deal with vendors and brand marketers, the food sector has to settle for just 15-19%.

The lifestyle garments and related accessory retailer Shoppers' Stop has four in-store private label brands that contribute approximately 25% to its turnover, growing 5% over the previous year. The private labels of a Delhi-based apparel retailer Ebony Retail contributed approximately 21% to total sales last year.

In grocery, FoodWorld's private label brands account for around 21%

of total sales. It is reported that the company plans to increase the share of its store brands to 27% of total sales by the time the first phase of the private label initiative is over. FoodWorld expects to extend its private label brand to 38 sub-categories from the 22 it currently has.

Westside, the apparel retailing initiative from the house of Tatas, is a success story with a strategic approach to private brand retailing (approximately 80% to 85% of the merchandise retailed comprise its own brands). The store is said to be struggling in the area of men's apparel, which is truly brand-led, and is said to be contemplating accommodating a few 'must have' men's brands in its outlets in addition to its core private labels.

Key Concerns in Own-Label Branding

1. As there is scope for increasing gross margins considerably, retailers are prepared to invest in private label brands (notwithstanding the high marketing costs).
2. Retailers need to ensure that the private label strategy is aligned to the store's overall marketing strategy.
3. They have to ensure high standards of quality in order to ensure that shoppers accept their private labels.
4. It is advisable to fill existing merchandise gaps with private labels so that retailers don't take competition from national brands head-on.

Questions for Discussion

1. How far can own-label brands go in India?

2. As far as Indian supermarkets are concerned, which products are less suitable for the private label formula?

3. It is not easy for multi-brand garment retailers to establish private label brands. Discuss.

4. Is cross-categorization (supermarkets getting into retailing own-label clothing and vice versa) a possible option in developing own-label brands in India? Discuss.

CHAPTER 9

Supply Chain Management in Retailing

CHAPTER OBJECTIVES

1. To define the supply chain process in the retail environment
2. To elaborate on the channel elements and the value contributions of channel enablers
3. To focus on the details of logistics and the functions of back-end merchandise management
4. To explain the relevance of the current concepts in supply chain management to optimize efficiencies

Supply chain management (SCM) is an end-to-end process in merchandise planning and movement, from planning the inventory (preparing the purchase order) to the point of reaching the merchandise to the customers. SCM is an integrated process where every activity is interlinked with the system for information throughout the cycle-time of each step of the process so that timely action can be taken.

Previously, individual activities of the SCM process — for instance, warehousing, distribution, transportation (inbound and outbound) etc. — were done separately. Later, the process moved on to logistics where every activity was carried out in a logical sequence following a specific timetable. Now, an information backbone supporting the SCM process has helped retailers in greatly reducing cycle times and attaining efficiency.

Efficient Inventory Planning: Efficient inventory planning enables the retail organization achieve its strategies and benchmarked standards of customer deliveries, at the same time reducing supply chain expenses. Inventory planning has already been discussed in the chapter on merchandising.

Forward planning is done by forecasting sales and Beginning of Month (BOM) and End of Month (EOM) inventories for specific periods, and preparing the OTB (Open to Buy) plans. Efficient inventory planning optimizes purchasing controls through OTB so that the planned stock turns are achieved for the store with just-in-time inventories for freshness and achieving customer satisfaction through the seven 'rights' of merchandising (*see* **Chapter 8**).

Pre-Purchase Order (PPO) and Purchase Order (PO): The PPO is an instrument through which the tentative plan of order placement to the vendor is done for the whole season as soon as the inventory planning is completed. The Purchase Order is the confirmed order for supply.

INTEGRATED SUPPLY CHAIN

The end-to-end integration of all supply chain elements and functions are achieved by applying interlinked packages for perfect information management. The integrated supply chain starts from the design stage at the vendor level to the time when there is consumer response at the retail stage. The benefits of having an integrated supply chain are many, including achieving the best delivery performance, reduction in inventory, faster fulfillment of cycle time, accuracy in forecasts, lower supply chain costs, improvement in overall productivity, improvement in capacity utilization, and so on.

Vendor Management: Efficient vendor management involves selecting the right vendors capable of giving the right quality of merchandise and meeting delivery deadlines. Besides, they should be able to deliver the right quantities as well, so that the retailer can get the right 'hit ratio'. The right hit ratio measures the gap between delivery and purchase orders and helps eliminate backlog in deliveries. In a chain store scenario, vendors directly delivering to stores is an important element in attaining good supply chain efficiency.

The vendors directly manage inventories in a few retail organizations. Vendor Managed Inventory (VMI) is ideal for retail organizations as it totally eliminates inventory-carrying costs. Here, vendors manage the inventory at every store, monitoring the flow of information and ensuring just-in-time deliveries. The vendors are able to take back slow-selling and non-moving merchandise, thus reducing the scope for mark-down losses for the store.

Electronic Data Interchange **(EDI)** helps in establishing an efficient information flow on stock movement, and the vendors get to know of sales and inventories instantaneously. Reorder supplies are immediately planned and executed by the vendors following acceptable norms. This process eliminates the time taken to exchange documents for placing orders, thus achieving just-in-time inventory management. EDI is done through web-enabled servers or with the help of the organization's ERP (Enterprise Resource Planning) package that interacts with the vendors' systems.

Warehouse Management: The retail warehouse or the distribution centre (DC) performs the functions of receiving the ordered stocks; checking for the right quality, quantity and price; temporary storing and docking; tagging the merchandise with both the MRP and security tags; preparing and readying the merchandise; transporting the merchandise; receiving goods returned from retail stores, if any; and sending returned merchandise to vendors back as returns or for refinishing.

A *Goods Received Note (GRN)* is prepared when the merchandise received at the warehouse from suppliers/vendors is checked and matched with the relevant purchase order (PO) after certifying all the elements of quality, quantity, etc. The GRN is then automatically recognized by the system after authorization for payment to the vendor by the accounts department. The merchandise is then docked and tagged with bar codes and price tags if applicable. If the bar coding for MRP has already been done by the vendor, it saves a great deal of time for the retail organization. Then, only the security tagging needs to be done at the warehouse.

Inter-Transfer Note (ITN): This is made when the prepared and readied merchandise is supplied to the retail stores. The reverse ITN (ITN out) is prepared when goods are sent back to the warehouse by the retail store. Goods that are returned to the warehouse are then sent back to the suppliers and vendors. The system recognizes the same and raises a debit note to the vendors.

Transportation is done according to timely delivery schedules so that replenishments are delivered as per the plan. Cost efficiency and reduction in delivery time are critical success factors in transportation.

Efficient docking with a plan ensures the best utilization of space. Docking also ensures that the First In First Out (FIFO) delivery plan is followed so that ageing of merchandise in the warehouse is kept to the minimum.

Material Handling Equipment in the warehouse should be tailored for specific varieties of merchandise. At a micro level of handling, most of the time garments are delivered by hangers and sometimes by the browser itself in a ready-to-sell state.

Value Chain: The entire SCM process is a value chain where bottlenecks,

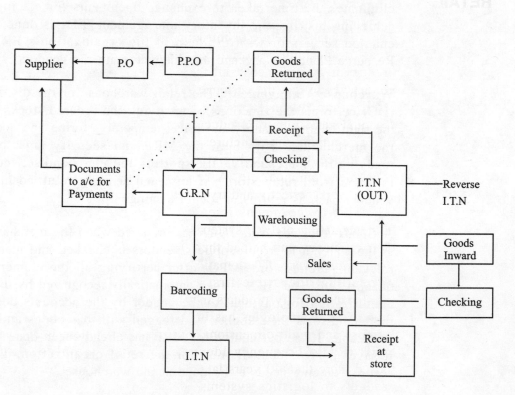

Fig. 14: *Retail Supply Chain Process Model*

value-adding factors and liability factors are identified and addressed, thus enabling the retail organization to have an efficient supply chain. The entire process needs to be audited to meet timelines, and may be reengineered to achieve cost efficiencies and reduce cycle times.

The supply chain is the heart of retail operations that ensures that the right product is in the right place, at the right time and the right cost.

EFFICIENT CONSUMER RESPONSE (ECR)

This is a demand-driven replenishment system designed to link all parties in the logistics channel to create a massive flow-through distribution network. Replenishment depends upon consumer demand and point of sale (POS) information. In a retail organization, an integrated supply chain — with the right application of packages enabling the free flow of information and consequently merchandise and services — elicits the greatest response from consumers since it addresses their needs appropriately.

RETAIL AUTOMATION AND SUPPLY CHAIN MANAGEMENT

The principal objective of introducing supply chain management (SCM) in a retail organization is to satisfy the customer at the right time with the right product at the right cost, all the time. Integrated systems help bring about efficiencies so that the customer is satisfied every time. The challenges that a retail organization faces are many: huge stock-keeping units (SKUs), seasonal variations of product lines necessitating the introduction of new SKUs, complex tax structures, the sheer geographic spread of the country (and hence complex logistics and replenishment periods), changing consumer demands, etc. A retail organization has to plan to make this system work perfectly and try to satisfy the needs of every customer without fail. This by no means is easy to achieve. Automation — through the implementation of ERP systems — has helped many organizations improve their efficiency and helped them grow.

The discovery of automatic identification technologies has been a boon to retailing; they were first introduced globally in the 1960s to assist logisticians identify products in the supply chain. The global development of such SCM technologies has been very rapid. There were barcodes, touch memory and multi-dimensional barcodes. Now there is an early technology RFID (Radio Frequency Identification) that is only starting to emerge. Indeed more than 40 years later, RFID promises to directly connect physical products to logistics systems as the only truly automatic identification technology. In India the development of SCM technologies has come a long way. Retailers in the organized sector are beginning to barcode all their products; organizations like Foodworld (RPG group) and Shoppers' Stop (Raheja group) have urged their vendors to supply merchandise only with standard barcodes.

The next phase will see the introduction of RFID technology to help track the product and customers' use patterns even post-purchase. P&G currently tags (RFID) a small number of cases and pallets of products as part of a trial with Wal-Mart stores in the USA. The company is currently focusing on the supply chain and has not even begun to think about what's going to happen to the items post-sale. The Federal Trade Commission in the USA held a forum recently to begin a dialogue on RFID, its uses and benefits, and potential concerns. There are privacy concerns stemming from the fact that companies will collect data about customers without their knowledge, and then may misuse that data. Indian organized retailing is just on the threshold of employing retail automation technologies enabled by UPC (barcodes of GS1 standards), as they do not now need to re-barcode merchandise supplied from various vendors (as has been the practice with many organized retailers).

Most retailers in the organized sector in India have to use retail software in their back end and front end operations and are constantly looking to upgrade their systems as they evolve. To help this growing retail sector get the best, many Indian software companies have developed software packages to suit the different and varied requirements of these retailers. Among the few who are in the market is Chennai-based Polaris Retail InfoTech Ltd, a subsidiary of Polaris, which has entered the market with its software, Retail Excel. Reputed organizations like Wipro Infotech, Tata Consultancy Services and NCR Technologies have created robust retail automation software. The Chennai-based T.V. Sundaram Iyengar & Sons are currently test-marketing their new point-of-sale system for small and medium retailers in grocery and other related segments. The Bangalore-based VMoksha Technologies has developed software for the retail segment while Pune-based Zensar Technologies has tied up with the RPG group for retail software. The list of those developing retail software is growing by the day. There are many other packages like MS Retail, Shopper, Retail Pro, Retail Magik, etc. that help enable the fast implementation of retail automation in India available in the market. Not to mention large ERP packages like JDA, SAP Retail, Oracle Retail, etc.

Let us now take a look at how two organized-sector retailers tackled the challenges of establishing efficient supply chains:

Example 1 — TANISHQ

Tanishq is a division of Titan Industries Ltd, India's largest watch maker. It is India's only fine jewellery brand with a national presence, and an acknowledged leader in the branded jewellery market. Tanishq is sold exclusively through a company-controlled retail chain with over 108 boutique stores spread over 61 cities. This network is supplied and supported by a network of 32 CFAs (Clearing and Forwarding Agents). With the network of boutique stores poised to grow, the Tanishq management had to increase visibility along the supply chain, CFAs and boutiques across the country. The Tanishq team picked Wipro Infotech, India's premier IT solutions company, to put together the solution. The Wipro Infotech team designed a web-based solution, Goldmine, to facilitate the flow of information between various distribution entities. Goldmine offers a platform for the sales, management and factory teams of Tanishq to monitor key activities and parameters along the distribution chain. It also serves as an integration platform to pull together existing information systems in the company such as SAP/Oracle, DOS-based point-of-sales systems in boutiques, without modifications. Wipro Infotech developed the solution using the .NET framework with an ASP .NET presentation layer.

Challenges addressed: The most significant supply chain management issues addressed by Tanishq are in the areas of reducing cycle time, increasing efficiencies and reducing costs in the areas of tracking movement of goods and sales indenting, order status, sales visibility, communication (reports) and exception reporting.

Goods in transit: The new system provides details of goods that have been dispatched from the factory to the CFA and then to the boutiques. This functionality also enables tracking of stock return cases from the boutiques to the CFA. And from there on to the factory. This helps the organization track goods in transit and monitor loss of goods effectively if any.

Indenting: The ordering of goods by the boutiques is automated. They can refer to online product catalogues and price lists before placing orders. Goldmine enables online indenting for replenishment, shop-specific indenting as well as customer-specific indenting. Such online indenting is based on norms set by the administrator for each variant. Hence, the company can enforce prudent credit norms through Goldmine at the point-of-sale system. Say a boutique has a great track record, selling Rs 20,000-25,000 worth of bangles, but not up to the Rs 50,000 level it had reached in the past, the company can set prudent indenting levels for gold for that boutique. This information is transmitted to the point-of-sale system via Goldmine and is actually enforced. Previously, under the manual system, the company had no means of systematic enforcement of such norms.

Order status: This functionality provides visibility on the status of orders placed by boutiques. This is made possible by the daily synchronization between the Oracle system at the factory and the web-based solution. Boutique users no longer have to send emails or call up anyone to find out the status of their orders. They get it at their own convenience from Goldmine.

Sales visibility: With sales information flowing in from the boutique into Goldmine, visibility of sales from each boutique is improved. Management can now track the effectiveness of marketing programmes and promotions at the boutique level, according to category and price band. Bestseller information for all boutiques is currently available on demand.

Communication and exception reporting: Goldmine provides a platform for dissemination of information through content uploads, bulletin boards, and so on. Information on local gold rates (the most important component of material cost), market information, promotion scheme details and product catalogues are transmitted in real time. The company has over 40,000 product variants, so this system capability is crucial. The system also provides for discussion on queries raised by users at the boutiques for producing and modifying new and existing products. Discussions between factory users and boutique users are tracked and an escalation mechanism with alerts is in place in case queries are not handled promptly.

Future plans: As Goldmine builds up the supply chain database, Tanishq intends to build a data warehousing application enabled with advanced data mining using SQL server. This will facilitate the use of relevant business intelligence in real time in the boutiques during a customer touch. Market leader Tanishq will set its benchmarks in retail automation and its applications for many in the industry to follow in future.

Example 2 — SHOPPERS' STOP

Shoppers' Stop has implemented the US-based retail ERP system JDA. JDA facilitates the integration of all retail functions in Shoppers' Stop efficiently.

Efficiencies in the buying process: It is JDA's merchandise management system that now performs the buying process and merchandise management control practices. Pursuant to range width and assortment plans, purchase orders are issued to suppliers through the central merchandising function. The actual delivery of stocks is then controlled on a weekly basis through the delivery authorization process mechanism. The delivery authorization number acts as a tool to control the overall inventory position. The delivery authorization is issued to vendors on a weekly basis based on the previous week's actual sales and on the forward sales plan (forecast). The vendors then despatch the goods to the distribution centre based on the purchase order and delivery authorization. Every distribution centre gets a copy of the delivery authorization issued for the week. At the distribution centre support is provided by the 'warehouse management system' (WMS) of JDA, which manages the warehousing function most efficiently.

The challenges at Shoppers' Stop are the spread of the 21 stores across the country in varying large sizes, ranging from 25,000 sq ft to 55,000 sq ft, the large SKU base, etc. Also, it has more than 300 suppliers who supply stocks to three distribution centres, which then redistribute merchandise to all the stores. Variety, colour and size of merchandise play a very important role in delivering a great shopping experience to the customer.

Profitable growth: Shoppers' Stop views SCM as an enabler of profitable growth; it firmly believes that ERP, if used well, can cut costs greatly by reducing cycle times and inventory levels. One of the key drivers of the profit-driven operation is the significant development in the retailer-supplier information integration in the supply chain — the emergence of retailer control over the movement of suppliers' goods into the retailer's distribution centres. This has led to more complex relationships involving suppliers, third-party distributors and retailers through supplier-retailer collaboration where major suppliers and retailers have the opportunity to exchange timely information on consumer demand and put into practice the most appropriate product flows.

SCM at Shoppers' Stop: SCM at Shoppers' Stop coordinates and integrates all activities associated with moving products, services and information into seamless processes linking all the partners in the chain, including the various departments, vendors, transporters and other service providers. The system facilitates perfect supply chain coordination with an able information system that controls all SCM activities. SCM at Shoppers' Stop begins and ends with the customer. The guiding philosophy is to improve the organization's performance by managing constraints and uncertainties inherent in the earlier system. The focus is on using new tools and techniques. The first step in SCM is merchandise planning and sourcing.

In Shoppers' Stop, SCM is seen from a strategic perspective rather than just as an operational issue. Core supply chain issues such as month-end sales peaks, forecasting inaccuracy, constraint-based planning and so on continue to create problems for Indian retailers even after ERP implementation. Many organizations implemented SCM as a tool to contain costs and identifying means for reducing pressure on margins due to competition. The mindsets of organizations underwent a transformation when they accepted to consider the use of such integrated SCM from end-to-end. The first step in SCM is merchandise planning and sourcing. The range width and assortment planning process is used to develop meaningful sales and space plans. The planning process starts six months before the actual beginning of the season to fill an agreed amount of footage with a product that matches customer demand. The challenge is to develop a balanced range which provides the appropriate mix of colour, price, styling and fabric so that the customer is given the best possible choice at all times. Also on the agenda is having a mix of own-label products and brands in such a way that it aligns with the company's strategic goal of increasing own-label participation to drive store loyalty through exclusivity, and complementary to overall brand strategy. Once the range width and assortment planning is done, the next challenge is to source the merchandise. The buying department then decides on suppliers who will supply the necessary merchandise as per the plans.

While selecting suppliers, various parameters are considered, such as past history, quality, hit rates in supplying goods on time, margin and vendor's cooperation in crisis situations, manufacturing capacity, future capacity expansion plans, financial capabilities to invest for growth etc. The greatest challenge is to get the act together and seamlessly integrate the parts in such a way that the effectiveness of the whole chain is more important than that of an individual link of the chain.

Future plans: Future projects at Shoppers' Stop include Automatic Data Capture (ADC) at the distribution centres. Every product has a different barcode and since every barcode is number-based, there are chances of errors in operations, resulting in stock inaccuracy. Shoppers' Stop has already set up the ADC for the cashier and stock-taking process. It further plans to use it for the stock-receiving process and stock replenishment at distribution centres. The company is also in the process of testing a consolidated intake model, which, in time, will add value to the total SCM. For this the company plans to take the services of a 3PL (third party logistics) company which will do milk-runs on a daily basis and collect stocks as per delivery authorizations and deliver them to the distribution centres. Another endeavour is to integrate suppliers into Shoppers' Stop's supply chain through electronic data interchange (EDI) and the Internet. Shoppers' Stop is investing in B2B (web-enabled procurement solutions) to achieve this. The idea is to disseminate and seek information faster at minimal cost and do online transactions with business associates to speed up the transaction processing. The first phase of this project is already implemented and major vendors are now connected to Shoppers' Stop's B2B web site.

SCM is a key factor in improving overall efficiency, and creates an opportunity for enhanced sales and customer satisfaction. Shoppers' Stop has already initiated progressive steps in the management of its supply chain in line with its mission of 'Nothing but the best'.

SUMMARY

- Supply chain management forms the heart of retail operations. It reduces cycle times and speeds up operations. It enables the supply of the right merchandise to the end-consumer at the right time. An efficient supply chain management system reduces operations cost substantially.

- Information management is the key to attain efficiency in supply chain management. Using the right technology, information flow will help dynamic decision-making across functions.

- A planned and documented process flow will ensure efficiency in the supply chain. Processes need to be audited to improve cycle times and attain cost efficiencies. Innovative and new technologies should be adopted as soon as they are available.

- The efficiency of the entire supply chain process depends on how retailers seek, understand, assimilate and respond to consumer responses.

- Retail automation plays a significant role in ensuring timely operational deliveries and achieving efficiencies.

Questions:

1. Supply chain management is a progression in the value chain from sourcing to satisfying customer needs. Discuss.

2. Describe the significant benefits of vendor managed inventories in retailing.

3. Explain the key documentation involved in an efficient warehouse management system.

4. Discuss the advantages of retail automation in supply chain management.

Cross-docking in the Retail Supply Chain

Cross-docking is a process by which finished goods from the manufacturing source are taken and delivered directly to the customer with little or no handling involved in between. Cross-docking is applied to a number of circumstances in the material handling process. In manufacturing cross-docking is used to consolidate in-bound supplies which are then prepared to support just-in-time assembly. In the distribution scenario, cross-docking is used to consolidate in-bound supplies of products from different sources/suppliers which are delivered when the last in-bound shipment is received. In transportation, cross-docking is used to consolidate shipments from many suppliers, often in Less Than Truck Load (LTL) batches, in order to achieve economies of scale. In retail, cross-docking involves receiving merchandise from multiple suppliers and consolidating by way of sorting them to out-bound shipments to different stores.

Cross-docking involves the reduction of handling and storage of inventory and the conventional process of filling the warehouse with inventory before shipping it to various locations is virtually eliminated, when an organization uses the cross-docking concept. In essence, cross-docking means receiving goods at one end and shipping out through the other instantaneously without allowing storage. Thus cross-docking brings about a paradigm shift from "supply chain" to "demand chain". For example, the merchandise coming into the cross-docking centre is already pre-allocated for a replenishment order generated by a retailer in the supply chain. Thus cross-docking enables the retailers to streamline the supply chain from the source point to the point of sale. Cross-docking always helps reduce direct costs incurred as a consequence of holding excess inventory by eliminating unnecessary handling and storage of merchandise. As products would move continuously, cross-docking would result in almost nil product damages and nil losses due to product obsolescence.

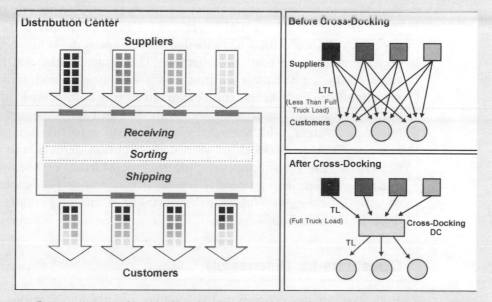

In a conventional distribution and logistics function goods are received and stored in a distribution centre and often these goods remain there until ordered by the store. In such a scenario shipments ordered are often Less Than Truck Load. Cross-docking now allows for continuous movement of goods as they are pre-assigned to a store and the distribution centre also sorts merchandise to be shipped to a consolidated batch including many orders from many other suppliers to the stores. This often provides for Full Truck Loads (FTL). Cross-docking works seamlessly with one set of workers receiving goods on pallets in lanes corresponding to the receiving doors, a second set of workers sorting pallets into shipping lanes from which a third team loads them into outbound vehicles.

Wal-Mart is said to use the concept of cross-docking efficiently and the company delivers about 85% of its merchandise using the cross-docking system. The system runs in such a way that shipments typically spend less than 24 hours in the distribution centers, sometimes even less than an hour. Goods are continuously replenished to Wal-Mart stores within 48 hours by using the cross-docking system without having to store merchandise anywhere. The company-owned transportation systems also help Wal-Mart in the speedy replenishment process which facilitates just-in-time replenishments where goods from the warehouse are moved to the store in less than 48 hours every time. The cross-docking locations are also planned in such a way that distances are managed with ease to achieve such time-bound goal for replenishments. Cross-docking allows Wal-Mart to replenish their shelves 4 times faster than its competition.

Wal-Mart has invested a great deal in this unique cross-docking inventory system which has enabled the company to achieve economies of scale and reduce costs considerably. The company also has invested in state-of-the-art technology that can track stocks and movement of merchandise. This keeps the organization up-to-date with information pertaining to sales and inventory. Wal-Mart had implemented a satellite network system which enables sharing of information among the company's wide network of stores, distribution centers and suppliers. Cross-docking techniques adopted in Wal-Mart have been delivering optimal efficiencies and results for the organization. The implementation of cross-docking at Wal-Mart has become a model globally for other organizations to follow.

Questions for Discussion

1. Explain the cross-docking system and its applications in supply chain management.
2. What are the benefits of cross-docking?
3. How does cross-docking work better than material handling in the conventional distribution system?
4. How does cross-docking help Wal-Mart in achieving efficient replenishments?

CHAPTER 10

Retail Marketing and Advertising

CHAPTER OBJECTIVES

1. To introduce the concept of strategic retail marketing in India
2. To provide information on 'store positioning' and to discuss the current positioning platforms of various retail organizations in India
3. To provide insights into the elements of the retail marketing mix
4. To explain concepts such as Customer Relationship Management and their applications in the Indian retail marketing scenario
5. To give details about the direct marketing and micromarketing efforts undertaken by some Indian retailers
6. To provide a good understanding of retail advertising and communication

RETAIL MARKETING STRATEGIES

In Indian retailing the current marketing challenges are in two major areas:
- Creating footfalls in the store.
- Converting browsers into buyers.

Creating footfalls in the store starts with building the store brand, positioning the store, profiling target customers and understanding their buying behaviour, defining the retail marketing mix, creating customer relationship and loyalty, and direct marketing, effectively planning and implementing store events and promotions.

Micromarketing is a significant marketing strategy as it totally focuses on the target consumer.

Building the Store Brand: The store brand is built on such parameters as merchandise category, price/quality, specific attributes of benefits, lifestyle/activity, etc. It is essential to select and define the target market to comprehensively define the brand proposition to the consumer.

The brand conveys the value proposition to the customer. For instance the brand Shoppers' Stop signifies a one-stop shop for lifestyle garments and, its 'Feel the Experience While You Shop' theme conveys that it stands for free access and experiential shopping. The name Big Bazaar itself tells the consumer what the brand is about: very large, with diverse and genuinely 'value for money' merchandise. The store brand is thus a great differentiator, occupying a distinct position in the mind of the consumer — in short, 'store positioning'. A strong store brand guides the overall business strategy of the organization and acts as an ambassador for entering new markets, which some Indian retail organizations are currently doing.

STORE POSITIONING

As an expert aptly puts it: "Store positioning is not what you do to the store; it's what you do to the mind of the customer!"

So what does it take for a retail store to create an identity for itself in customers' minds and differentiate itself from the clutter? Here are some ways in which they can stand out:
- A store can be exciting to its customers with its merchandise, its range of services, service delivery standards, ambience and convenience. An expensive, unfriendly and even repulsive store creates a negitive positioning that is hard to shake off.
- Retail stores could position themselves in the minds of their customers on various platforms derived from the retail mix. The most common ones are

merchandise and related attributes such as category and range distinction, price, store design and ambience, customer service and related processes.

➢ Factors like convenience of location or fashion trends are also used to position a retail store.

Such attributes are chosen according to their importance to the customer. The more the relevance of such attributes to the consumer, the better they are imprinted in their minds.

Toys 'R' Us, the multinational toy store has a *'single line* (largest and the best) and *price off'* positioning. This has worked successfully since 1948 when it was started by Charles Lazarus at the age of 25. The organization's positioning has consistently met customer expectations. A few instances in the Indian context are presented below.

Dairy Farm International's Health&Glow store in the south, is positioned as the *'Look good. Feel good'* store. The brand signifies health and beauty and the logo — a guardian angel flying into a 'G' — conveys the impression of health and vitality. Health&Glow offers its customers a unique experience by offering a select range of quality health and beauty merchandise and complementing its proposition with trained consulting staff.

Barista is positioned for a new experience in the store environment. It is creating a unique positioning whereby *the consumer owns* the store. That is, it wants to create a place where a consumer is recognized by name, where his tastes and preferences are known enough to make him feel at home, where he can freely interact and have meetings and where he can savour the aroma of coffees from across the globe and at a reasonable price. Barista boasts that it isn't just in the business of coffee; it is also selling an experience. Its slogan: "It is not in the coffee business, serving people, but it is in the people business, serving coffee!"

Planet M is positioned as *the music store of the universe*. It strongly believes in propagating and selling both popular and niche genres of music — an unmatched width of offerings in the right depth. Whether it is through frequent performances by artistes in the store, or its associations with concerts, Planet M tries to bring music-loving customers as close as possible to the music they love. Planet M has been associated with Classical Nites (Pandit Hariprasad Chaurasia, Ustad Amjad Ali Khan, Pandit Jasraj, Pankaj Udhas etc.), power-packed international performances (Right Said Fred, Stereo Nation, Karnatic Lab, Maroon Town, Revolution etc.) and of course popular rock bands like Parikrama.

Wills Sport, the trendy retail store selling an exciting range of leisure wear, is positioned as the store where the customer would *enjoy the change*! Customers can pick a complete wardrobe with the assistance of fashion-literate staff, who are trained to be unobtrusive yet helpful. A Wills Sport customer can exchange a garment bought at any Wills Lifestyle store at an outlet anywhere in India, without a cash memo or even a price tag.

Does the Store's Positioning Stand the Test of Time?

Shoppers' Stop has the '*Feel the experience while you shop*' positioning, which has now been challenged by Lifestyle's promise to differentiate the shopping experience with the '*Stay True. Don't Blend In*' positioning. It almost has the same sprawling space, ambience, brands and similar categories of merchandise. Shopper's Stop's positioning was freedom for the customer to move around and freely access merchandise, a liberal returns and exchange policy and the choice for the customer whether to buy or not to buy. But these are no longer considered special and a 'given' in any department store. The country's first large format retailer may have to enhance deliveries to suit such higher consumer expectations.

Does the Store Communicate What it Actually Delivers?

Wal-Mart's positioning is *Always Low Prices. Always Wal-Mart.* Tom Coughlin, president and chief executive officer of the Wal-Mart stores division says: "We want our customers to trust in our pricing philosophy and to always be able to find the lowest prices with the best possible service. We're nothing without our customers." And that's what they continue to do in Wal-Mart: work diligently to find good deals to pass on to their customers, always being true to their claim of delivering exceptional value. It is not a 'sale' but the 'great price' that the customer can count on. The company has stuck whole-heartedly to its positioning of bargain prices.

Customers Look for Benefits and not the Features of the Store

Nordstrom has positioned itself as the *customer service company,* offering the best possible service, selection, quality and value. Its culture always encourages its employees to make extra efforts to give unequalled customer service — "Not service that used to be, but service that never was."

Nordstrom sales associates are empowered to do virtually everything they can to make sure a shopper leaves the store satisfied, carrying home the right item in the right size in the right colour at the right price. Follow-through after the sale is a way of life at Nordstrom. When a customer receives a call over the phone after a few days of purchasing shoes from the store to find out how they are working out, you can only imagine the quality of service it provides.

So, positioning is how the consumer perceives the brand in the market. Strong brands have a clear, often unique position in the target consumers' minds. Positioning can be achieved through several means, including brand name, image, service standards, product guarantees, packaging and the way in which they are delivered. In fact, successful positioning usually requires a combination of these.

Business strategists talk about the first-mover advantage in positioning. In terms of brand development, by being a first mover, it is possible for the first successful brand in a market to create a clear positioning in the minds of target customers before the competition arrives on the scene. This is true in the case of Shoppers' Stop, which pioneered organized garment and related accessories (department store) retailing in India through a large format.

From Mind Space to Heart Space: All the above instances drive home the message that the positioning of the retail store has to be consistent, without any aberrations. Positioning deliverables have to be integrated with the culture and philosophy of the organization. That's the key to creating an image for the store, helping customers to identify with it and say with pride: "That's My Store!"

Target Customers and Buyer Behaviour: Retailers who seek to understand their customers better always study buyer behaviour in detail and attempt to find out what customers do while in the store or at home.

A food retailer for instance needs to know how his customer lives, how he uses the products he buys and what his consumption patterns are. If an apparel retailer wants to find out what type of clothes its typical customers really want to buy, it might want to get into consumers' closets, literally. Retailers can ask customers to show them how they put together their wardrobes, how they use the clothes that are in fashion and for how long, and on what occasions they buy clothes. Such an exercise helps retailers to find out how consumers mix and match items, which items they choose to keep in their closets during which season or year and why.

RETAIL MARKETING MIX

The retail marketing mix consists of the following elements:
(1) *Product Offerings*: This refers to the product mix that the store retails for customers after a careful study of what their needs and wants are. By matching customer preferences with an assortment of merchandise offered within the store's categories, the retailer gets an ideal basket size per customer. The basket size contains the mix of items a customer buys during a visit.
(2) *Place*: This is the location of the store and its catchment boundaries. The key to optimizing the element of 'place' in the marketing mix is to undertake local marketing efforts besides the national marketing plan.

Determining the market share of the store in the catchment area gives an indication of its performance and efficiency.

(3) *Price*: Price is an important element in the marketing mix as customers are very price-sensitive. Pricing is of different kinds:

Maximum retail price (MRP) on items generally means full pricing.

Promotional pricing involves a temporary reduction in the price to the customer during a particular season, while closing a particular line, or to clear saleable defectives and shop-soiled merchandise.

Loss leader pricing is a tactic used to sell at cost or a little above cost a few critical items to get more footfalls into the store.

Odd pricing is the way footwear organizations like Bata price their products in India — at levels like Rs.129.95, 149.95 etc.

Price bundling is the reduced price offered for a bundle or a predefined group of merchandise when bought together by the customer.

Everyday low pricing (EDLP), which is not a familiar concept in India, is pricing different kinds of merchandise on a lower scale everyday. If pricing is innovative and exclusive to the identity of the store, offering the right value to the buyer, it will bring in more and more customers and help the retailer to retain them as well. (Pricing has been discussed here as part of the marketing mix. Pricing strategy is dealt with in detail in Chapter 6 — *Retail Strategies)*.

(4) *Promotions and Events*: These help the store to achieve its short-term goals. Promotions may be price-led or occasion-led, in which case special merchandise is offered by the store only for the occasion (example: *Dandiya*). Most retail organizations run promotions during festival seasons like Diwali, Christmas, New Year, Valentine's Day, Id, and so on.

Sometimes promotions are driven by brands in cooperation with the retailer. Retail events are gaining significance in India with retailers preferring them to direct price-offs. However, if run very frequently promotions may prove detrimental to the image and positioning of the store.

(5) *People*: There are two kinds of people as far as the retail marketing mix is concerned: *People to Serve* (customers) and *People that Serve* (employees). It is customers who determine whether the retail store is selling the right products and services. People that serve the organization are the ambassadors or the face of the retail store. Excellent delivery standards — which go hand-in-hand with the image and positioning of the store — can be achieved only if the staff are trained well.

(6) *Presentation*: Presentation is the way products and services are grouped and presented in a retail store. Such presentation should conform to the

store's positioning and customer profile. For instance, a boutique selling designer garments needs to present its merchandise in exclusive splendour — it cannot use ordinary furniture and fixtures. Attending on customers in the boutique ought to be done on a very personal basis, as a mass approach will turn them away.

CUSTOMER RELATIONSHIP MANAGEMENT

Customer relationship management or CRM has become the buzzword in India with every retailer in the organized sector trying to create long-lasting consumer stickiness for his retail store.

However, an organization has no business 'managing' customer relationships. Does the customer not have the right to manage his relationship with the retail organization? So, it should actually be *Customer Managed Relationship* and not Customer Relationship Management!

Customer Defined Relationship: Organizations define their relationship with the customer based on the frequency with which he or she uses the organization's services or the quantum of his purchases. It is sometimes defined by awarding colourful cards to the customers — Blue, Silver, Gold, Platinum, etc. So, the relationship here depends on the customer's capacity to spend and not on the organization's ability to serve him. In fact, it is the customer who also has to define the class of service that is extended to him or her — whether it is Blue, Silver, Gold or Platinum! Hotels and restaurants are graded. Educational institutions too are graded by Boards of Accreditation, like the National Bureau of Accreditation of AICTE for management institutes.

In fact, there should be an audit process in place for the retail organization's performance parameters such as merchandise availability, policies and procedures, compliance with legislation, customer responsiveness, customer facilities offered, instances of gaps between promises and fulfillment, quality of services extended and so on. It is consumer panels that must grade retail organizations. This may seem like a wild idea, but if implemented it will make retailers pull up their socks and extend the best possible service, vying with each other to attract customers. This is the first step towards letting customers manage their relationships with retail stores.

Customer Owned Relationship: Will retail stores allow customers to own their own data? Customers will be amazed if retail organizations send them details of their purchases every month in addition to what they currently provide as points statements! Alternatively, retailers can e-mail a copy of the cash memo to the customer if preferred, as and when the transaction is complete. This can be easily done as POS software packages nowadays support an automatic hook-up to e-mail servers when the cashier completes the 'end-of-day' or 'day-close' process.

Farmacross, a pharmacy retail chain in Mumbai that was commissioned recently, has set up a kiosk in a customer society connected to the store in its catchment area. Customers can use the kiosk to order their requirements from their own 'domains' and the store gets ready to deliver the merchandise to the customer's door as soon as the order is clicked. To enable prescription drugs to be retailed, there is also a hook-up to the doctor's terminal for prescriptions! The kiosk within the customers' domain enables them to store and use their own data effectively as and when required. The customers are thus empowered with ready access to information that may help them judge the efficiency of the store's deliveries and whether they want to stick to it.

Customer Decided Relationship and Loyalty Benefits: (Is the store loyal to the customer rather than the customer being loyal to the store?)

Customer preferences and choices are dynamic in nature. Since customers have become shrewd now, they try to get the maximum advantage. They are better informed and expect the retail organization to be loyal to them, demanding that it fulfil their expectations like:

- Emotional Benefits
- Information and Knowledge Benefits
- Conditional Benefits
- Financial Benefits
- Service and Errand Benefits, etc.

Some gaps are common, resulting in the retailer not being loyal to the customer. Like:

— When the retailer makes a tall claim that is not fulfilled and when promised benefits are not delivered.

— When benefits are conditional and complicated for the customer to attain.

— When the points allotted are not commensurate with purchases.

— When not enough information is provided by the retailer or when the customer is not informed on time.

— When the customer sees competitors offering better value consistently.

— When there is monopolistic behaviour by the retailer.

— When the retailer does not respond to the customer instantaneously with commitment.

CMR — an anagram of CRM — is a simple concept and is customer-managed. Every retailer must have end-to-end processes — in terms of information, operational metrics, business outcomes and service offerings — in accordance with consumer expectations.

DIRECT MARKETING

Direct marketing enables retailers to establish personal contact with the customer. The retailers can then have a database of buyers along with their buying occasions and preferences thus ensuring that they can have effective and timely communication directly with consumers. It also provides a key differentiating factor: along with the information direct marketing will ensure efficient communication that will persuade customers to respond instantaneously. The different types of communication in direct marketing are:

(1) *Direct Mail:* This generally has two forms. One is well-designed with proper copy and layout while the other is a simple letter to the customer conveying the required information. Mailers are generally attractive and inviting to read, with highlights of offers and promotions.

(2) *Catalogues and Mail Order:* These are not so common in India. We are yet to come across an Indian retailer in a brick-and-mortar format who does direct marketing by way of catalogues and mail order. However, Otto Burlingtons in India does catalogue and mail order retailing.

(3) *Telemarketing:* A few retailers in India also make telemarketing efforts too along with their brick-and-mortar operations. They use call centres that perhaps handle more queries and responses than proactive marketing.

(4) *Electronic Retailing:* This is yet to take off in a big way. Right now there are a few brick-and-mortar retailers dealing in books and music who sell merchandise through their internet sites as well. Fabmart, a food retailer that was doing e-retailing in south India, has set up brick-and-mortar operations to complement its internet efforts.

MICROMARKETING IN RETAILING

Contemporary marketing in most organized retail establishments in India are generally thematic or tactical. For consumers, the buying process has two stages: choosing a store, followed by a brand. Thematic initiatives communicate what the retail store stands for, trying to put forth the positioning idea/platform on which it is built — say, on the platform of sheer experience or on multi-brand convenience — in order to entice customers into stepping into the store (to generate the required footfalls). Tactical efforts aim to convert browsers into buyers.

Shoppers' Stop, for instance, has positioned its store on the 'experience' platform. Subhiksha in the south relies on the 'less than MRP' platform, Pantaloons on 'family culture and value' while Bata has chosen 'quality

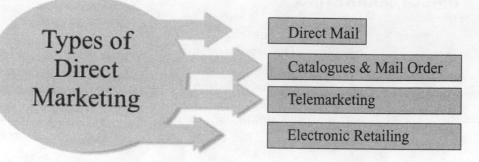

Fig. 15: *Different Types of Communication in Direct Marketing*

footwear at affordable prices'. The tactical promotions of these retail outlets have always consisted of value additions to select merchandise applicable for a short span of time, discounts during sales, or a sweepstakes temptation during festivals.

Mass Approach: When a larger target audience is addressed with a wide assortment of merchandise, retail stores take the mass approach. In both these thematic and tactical efforts, customer segmentation is generally according to socio-economic, geographic, demographic and psychographic categories and reached through common media vehicles. These vehicles reach much more than the targeted customers, and this may result in a lot of spill. For example, in geographic segmentation, there can be a local market focus if the catchment of the store is to be addressed. In psychographics segmentation there may be an appeal to the lifestyle of the consumer to promote the store's offerings. All these segments are generally addressed en masse.

What is Micromarketing?

Micromarketing hits the bull's eye of the target customer. It has a narrow marketing focus and has two forms. One uses the data captured on the customer to analyse his visit patterns and buying behaviour, to carry a marketing message that is tailored specifically to him. The second aims to tailor the product/services mix more closely aligned to the needs and preferences of customers.

Micromarketing is the outreach to consumer clusters of the local market. It does so by identifying specific needs and wants and customizing merchandise and service offerings even at an individual level. This allows the retailer to capitalize on the differences in consumers and competition too.

Portfolio Approach: Micromarketing is hence a portfolio approach, catering to well-understood specific segments with clearly focused categories.

So, What is the Role of Micromarketing in Indian Retailing?

Micromarketing can enable Indian retailers to come up with tactical programmes that cater to the needs of specific individual customers or customer groups by identifying meaningful clusters. For example, in the case of individual customers, a loyalty programme can track purchases and analyse them to provide a meaningful interpretation of his/her tastes and preferences.

Micromarketing identifies very specific target segments such as 'teeny-boppers' in the youth segment or 'hikers' in the leisure category, meets them in their domains, say colleges, and addresses them in their own language. It creates micro clusters of these teeny-boppers or hikers, and attempts to find out their locations, age groups, spending details, lifestyle, leisure activity, preferences of shopping locations, buying behaviour, etc. The retail organization then matches these specific consumer characteristics with what it offers and when. Micromarketing here involves a specific merchandising strategy for these clusters by building special SKUs. Teeny-boppers can perhaps lay their hands on a 'mix and match' of their attire with a package deal or stroll into the 'capri corner' created for them. Or hikers can find a complete kit for their hobby!

MICROMARKETING AND EFFICIENT CONSUMER RESPONSE

Efficient consumer response involves meeting customers' needs and expectations, and planning a strategy of deliveries. Micromarketing enables retailers to implement these processes with precision. We will now see how micromarketing helps in the development of an efficient consumer response (ECR) model for the retail store and how it eventually enables the store to build its business objectives:

- *Providing Strategic Direction*: Micromarketing creates consumer value by analysing the dynamics of the store's consumer clusters and provides need-based product categories, thus giving a strategic direction to the business.
- *Planning the Right Merchandise Mix:* Micromarketing helps the store optimize the assortment mix, not only by fulfilling the needs of the target customers but also by having the right inventory levels, thus ensuring a viable revenue stream.
- *Planning Efficient Pricing*: Micromarketing enables the retail store attain

a high degree of efficiency in pricing — that is, the customer gets the best value for money.

- *Deciding the Store's Promotions and Events*: Micromarketing facilitates the development of focused promotional programmes and adherence to planned merchandise category objectives. Thus it avoids spill while achieving economies in communication and an optimum level of footfalls and conversions.
- *Enabling Customer Relationship Management*: Micromarketing goes a long way in capturing and analysing data on customers and leveraging it to build relationships with them through interactive communication.
- *Facilitating Consumer Value Measurement*: Micromarketing employs proper feedback mechanisms for the store to assess value addition against the cost for consumers after every programme. It can then effect course corrections, thus ensuring customer delight every time and trigger repeat purchases.

Micromarketing thus brings the retail store closer to consumers who are understood thoroughly. The risk of large unsold inventories is nearly eliminated. As communication is direct and interactive, there is very little room for misunderstanding or a communication gap. Acquisition, maintenance and retention of customers through loyalty programmes can be very cost-effective. The single most important differentiating factor in today's organized retailing is micromarketing, as knowing the customer better and better means keeping him for ever and ever!

ADVERTISING IN RETAILING

Advertising in retailing, like FMCG sales, involves both above-the-line (media) and below-the-line communication. The advertising mix of the retail store consists of:

(a) Point of sale (POS) advertising.
(b) Sales promotion (explained as part of the marketing mix).
(c) Publicity.
(d) Personal selling.

POS Advertising: This is more relevant to the retail store's communication strategy than above-the-line media communication. It is an interesting point that the point of sale itself forms a communication medium as advertising can be done within the store.

POS advertising is in the form of materials and activities. POS materials include festoons, buntings and posters that can be used within the retail premises. POS activities consist of displays, visual merchandising, display contests, shelf-on-hire (SOH) for brands, etc. POS advertising is very cost-effective and addresses the right target customers as they come into the store itself. There are separate places within the store earmarked for in-store branding and signage effectively used for advertising within the store. This is commonplace in convenience stores and food supermarkets.

Sales Promotion: Sales promotions are done with special communication and displays. It uses copy similar to those used in media advertising and other props and materials so that it immediately attracts the customer's attention when he or she enters the store.

Sales promotion need not necessarily involve price-offs every time. The promotion may be for a new product line or a new category that has hit the shop-shelves by way of displays and special product corners. For instance, the bookshop Crossword has a special sales promotion podium for the latest arrivals with sections like bestsellers, recommended reading etc. Sales promotion communication takes place by shelf-talkers thematically designed for the promotion. The theme is extended even to the uniforms that store sales personnel wear.

Publicity: Publicity is the non-paid advertising mileage that the retail organization gets through free write-ups in media about the store's latest arrivals, sales promotions or any event that the store or brand has organized to achieve its sales objectives. New store launches get a great deal of publicity by way of television interviews of the CEO, interviews on FM radio channels, and interviews and write-ups in the press. Most organized retailers employ PR agencies as retainers. Innovations and exclusive programmes are generally accorded the greatest media hype by public relations.

Personal Selling: Sales and service personnel in the retail organization are its ambassadors, and communicate the value proposition of the entire store. Well-trained sales and service associates who advertise the store by their extraordinary selling and service skills are assets to the retail organization.

Personal selling helps in cross-selling complementary items to the customers, up-selling to achieve higher volumes and selling add-ons to increase average ticket size. Sales associates can do personal selling by making suggestions to customers on what they need to buy for specific needs.

SUMMARY

- Retailing in India is growing fast and soon there is going to be a scramble for the customer's wallet share. Hence retailers here need to plan their strategies to differentiate themselves.
- Retailers should not stop with just attempting to get a share of the customer's wallet, but also need to get the customer's mind space through their positioning efforts.
- If retailers follow customer relationship management practices genuinely, they would be able to convince customers into making space for them in their hearts and be loyal to their product offerings.
- Innovative advertising, communication and promotions help customers make purchase decisions easily. However, retailers must also deliver what they promise.
- Point of Sale communication is very significant in retailing. It is through POS reminders that browsing is converted into buying.

Questions:

1. Outline the importance of building a store brand, explaining the elements that contribute to the same.

2. Explain 'store positioning' with examples.

3. Explain each element of the retail marketing mix.

4. How is the new perspective of 'customer managed relationship' distinctly different from 'customer relationship management'?

5. What are the different types of direct marketing? Explain each with examples.

6. Elaborate with examples how the portfolio approach in micromarketing differs from the mass approach.

7. How does micromarketing enable efficient consumer response?

8. Write notes on the elements of the advertising mix in retailing.

Predatory Pricing

In general terms, predatory pricing is a situation where a dominant firm charges low prices over a long enough period of time so as to drive a competitor from the market or deter others from entering and then raises prices to recoup its losses. While price/cost comparisons are an important element in determining unreasonably low prices, they are not necessarily determinative unless the price is clearly above cost. Predatory pricing occurs when a company sets an unrealistically low price for the purpose of forcing a competitor to withdraw from the market. This leaves the company with less competition, which means it can disregard market forces, raise prices and exploit consumers.

Price cutting or underselling competitors is not necessarily predatory pricing, but when such techniques are used by a business with substantial market power for the purpose of getting rid of competitors, it is considered to be a misuse of that market power.

In many countries, legal restrictions may preclude this pricing strategy, which may be deemed anti-competitive. In the United States predatory pricing practices may result in antitrust claims of monopolization or attempts to monopolize. Businesses with dominant or substantial market shares are more vulnerable to antitrust claims. However, because the antitrust laws are ultimately intended to benefit consumers, and discounting results in at least short-term net benefit to consumers, the US Supreme Court has set high hurdles to antitrust claims based on a predatory pricing theory. The Court requires plaintiffs to show likelihood that the pricing practices will not only affect rivals but also competition in the market as a whole, in order to establish that there is a substantial probability of success of the attempt to monopolize. If there is a likelihood that market entrants will prevent the predator from recouping its investment through supra competitive pricing, then there is no probability of success and the antitrust claim would fail. In addition, the Court established that for prices to be predatory, they must be below the seller's cost.

Law against predatory pricing in Canada: The criminal sanction against predatory pricing has been part of Canada's competition law for over 50 years. Section 50(1)(c) of the Competition Act, as the provision is now known, rejects the concern that certain unfair pricing methods should not be used in the short run to diminish competition and the benefits which flow from it in the long run. This type of undesirable pricing behaviour is known as "predatory pricing." Placing a criminal ban on a range of price competition, as section 50(l)(c) does, carries with it the risk that business persons may, because of uncertainty about the application of the law, refrain to some extent from engaging in price competition which would be healthy and beneficial. This is heightened by the globalization of markets and increased foreign competition. It is important to ensure that the enforcement policy for predatory pricing does not have a chilling effect on price competition.

The Statutory Provision: Section 50(1)(c) of the Competition Act states: "Everyone engaged in a business who engages in a policy of selling products at prices unreasonably low, having the effect or tendency of substantially lessening competition or eliminating a competitor, or designed to have such effect, is guilty of an indictable offence and is liable to imprisonment for a term not exceeding two years." As set out in section 1.1, the Competition Act's purpose "is to maintain and encourage competition in Canada" (emphasis added). Section 50(1)(c) of the Act is consistent with this purpose by prohibiting those forms of pricing behaviour which, though they may provide short-term benefits to buyers in a particular market, are designed to frustrate and interfere with the process of competition in the longer term, an outcome ultimately detrimental to consumers.

Strictures against predatory pricing in Australia and China: Trade Practices Act provides strictures against predatory pricing in Australia. Predatory pricing is unlawful under section 46(1) of the Trade Practices Act, which prohibits businesses that have substantial market power from taking advantage of that power to eliminate or substantially damage a competitor, prevent the entry of a person into a market, or deter or prevent a person from engaging in competitive conduct in a market.

In 1993, the Standing Committee of the People's Congress adopted "the Law of the People's Republic of China for Countering Unfair Competition", which indicated a new stage in the development of legislation on competition in China. China's Unfair Competition Law is drafted based on the summary of various issues occurred in acts of unfair competition by Chinese companies in their business operations and transactions, the experience of enforcement with respect to countering unfair competition and successful practice and examples of other countries. And the purpose of the Law is to safeguard the healthy development of China's economy and to protect the lawful rights and interests of operators and consumers. Acts of unfair competition prohibited by the Law are summed up as follows:

1. To deceive consumers by passing off a register trade mark of another person, using without authorization, specific name, packaging, decoration of well-known goods, forging or falsely using symbol,

etc.;

2. To abuse administrative powers; (Art. 7)
3. To force others to buy goods designated by public utility enterprises or enterprises having monopoly status;
4. To make tie-in sales;
5. To sell with prizes attached by fraudulent methods;
6. To buy or sell goods by means of bribery;
7. To submit tenders in collusion with one another;
8. To damage competitor's reputation by falsehood;
9. To squeeze competitors out by selling goods at price below cost;
10. To infringe other's business secrets.

In China, Industrial and Commercial Administration Department is the agency to enforce the law for countering unfair competition. The punishment rendered against activities of unfair competition are: e.g. ordering to stop illegal acts; confiscating illegal proceeds; imposing a fine of less than 3 times the amount of illegal proceeds; revoking the business license or being prosecuted for criminal liability. After the promulgation of the Law, the industrial and commercial agencies have handled more than ten thousand unfair competition cases overall in China. The Chinese government will strengthen the enforcement and complete its competition policy and law step by step in order to protect the fair competition in China's economy.

In India even though the Competition Act was passed by Parliament in December 2002, for nearly five years now the Indian government has been unable to bring into force the substantive provisions of the act. Explanation (b) to Section 4 of the Competition Act defines "predatory price" as the sale of goods or provision of services, at a price which is below the cost, as may be determined by regulations, of production of the goods or provision of services, with a view to reducing competition or eliminating the competitors.

The implementation of the Act, and the appointment of the chairman and all but one of the ten members of the proposed Competition Commission of India (CCI), was stalled by a writ petition in the Indian Supreme Court which contended that the constitutional doctrine of separation of powers required that the CCI be headed by a judge chosen by the judiciary and not a bureaucrat chosen by the executive. In the event of the retail sector opening up in a big way if the beneficiaries have to be our consumers, then the Government of India should notify the Act immediately.

Questions for Discussion

1. What is predatory pricing and how can it affect healthy competition among retail stores?

2. What are the steps taken by the governments in various countries to prevent predatory pricing as a retail strategy to edge out competition?

3. What are the steps that the Government of India should take to prevent predatory pricing in retail?

CHAPTER 11

Franchising in Retailing

CHAPTER OBJECTIVES

1. To provide a clear understanding of franchising as a form of retail business
2. To enlighten students of franchising practices in India
3. To outline the different types of franchising
4. To provide insights into the types of franchise agreements
5. To identify the success factors of retail franchising operations in India

INTRODUCTION TO FRANCHISING

Franchising is a form of business that is quite popular in retailing. It is used by organizations to expand their business through partners who in general terms are given the right to run the organization's business. The organization becomes the franchiser and the partner is the franchisee. In a franchise arrangement the franchisee pays the franchiser a sum of money or a percentage of the income; the franchisee is allowed to exercise the rights under the franchiser's guidance. In the event of a franchise start-up scenario, the franchiser often covers the franchisee with a guaranteed income. Franchising is one of the best methods employed globally to expand retail businesses across borders or within one's own country.

Franchising is a growing business globally, and it is known to generate win-win business partnerships. Franchising also increases employment, earnings and entrepreneurship. It is a particularly good developmental tool in countries where financial resources are inadequate and the need to stimulate individual initiative is acute. Franchising helps a great deal in promoting sharing of technology, trademarks, marketing, intellectual property and business design rights. It also has the effect of creating relationships between one economy and another, which benefits developing countries, or countries that are shifting to a market economy.

Franchising has a two-fold purpose: it enables the franchisee reduce risks since he operates with the proven knowhow and brand of the franchiser. The franchiser too benefits as he is using the franchisee's resources to expand his business. In short, franchising in retailing involves creating a network of interdependent business relationships that allow many to share a store brand, a proven rollout system and a successful method of doing business. Thus, franchising is a strategic alliance between groups of people who have specific relationships and responsibilities with the common goal of dominating markets getting and keeping more customers than their competitors.

FRANCHISING IN INDIA

There has been an influx of foreign brands into the country since India is considered to be an ideal place for new business ventures because of its established democratic system and rich history. Rapid changes in consumer attitudes in our country — though many people live in villages and have limited purchasing power — have encouraged many global brands to set up shop in India. India has a large and growing middle class and a wealthy segment of consumers. Franchising allows India to build its retail infrastructure and develop its domestically-oriented businesses in a way that is efficient and profitable for the national economy.

The Indian franchise economy accounts for five percent of the country's GDP and will make the economy grow because it encourages private enterprise with no danger of flight of capital. At the same time, it offers the potential to establish products and services that meet global standards. Today the organized Indian retail franchise market is estimated at approximately Rs. 10,000 crores (US $ 2.5 billion).

However, despite repeated attempts by industry experts in India to convince policy makers to allow foreign direct investment (FDI) in the retail sector, that hasn't happened. There has been vigorous opposition from small traders who fear that foreign retailing companies will take away their business leading to the closure of their shops and resulting in considerable unemployment. Given the political clout of the small trading community because of their enormous numbers, the government has barred FDI in retailing since 1997. Hence, at present, foreign retailers can only enter the retailing sector through franchising agreements, except single brand retailing.

There are two major types of franchising that are prevalent today in retailing — product/trade name franchising and business format franchising.

Product/Trade Name Franchising

Here the franchisee requires the trade name, trademark and or product from the supplier or manufacturer. For example Arrow, Scullers, Tommy Hilfiger, etc. are brands franchised in India. Walt Disney has been successful in having its label on all sorts of goods for children, like clothing, toys and school equipment.

Business Format Franchising

This format of franchising permits the franchisee to use the franchiser's products/services, trade name, trademark and, *most importantly, the prescribed business format*. In India, business format franchising is done in the case of McDonalds, Bata, KFC, etc. These franchisees have the identity of the franchiser company in their retail environment, right from store design to service standards to deliveries. A lot of local franchises have also become established, like Nilgiris — the food retailing chain in the south that currently has ten franchised stores. Pizza Corner, the chain of dine-in restaurants and delivery outlets, plans to open another 100 franchised outlets over the next five years.

TYPES OF FRANCHISE AGREEMENTS

The following are the key methods of franchise arrangements made globally. Let us analyse their pros and cons:

Direct Franchising Format: The direct format of franchising is a simple arrangement where the franchiser grants the franchise to a franchisee by the execution of a contract. Under this arrangement the franchiser has direct control over the franchisee and the dos and don'ts are clearly specified. The franchiser here grants the franchise along with operating guidelines and the policies of the franchiser. The consideration payable to the franchiser is usually in the form of a periodic royalty. The franchiser provides assistance to the franchisee by offering all the standards and process manuals, shares expertise by offering transfer of knowledge and technology and handholds the establishment of the network. The franchiser monitors and controls the operations too. The singular advantage is that of getting a readymade and established business format that can be replicated. The flip side of this format is that franchisees will have to work strictly within specified compartments with little room for flexibility in operations; every local adaptation of the format will have to be approved by the franchiser. In the case of foreign franchisers, franchise agreements arc governed by the laws of countries to which the franchiser and franchisee belong.

Subsidiary Franchising: Wherever laws and regulations allow foreign organizations to set up their subsidiaries in India, franchising is done through a subsidiary. The franchiser controls the subsidiary directly. The major advantage of this approach is that the franchiser is present in the country as a corporate body. The contract will in this case be a domestic contract and thus subject to local laws. Most of the foreign automobile companies work this way; franchise rights for retailing and dealerships are given to others by the subsidiary office in India, which controls all the processes in retail and distribution. Here the subsidiary office enters into an agreement with the franchisees.

Regional/Area Franchising Or Multiple Franchising: Here the franchiser offers franchise rights to a franchisee only for a region or an area. There are separate franchisees for each area or region in the country. This kind of arrangement is also known as multiple franchising when more than one franchisee is given the franchise rights for the same brand. An ideal example is McDonalds in India where franchise rights are given to different organizations in every region. Such agreements offer the franchisee the right to open a multiple number of outlets according to a predetermined schedule and within a given area.

Unit Franchising: The franchiser offers rights to a franchisee to open and run just one store through an exclusive agreement. This arrangement involves many franchisees. Managing many franchisees across the country may be an uphill task for franchisers. Further, it is very difficult to monitor compliance to specified standards and processes. The strength of this format is that each franchisee pays full attention to his store and its performance. In India, Himalaya of Bangalore has adopted the unit franchising method for its ayurvedic concept stores. Many of Titan Watches' 'World of Titan' stores fall under this category too.

Master Franchising: In this arrangement, the franchiser grants the franchise rights to an entire country or territory. The franchisee is permitted to open franchise outlets itself and/or grant sub-franchises to others. In this case, two agreements are generally involved — one that is entered into between the franchiser and master franchisee and the other between the master franchisee and sub-franchisees. Many footwear store brands are franchised in this fashion. The major advantage of this kind of franchising is the rapid increase in scale following specified standards and processes. Further, local sub-franchisees are familiar with the local market and business viability can be ensured.

FRANCHISE OPERATIONS ARRANGEMENTS

Franchiser Owned and Franchisee Operated: The franchiser owns or has the property lease so that it is sure of the location's security for a long time and lets the franchisee operate the business for a consideration. The capital investments are made by the franchiser, but the operations are handled by the franchisee who follows the norms and standards agreed upon. Commissions are generally lower in such arrangements. Fuel retailers like Hindustan Petroleum Corporation (HPCL) and Bharat Petroleum Corporation (BPCL) operate many of their outlets through such unit franchise/dealer agreements.

Franchisee Owned and Franchisee Operated: In this arrangement, the franchisee is responsible for all investments, and the operations as well. Only the expertise and guidelines are provided by the franchiser. The product offerings are often sold on an outright or on a consignment basis to the franchisee. The franchisee gets more commissions under this arrangement compared to the franchiser owned and franchisee operated scenario. In India, Zodiac operates its men's retail outlets under this arrangement. Bata's franchisee agents across the country operate under similar terms. Arrow, which is a master franchise held by Arvind Garments in India, has such arrangements. International franchises in India such as Nike, Reebok and the homegrown ColorPlus use this franchise arrangement with their franchisees. This is the most popular method of running retail outlets in India.

KEY SUCCESS FACTORS IN FRANCHISING

Implementation of a Pre-Tested Model: Franchising will yield good results if done by organizations after creating a brand and testing it for its successful operations. Retail organizations ought to look at establishing a Company-Owned and Company-Operated (COCO) model successfully before seeking expansion by taking the franchise route.

Transfer of Knowledge and Relevant Inputs by the Franchiser: A well-known and trusted brand automatically draws customers. Another major benefit is the support given by franchisers, who provide their valuable inputs gained by their rich experience in retailing. This includes training, store design and advertising and promotion. In some cases, companies also provide minimum sales guarantees, though these are rare since they reduce the incentive for franchisees to sell. Another advantage for franchisees is that they have to interact only with one supplier, greatly simplifying business operations.

The Franchisee is the Franchiser's Face to Customers: The franchisee has to carry on his operations by playing the role of the principal brand. The store's image elements and product or merchandise portfolio have to be carefully maintained as any non-compliance to specified standards may disturb the customer's buying experience. This also includes the upkeep of various other standards specified in the areas of customer service, store presentation and identity, operating processes and store personnel skills and identities. All these will enable the transfer of the total brand experience to the customer. This seamless integration of the franchiser and the franchisee to present one single 'face' to the customer will ensure successful store operations.

Creating a Win-Win Situation by Reducing Risks: In a franchise arrangement, both the franchiser and the franchisee must stand to gain. The franchiser gets a partner in the franchisee to establish his business and shares with the franchisee such tested technologies, product offerings and processes that the franchisee can apply immediately to attain business growth. Sharing investments and returns through mutually agreed means will enable the growth of both the franchiser and the franchisee, covering the risks at the same time.

An Attitude of Ownership and Shared Responsibilities: Franchisees fail when the franchise retail business is not 'owned' by the franchisee. Many franchisees tend to treat the franchise as the franchiser's business; they often feel that the franchiser has the responsibility of ensuring success. Nothing should be left to chance: there must be clearly defined responsibilities for both franchiser and franchisee.

Periodic Performance Review: Regular reviews of performance and planning actions for implementation by both parties will ensure successful franchise operations. Besides, such periodical reviews will bring to light gaps in any area of deliverables on the part of either the franchisee or the franchiser that have to be dealt with urgently.

SUMMARY

- In the absence of FDI in retailing in India, franchising is the desired root for foreign multinationals to operate in India.
- Franchising is an effective method of rolling out retail stores in order to establish a retail network quickly in a country like India, whose geographical spread is vast.
- An ideal type of franchising needs to be chosen that is relevant to the kind of retail business and its objectives.
- A robust franchising agreement ensures a lasting relationship between the franchiser and the franchisee.

Questions:

1. Briefly describe the franchising form of retailing and its advantages in retailing in India.
2. Briefly outline the major types of franchising.
3. What are the different types of franchise agreements, their advantages and disadvantages? Explain with suitable examples.
4. Describe the key success factors of franchising in India.

RETAIL FRANCHISING

(i) ARCHIES GIFTS & GREETINGS — CREATING A LARGE NETWORK!

Archies was set up in 1979 as a partnership firm to carry out the business of manufacturing and marketing posters and greeting cards. The company pioneered the concept of branded retailing in India. The first exclusive store of the company was opened in 1987. In 1990, the business of the partnership firm was taken over by Archies Greetings & Gifts Pvt Ltd and the company was incorporated as a public limited company in 1995. Today Archies Gifts & Greetings is the market leader in the gifts and greetings business.

The business was started as a hobby. Archies were into their family business of sarees and from there they started the business of songbooks (lyric books) of English songs. They sold all their merchandise through mail order at that time. Then they started making posters, which were also distributed through mail order. Subsequently, Archies started getting queries from retailers who wanted to stock their products, so the wholesale network was started. The company then got feedback about the demand for greeting cards, and began to deal in them as well. After that, they started opening exclusive stores because cards had limited appeal at the time. The business was started in 1979 and the first store was set up in 1987. They then made their own model suitable for Indian conditions. They created a branded franchise because the scenario was conducive to franchised outlets in India. Today the company has a strong network of over 500 franchise stores, apart from six branch offices and 55 distributors located at 180 locations across the country. Archies' success was due to the creation of innovative products that were price-sensitive and of good quality, retail branding, and the creation of a countrywide retail network through the franchise route.

(ii) APOLLO HEALTH AND LIFESTYLES LTD. — PRIMARY FOCUS ON FRANCHISING

Apollo Health and Lifestyles (AHLL) is a 100 percent subsidiary of the Hyderabad-based Apollo Hospitals group. The group came up with the innovative concept of setting up specialty clinics — Apollo Clinic — across the country. These clinics offer a comprehensive range of day-to-day health services under one roof. These include specialist consultation, comprehensive diagnostic services, a range of preventive health check packages and a 24-hour pharmacy. There is also a telemedicine facility, connecting patients and enabling them to seek opinions from an expert panel of doctors from Apollo Hospitals, as and when required.

Apollo decided to foray into primary healthcare after recognising the phenomenal business potential of this segment. A KSA Technopak study of SEC A and B households revealed that an urban household spent 11 percent of its income on healthcare, of which 68 percent was on non-hospital expenditure. The organization's internal assessment also showed that the average healthcare expenditure per family per month was Rs 540 on consultation and tests alone. The estimated value of the Indian healthcare system is Rs 100,000 crore. Of this, hospitals accounts for about 30 percent. Effectively, this means that Apollo is looking at a market of around of Rs 70,000 crore. What's more there's a huge market opportunity in the day-to-day healthcare segment since the primary healthcare market in the country is not very organized.

Having set up company owned and run clinics, AHLL has now forayed into opening franchised clinics. The company already has 55 clinics operational in all the major locations of the country. It aims to have a total of 75 operational clinics by mid 2008, and in the medium-term plans to have more than 200 clinics by 2010, according to recent reports. It is learnt that the model is such that the franchisee has to invest in the clinic as well as manage day-to-day operations. Each clinic is set up on leased premises of approximately 4,000 sq ft and involves an investment of about Rs 2 crore and will be funded on a 1:1 debt equity ratio, it is learnt. AHLL will provide assistance and be involved in mobilising resources, selecting appropriate sites, site architecture and installation of medical equipment.

Going International in a Big Way: AHLL intends to use its expertise, standards and cost competitiveness to tap this opportunity. Its plan is to leverage opportunities in the international health market, primarily through the franchise route. It is in advanced stages of discussions to set up clinics in various countries, including Pakistan. In fact, in Pakistan, according to reports, the company is expecting to award the franchise soon and it can be either in Karachi, Lahore or both the cities. AHLL has successfully set up their franchised clinics in Riyadh, Saudi Arabia and Qatar in the UAE region.

A clinic in Nigeria is underway and it is soon to be launched. It is learnt that a proposal has been submitted in Yemen to establish a clinic there.

The organization plans to ensure consistently superior quality service in every sphere, ranging from personnel and infrastructure to equipment and operating procedures, and these will be transferred to the franchisees. While the services will essentially be the same as those offered in India, there will be customisation with respect to local needs and social norms as indicated by the demand studies and research. AHLL will provide its expertise; its scope of services will include providing strategic inputs in the area of business development and marketing as well as knowhow and technical services in recruitment, training and non-negotiable service quality standards.

The following critical success factors are looked into while establishing Apollo Clinics:

- Accredited staff and management.
- High-tech equipment and high technology usage.
- Stringent quality control of processes and procedures.
- Strong relationships with doctors, smaller hospitals and insurance companies to ensure adequate referrals.
- Extensive client base.

(iii) BPL MOBILE GALLERIES — THE FRANCHISEE PAYOUT MODEL

BPL went in for franchising by establishing BPL Mobile Galleries (BMG). The company always intended the galleries to be service touch-points where sales also happened. Clearly, the focus is on customer service. So while designing the payout, kept the following in mind:

1. BPL did not want any fixed payout; typically it was a minimum guaranteed commission.
2. It wanted revenue-sharing arrangements for genuine involvement of franchisees.
3. The payout should be weighted towards service elements more than sales commission.

Based on the above, the only quantifiable elements in its business that could be linked to service were billing and collection. Even though collection is a reflection of billing, it decided to compensate the franchisee on both. This was done to ensure that the franchisee did not become lop-sided in his focus, that is, he did not become a collection agent only or just a sweet talker with no focus on collecting the company's money. It also put a nominal debit on outstanding beyond a specified period. The logic here was that if the subscriber got good service, why should he not pay on time for the services availed?

To come to actual amounts of billing and collections, the company had to take a systematic approach, as it would be too erratic otherwise. In its billing system, the company classified each customer according to his primary address in the gallery area as a cost-centre. Now, the customer is mobile; he can be anywhere in the network and pay his bills anywhere or avail the services of a gallery anywhere. However his bill transactions will always be reflected in the particular cost-centre. All the payment credits would only be reflected in his cost-centre. It has attached cost-centres specific to the location of the gallery to the franchisee. This ensures that it can keep track of billing, collections, outstanding for each franchisee.

Further the customer is not hassled by being attached to a particular gallery; he can go to any gallery anywhere in the circle. The franchisee does end-to-end servicing for the customer, right from acquisition, credit verification, bill deliveries, voluntary and involuntary collections up to specified period, online or over-the-counter resolution of requests, complaints and queries, retention activities, etc. This means the franchisee has to have gallery staff and field staff accordingly.

The payout on billing varies from one percent to 1.5 percent and on collection varies from two percent to three percent. The debit on outstanding amounts varies from one percent to 1.5 percent and the period of outstanding amounts varies from more than 60 days to more than 90 days. On sales the franchisee earns as per the existing Terms of Trade as decided by the sales department. On MOTS (prepaid cards) sales the franchisee earns the retail margins, which again is decided by the sales department.

The system is slightly different in the metros. Since creating cost-centres and administering them is a concern, the galleries in the metros are pure retail outlets. This means the franchisee attends to only a walk-in subscriber and has no field staff. There are no cost-centre allocations. These BMGs are remunerated almost equally on sales and service. Sales are in similar terms as above with some exclusive promotion support. Instead of revenue sharing on billing, the franchisee gets different amounts for different service assignments he does from his gallery, without any debits for any defaulted assignments. For example, the franchisee gets Rs 150 for each roaming he assigns from his gallery. The franchisee also gets one percent on all cash and credit card collections and no commission for cheques collected. Earlier, Mumbai galleries were paid a minimum guaranteed commission, which has now been discontinued. The payout model of the BPL franchise has been a successful one and the organisation has more than 100 at present (including a few of its own).

With effect from Mar '06, all BPL Mobile Galleries of Maharashtra & Goa, Tamil Nadu & Kerala were migrated to Vodafone (then Hutch) with the only exception of Mumbai. Over a period of time all the franchising models of the three circles were also migrated to the existing Vodafone (then Hutch) model.

The current model of franchising pays back a percentage of revenue to the franchisee or an assured ROI on the investments made (whichever is higher). There is a cap on the earning in case the returns are very high. The franchisee is not involved in running the day-to-day operations; he only manages the environment, as and when required. The entire management of the Vodafone Stores in these circles is the direct responsibility of the company. The Store in-charge is on the company payroll while the rest are outsourced from an established agency. All expenses are either borne by the company directly or reimbursed to the franchisee.

In Mumbai, the franchising format remains the same, except the company has taken over the lease of all existing and new premises from the franchisees. The company recovers the amounts spent on the rental by deducting a fixed amount from each postpaid sales commission payable to the franchisee.

Franchising has been more successful in the United States compared to independent businesses. The same trend can be replicated in Indian provided the right modalities are worked out and agreed upon. The key challenges in successful franchise operations in India includes larger commitments from the parties involved, greater handholding through turbulent times by the franchiser and having a consumer-oriented perspective to the relationship between the franchiser and the franchisee with common goals and understanding.

Questions for Discussion

1. What in your opinion are the reasons for an entrepreneur getting into franchise operations in India?
2. Discuss the different franchise models that can work in the Indian scenario.
3. Elucidate the relevance of creating pilot models before franchising in retailing.
4. Is franchising a desired route for foreign multinationals that want to operate in the retail sector in the absence of FDI in retail in India? Discuss.

CHAPTER 12

Retail Management Information Systems

CHAPTER OBJECTIVES

1. To provide an overview of the recent international developments in retail technology and automation
2. To enlighten the reader about the benefits of retail technology
3. To discuss the applications of current retail technology in India
4. To discuss the role of retail technology in various retailing functions
5. To provide the reader with insights into retail technology as an enabler of efficient management information systems for effective decision-making

RETAIL TECHNOLOGY AND AUTOMATION

Technology has enabled retailers to function efficiently in every area. In this chapter the focus is on the role of technology and management information systems in all the key functions of retailing.

Point of Sale (POS) Technology: The customer check-out process has now been simplified to the extent where buyers can just walk through the store. A recent film shows a customer apparently 'shoplifting' and walking away from a supermarket. But in reality he was carrying the stuff that he bought through sensors that scanned at an instant all the merchandise he had. And in no time another sensor identified him, and consequently took payment from his credit card too! This demonstrates what innovations can do in the retail sector. Just imagine how it can alter the current cumbersome process of a customer entering the store with a shopping list and waiting until the salesperson wrapped up the merchandise for delivery behind a counter. Point of sale technology not only enables fast cashiering and efficient customer checkout, it effectively captures customer data and stores information for integration with the back-end technology to track customer purchases.

The past decade has seen so much improvement in retailing in India that we can say that we have leapfrogged into the future. What took a long time to develop in the mature markets in the West has been quickly adopted in India. Like the changeover from black and white TV to colour, which happened so fast in the country unlike in the West. Customer convenience, business viability and having that singular edge have been the major factors driving technology in retail, especially in the areas of operating processes, inventory management and customer relationship practices.

THE ROLE OF RETAIL TECHNOLOGY IN STORE OPERATING PROCESSES

Increased competition has led to tighter margins and greater pressure on profits. Operating expenses such as rent, payroll, utilities, etc. have steadily risen as gross margins have declined. The challenge of the future will be to increase the bottom line, not through increases in margins but from operating efficiencies.

According to experts, the two major technology innovations in the retail business have been the bar code and the shopping cart. Customers now also have free access to merchandise and information. Electronic Data Interchange (EDI) — which facilitates direct computer-to-computer transactions from the store to the vendors' databases and ordering systems — has enabled just-in-time inventory management. Product information kiosks and hand-held shopping assistants have enabled customers to find information on their own without having to ask questions or allowing anyone to invade their private space while shopping. Wireless portable data transfer (PDT) units help in stock takes and download the data into the database at the back-end office. Automatic replenishment through the merchandise management system tracks the merchandise sold and replenishes them in the inventory in an amazing manner through an efficient supply chain management system. Global product identification is enabled by the Universal Product Code (UPC), and its special bar code and unique numbering pattern help track inventory even across continents.

In the area of space management, organizations like AC Nielsen have mapped planograms with even margins in an attempt to integrate store space planning with optimal financial productivity. AC Nielsen's decision support services enable organizations to leverage their robust market and consumer information for tailored, rapid and well-informed decision-making. They support sophisticated multi-dimensional reporting, data navigation, analytical modelling, graphical presentations and expert systems tools.

Because of the low-margin nature of the business, retailers will have to focus on operational efficiency in order to create competitive differentiation. Such technology-based systems will be adopted rapidly in India. In the case of store security systems, the rate of innovation has been rapid. There are systems that work very efficiently with unseen and camouflaged tags. For instance, there are tags that spill indelible ink on anyone who tries to remove them forcibly, like shoplifters. Every professionally managed store has comprehended the need to save money by preventing shrinkage.

RETAIL TECHNOLOGY AND CRM

Customer service is supported by customer database programs that allow the retailer to identify which customers purchased what items and when. These systems link every SKU to a customer's name and address and allow relevant queries to be run: for example, a high-value basket query or a lost customer query. The database can produce a list of all customers according to what they spent in the past year, the number of times he or she shopped during a specific time-frame and so on. The Customer Relationship Management (CRM) software allows retailers to track customers and their purchase behaviour, thus allowing communication and promotions to be planned. With its signature-capture technology, CRM helps at the POS to gather all the information about the customer and ensures that his payments are easier too.

HUMAN RESOURCES & EXECUTIVE INFORMATION SYSTEMS

Technological innovations in the area of human resources management have made staff scheduling easy, especially in large retail formats. They have also enabled performance-linked incentives to be computed on an automated system and track achievements. CD-ROMs played on the shop floor have made training retail staff much easier. A few years ago the Bangalore-based branded fine jewellery retailer Carbon — realizing the problems involved in training employees in almost 38 retail counters across the country — developed an innovative induction training CD packed with product information and specific jewellery retailing skills provided by their area heads. CEO Mahesh Rao says: "We speak to our new employees in any location directly. We are able to show pictures of our state-of-the-art manufacturing facility at Bangalore to even those in Assam and north-eastern states through the CD along with product information and deliver basic retail selling skills until they visit us or we meet them personally."

A Human Resources Information System (HRIS) facilitates implementing the Performance Management System for retail personnel so that they can serve customers more efficiently.

Executive Information System (EIS) is a program that helps retail executives look at key data for effective decision-making and arrange it in any form they wish. For example, a chain store can easily compare, say today's sales, to the figure on the same day last year. If today's sales are down compared to that on the same day last year, EIS will help analyse each store's figures to pinpoint those that are lagging behind. After finding a store whose sales are down, one can drill down to the figures of each department or any rung in the merchandise hierarchy. After finding a department that is lagging behind, one can drill down further to the various classifications, then the SKUs in each class, and compare this year's inventory to last year's — all in a matter of seconds. EIS also helps produce graphs that help retail executives make quick business decisions.

RETAIL AUTOMATION IN MERCHANDISE AND SCM SYSTEMS

The application of merchandise and supply chain planning allows the retailer to draw up store merchandise and supply (including re-orders) plans and monitor performance against them. Basic planning typically involves sales and inventory plans for each store in the chain, for each merchandise category by month. The information feeds an open-to-buy application to control purchases by merchandise category so that planned sales are achieved. The technology automatically calculates re-order requirements and creates purchase orders. Purchase orders may be suggested manually

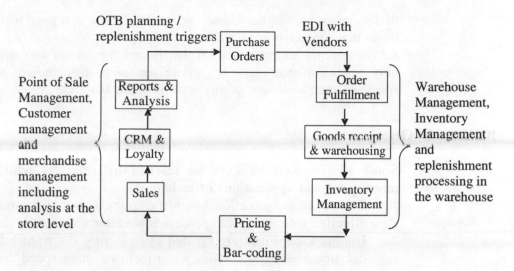

Fig. 16: *Merchandise Management Cycle*

(the system helps review them before communicating them to vendors), or automatically communicated to vendors. This application is typically part of Purchase Order Management.

Price and Promotion Management

Price management allows the retail back-end system to mark down prices for groups of items, based on select criteria — for example, all items related to a specific season. Markdowns can be permanent or temporary (during a promotional event). *Promotion management* allows retailers to plan promotional events, which may include temporary price changes. The application tracks the performance of the promoted items during the event for future decisions.

Management Information Systems and Analysis

Reports provide performance information that allows the retailer to manage the operation more effectively, such as how sales in a category match up to the plan. Key types include exception, interactive, and ad hoc reports.

Exception reports highlight only those items that require action. For example, an out-of-stock report will highlight items that need to be re-ordered immediately.

Interactive reports enable the system to query the information in the report and drill down to the relevant detail. For example, inquire on sales performance by category, and then click on the category to drill down to items that are performing well or poorly.

Ad hoc reports are requested on the fly and the format and criteria are used only once. For example, a request to see the performance of all SKUs in a specified merchandise category with specific features.

KEY LESSONS

Some key lessons have to be learned by retailers while discussing innovations and applications of technology:

1.   The retail organization has to be quick to identify and adopt cost-effective technology for process innovations.
2.   Unique capabilities are created by selecting the right information for decision-making and acting upon them to attain speed and accuracy.
3.   Business needs should drive technology and not the other way round. (Most Indian retail organizations use less than 50% of their ERP capabilities.)
4.   In-store technologies should be deployed for customer convenience and to stay ahead of the competition.
5.   Current innovations may become obsolete tomorrow. So review the performance of such innovations and work on scalability.
6.   Remember, customers adopt new technology and processes quickly and hence their expectations keep going up. The pace of innovation should be commensurate with consumer expectations.
7.   Merely employing technology does not guarantee success. Integrate innovations with technology as an enabler.
8.   Above all a retail organization should possess thorough know-how with common sense, interpersonal skills, a problem-solving attitude and a clear vision for the future.
9.   Lack of execution or implementation skills in an organization have rendered the best of innovations futile.

With the 'Veri Chip' being planted into mankind with advanced biosensor capabilities energized by radio frequency, changes in retail consumer interaction are imminent. This will lead to thorough customer intimacy. While the 'Veri Chip' will speak for customers, it is left to the retail organization to chip their customers together to find a winning formula.

SUMMARY

- Retail efficiencies can be achieved by using the right technology. Every function in retailing can reduce fulfillment gaps, cycle times and achieve great efficiencies.

- A few Indian retailing organizations have implemented ERP packages to achieve better resource utilization through automated processes.
- The future of retailing depends on reducing the gap between a retailer and the customer in terms of understanding and delivering product offerings, communication, deliveries of service, etc. It is through technology that the retailer can understand all these in the right perspective. Intelligent analysis of data will enable a better understanding of the customer.
- Innovation is the key in retail technology applications as consumers adapt to technology developments fast.

Questions:

1. Discuss technology's contribution to customer convenience at the point of sale.

2. Describe briefly the benefits of retail automation.

3. Discuss the role of retail technology in attaining efficiency in store operating processes.

4. Discuss retail technology as a great enabler in the following key functions of retailing:
    — Customer Relationship Management
    — Human Resources Information and Executive Information Systems
    — Merchandise and Supply Chain Management
    — Pricing and Promotions Management

5. What are the key lessons to be learned by organizations while applying technology in the retail business?

Retail Technology: Enabling Efficient Processes in Indian Retailing

As modern retailing in India is growing, many retail organizations are busy chalking out their strategies to quickly grab a heart-share of customers, notwithstanding their mindshare! Experts say that two key factors shall contribute to gaining customer stickiness in a large measure – one, a seemingly well planned merchandise mix for the customer, offered without any disappointments in the right time, in the right place, in the right price and in the right quantities and two, how well the retail store serves its customers pursuant to their expectations. If these two factors are focused on with meticulous attention, the retail customer would not turn away to any other place for satisfying his shopping needs and pleasures too. It seems so much simple but in practice, a retail organization has to exercise all its erudite methods of knowing every customer and putting together a merchandise mix for selling from their shelves. In addition to knowing the customer well, a retail organization ought to foresee styles and obsolescence, trends, etc. besides understanding even diverse things as palate desires and their dynamism too! At times the store's merchandising team will have to delve into the history of shopping habits for tracking repeat purchase trends. The other aspect of service too is related to understanding what those customers of varied dispositions would expect. It is said that more often a customer expects to be delighted with unexpected offers from the store and pleased with an 'extra mile' service!

An efficient enabler of achieving efficiencies in merchandising and customer service is undoubtedly retail technology. Deploying the right retail technology will help retail organizations have a proper merchandise plan pursuant to the needs of the customer. A base stock plan and a planogram (a planogram is a mapped shelf stocking plan in a retail store with its defined quantities and shelf location specifications) is well engineered by proper technology support. Replenishments are done in a retail store as a consequence to managing a well-defined demand chain process enabled by the right technology that can ensure very minimal stock-out scenarios. Shelf fill rates are monitored by the merchandise management system thoroughly and so there are no vacant shelves to disappoint customers. As retailing is a game of turning stocks over as frequently as possible to gain the maximum Gross Margin Returns on Inventory (GMROI), technology helps a store have performance measures worked out to the detail of an SKU (Stock Keeping Unit) level. Great advancements have taken place in deploying innovative technologies to help retailers' analytics work in their business. Wireless networking technology applications enable retailers to even identify customers when they are inside the store and remind the store personnel of their past purchases too! Other developed radio frequency ID (RFID) technologies like the wireless staff device provide information to the sales associate while technology enabled shopping carts will help customers get the right information.

A hi-fashion store in the West bears testimony to 'ultimate innovation' in technology applications to excite the customer! The enabling technology for the store is RFID tagging. All the store merchandise has its RFID tag. When scanned and detected, immediate access is provided to a database where there is rich stream of content for every garment, shoe, and bag. This is in the form of sketches, catwalk video clips, and color swatches. There is also up-to-date information on every item, such as what sizes or colors are currently available. This enables the sales associate to spend more time attending personally to a customer, and less time chasing to the stock room to check for available items. The store's dressing rooms are an amazing example of wonderful innovation. Each dressing room is a simple eight-foot-square booth with privalite glass walls that switch from transparent to translucent when a room is occupied! Once inside, the customer can switch the doors back to transparent at the touch of a switch, exposing themselves to onlookers waiting outside the room. Different lighting conditions allow the customer to view their selection in a warm evening glow or a cool blue daylight. The customer can gain direct access to the store database, as well as augment the experience of trying on and selecting clothes. Once inside the 'smart' dressing room the customer can directly access information that relates to their particular garment selection. As garments are hung in the closet their tags are automatically scanned and detected via RF antennae embedded in the closet. Once registered, the information is automatically displayed on an interactive touch screen, enabling the customer to select alternative sizes, colors, fabrics, and styles, or see the garment worn on the 'store catwalk' as slow-motion video clips. The dressing rooms also contain a video-based "Magic Mirror" which allows a customer to see an image of their back. As the customer begins to turn in front of the mirror the image becomes delayed, allowing the customer to view themselves in slow motion from all angles!

In Indian retailing, as technology has been undoubtedly recognized as a key driver of efficiencies, deployment of various applications has begun. Many retail technology organizations have been making a beeline to the CIO's offices of retailers to sell their offerings. Technology with its multifarious application capabilities can be a great attraction for retailers besides becoming a tool for attaining differentiation. Does technology bring best practices with it? The answer is a Yes in cases where the technology organization has developed applications for time-tested organizations that have been excelling in their retail business. Proven technology comes with its best practices and inherent capabilities, but care has to be taken to define a retail organization's business processes and see whether the chosen technology can customize itself to support the same. The risk that retailers may face currently in this growth phase especially when RFID innovations are taking place is that of the 'hype' created by many technology vendors to woo the retailers to use various applications. Most of the flashy technology of the store today is said to be sitting idle, abandoned by employees who never quite embraced computing elegance and are now too overwhelmed by large crowds to coolly assist shoppers with handhelds. Many gadgets, such as automated dressing-room doors and touch screens are believed to be ignored. The multimillion-dollar technology spend is said to look more like tech for tech's sake than an enhancement of the shopping experience and the store is promptly reevaluating its store strategy. We do have exceptional scenarios in India. An industry expert commented, "We have Maximum Retail Price (MRP) on all products we sell in India. That means a product cannot be sold above the MRP. What use do we have for the Price Optimization solution?" Well, the fact is that it can be used as a great tool to optimize margins while managing markdowns in a retail organization with respect to time frames.

Technology should be effectively used to avoid out-of-stock situations and to present the store in a well laid out 'planogram' identifying every now and then the areas of productivity in the matter of retail space, stocks, etc. and addressing promptly customer needs and queries. An efficient supply chain is integrated by information and technology should enable effective information exchange with vendors and process stakeholders. Innovations ought to be first applied to attain efficiencies in Indian retailing such as developing queue-busting techniques or efficient self checkout processes to address crowded cash tills during busy shopping hours. A phased technology need satiation will help retailers in India go a long way to establish their business process deliveries right!

Questions for Discussion

1. How does deployment of right technology help retailers in their growth?

2. Write notes on how retail technology and innovative retail solutions can bring best practices to retailing.

3. What are the factors that retailers in India need to consider while deploying retail technology?

CHAPTER 13

Retail Operations

CHAPTER OBJECTIVES

1. To provide an understanding of store operations
2. To enlighten the reader about the scope of functions in store operations
3. To explain the different store operating processes and their significance in running retail operations smoothly
4. To define the various store operating parameters in the areas of customer service, stock management, staff management and space management
5. To explain the process of designing performance measures and standards for retail store performance
6. To define a few activity reports to set goals for future action.

Retail operations enable a store to function smoothly (by virtue of defined processes) without any hindrances. The significant areas of retail operations consist of:

Customer Service and Accommodation: Customer service management has been dealt with in detail in Chapter 15. Service/customer accommodations include the store's policy on returning goods.

Retail Selling Process: This means ensuring efficient attending on the customer all the time he is in the store — when he enters it, selects the merchandise, pays for it and leaves. Steps involved in selling in the retail sales process are covered in detail in Chapter 18: *Role of Personal Selling in Retailing*.

Store Staffing and Scheduling: Human resource planning and management at the store level and scheduling the work timetable ensure efficient attending on the customer and service. *Managing Retail Personnel* (Chapter 14) dwells in detail on human resource management in retailing.

Retail Floor and Shelf Management: This is the process of planning and managing merchandise within the store, stocking and replenishing shelves and arranging products in a visually appealing manner to maximize sales (in-store merchandise receipts, stocking, etc.)

Store Administration and Facilities Management: Store administration involves proper planning to run the store besides ensuring compliance with the laws such as Shops And Establishments Act, Labour Act, etc. This process also includes the security aspects of the store, housekeeping and maintenance and its facilities like parking, playpen if any, toilets, etc.

Warehousing and Supply Chain Management: The process of merchandise re-orders, planning and organizing merchandise receipts, storage, transportation, information management in the supply chain, etc. are dealt with in detail in Chapter 9.

Loss (Shrinkage) Prevention: The process of loss prevention is a significant part of retail operations, which, if done efficiently, ensures better margins for the store. Electronic Article Surveillance (EAS) systems such as closed-circuit TV cameras, EAS tags etc. deter pilferage and shoplifting. This is covered in Chapter 8.

POS/Cashiering Process: Both front-end cashiering and back-end cash management, including banking, form an important part of store operations.

The process is greatly enabled by POS and back-end systems.

Visual Merchandising and Displays: These are done at the store level. They involve both conceptualization of themes and VM operations as well. These are elaborated in *Visual Merchandising and Displays* (Chapter 17).

In this chapter, we will see in detail the various operating parameters that help a retail store perform to its maximum potential.

STORE OPERATING PARAMETERS

Because of the growing use of technology, the retailer has access to a lot of information, which he should know how to use to measure his store's performance. Most of the time retailers are lost in the wilderness of information — especially thrown up by ERP packages (or POS software in the case of independent retailers) — and wonder what is critical to the success of their business operations. In front-end retail operations, it is very important to know how the store is performing at least on a day-to-day basis if not on an hourly basis. Anyone responsible for retail operations should have a ready reckoner called 'dipstick parameters' to measure retail performance.

Dipstick Parameters

Dipstick parameters enables retailers to find out about the health of specific areas of operation — customers, stocks, space, staff/employee, finance etc. — in an instant. Let's take a look at some of them:

Customer Transactions

How many customers came into my store compared to the corresponding period last year, and what percentage bought something (conversion rate)? Has the conversion rate gone up? How does my day-to-day average cash memo value or ticket size compare with the average value last month or last year? How much has this gone up during a promotion and hence what is the threshold cash memo size that I should consider to increase sales for the forthcoming promotion? The answers to these questions will help achieve the store's objectives.

Customer Conversion Ratio

$$= \frac{\text{Number of Transactions}}{\text{Customer Traffic}} \times 100$$

This percentage reflects the retailer's ability to turn a potential customer into a buyer. It is also known as the 'percentage yield rate' or the 'walk to buy ratio'. A low figure means that promotional activities are not being converted into sales, or that the overall sales efforts need to be assessed afresh. Unless automatic counting mechanisms are recording customer traffic, periodic surveys of customer traffic are required to arrive at a representative figure. Information on transactions can be gathered from cash register tapes which keep track of the time of the sale, or by having staff record the number of transactions for selected periods of time.

Returns To Net Sales

$$= \frac{\text{Total Returns and Allowances}}{\text{Net Sales}} \times 100$$

This percentage gives an indication of customer satisfaction by showing the value of returned goods and allowances as a percentage of net sales. An increase in this figure gives an early warning to the retailer. This could mean that customer expectations are not being met, and therefore the quality of the merchandise may need to be examined.

Transactions Per Hour

$$= \frac{\text{Number of Transactions}}{\text{Number of Hours}}$$

This helps retailers keep track of the number of transactions they are carrying out per hour, day, week or season. Hourly variations in sales activity could be important for setting store hours and staff schedules, particularly for cashiers. The information can be gathered with cash registers, which keep track of the time of the sale, or by having staff periodically record the number of transactions at selected periods of time.

Sales Per Transaction

$$= \frac{\text{Net Sales}}{\text{Number of Transactions}}$$

This measure gives the rupee value of the average sale, net of returns and allowances. It is used to study sales trends over time, or, in combination with other measures, decide whether a high volume of sales is more important than a high rupee value on each sale.

Hourly Customer Traffic

$$= \frac{\text{Customer Traffic In}}{\text{Number of Hours}}$$

Retailers use this measure to track total customer traffic per hour, day, week or season. This can be applied to an entire store or a single department to schedule hours and establish staff levels. Unless there are automatic counting mechanisms, periodic surveys of customer traffic are required to arrive at a representative figure.

Stocks

In order to determine the strength of your stock holding you need answers to this question. What is the average selling price[1] compared to the average stock price?[2] It's an ideal situation if both happen to be around the same value. This measure helps retailers find out if their store is overstocked or understocked in any category or even in an SKU.

---

[1] Average selling price is calculated by dividing the total value sold during a day or a period by the total quantity sold during the same day or period.

[2] Similarly, average stock price is calculated by dividing the value of the total merchandise in stock by the total quantity in stock.

Average Selling Price

$$= \frac{\text{Total Value of Goods Sold}}{\text{Total Quantity Sold}}$$

Average Stock Price

$$= \frac{\text{Total Value of Goods in Stock}}{\text{Total Quantity in Stock}}$$

Look at the stock-turn ratio. Turning stock around efficiently yields better profits: the more times a retailer turns his stocks, the more his margins. This can be found for any category or an SKU any time by checking the percentage sold from the stock of a specified category or SKU. For example, in the category where the dipstick is employed, if daily sales account for 2% of stock, it will take 50 days to sell all the stock. Then, dividing the number of days in the year (365) by 50, you get the number of stock turns for the year (7.3 times). This allows retailers to compare it with the store's target for stock turn and initiate corrective actions if needed. Remember, it is the gross margin return on inventory (GMROI) that matters.

Stock Turnover / Inventory Turnover Rate

$$= \frac{\text{Net Sales}}{\text{Average Retail Value of Inventory}}$$

Expressed as number of times, this ratio indicates how often the inventory is sold and replaced in a given period of time. Some retailers also use the ratio 'cost of goods sold' divided by 'average value of inventory at cost'. Both can be calculated for any time period. When either of these ratios declines, there is a possibility that inventory is excessive.

Percent Inventory Carrying Costs

$$= \frac{\text{Inventory Carrying Costs}}{\text{Net Sales}} \times 100$$

The importance of this measure (and the following one) has increased in recent years with the rise in inventory carrying costs due to high interest rates. This measure is also important to reduce stock obsolescence and to prevent blockage of working capital. Retailers use this measure to track the percentage of their net sales represented by the fixed costs of maintaining inventory.

Gross Margin Return On Inventory

$$= \frac{\text{Gross Margin}}{\text{Average Value of Inventory}}$$

Expressed in rupee terms, the gross margin return on inventory (GMROI) compares the margin on sales with the original cost value of merchandise to yield a return on merchandise investment.

Inventory can be valued at retail or at cost, but for many retailers inventory valued at retail is more accessible than that valued at cost. However, using inventory valued at retail may not give an accurate indication of investment cost.

GMROI can be dramatically altered by changes in inventory turnover and gross margin.

Markdown Goods Percentage

$$= \frac{\text{Net Sales at Markdown}}{\text{Total Net Sales}} \times 100$$

This is the percentage of marked-down merchandise to sales. If the ratio increases, the retailer may need to take a closer look at merchandising practices, particularly pricing. Markdowns may be symptoms of other problems, such as poor buying, advertising or store layout.

Shrinkage To Net Sales

$$= \frac{\text{Actual Inventory - Book Inventory}}{\text{Net Sales}} \times 100$$

Retailers use this control ratio to determine the percentage of net sales lost due to shrinkage. It does not indicate the cause of the shrinkage, but it does indicate the magnitude of the problem.

Space

Space productivity is critical to successful retailing, hence it is imperative to have parameters that measure space productivity. The top-of-the-mind dipstick measures are sales per square foot per day and margins per square foot per day. The performance of the store depends on the gross margin return on footage (GMROF).

As retailing is all about operating within a given space, its productivity can be measured according to any of the various retail elements, be it employees, stocks, customers or even the store's facilities, besides sales.

Occupancy Cost Per Square Foot Selling Space

$$= \frac{\text{Occupancy Cost}}{\text{Square Feet of Selling Space}}$$

Expressed in rupees, this measure translates occupancy cost into rupee value per unit of selling space. It gives an estimate of the amount of gross margin rupees each unit of space employed for retail selling must generate to cover occupancy costs. For a multi-unit retailer it is a helpful measure for comparing the performance of units at different locations. It can be calculated for any time period, such as a year or a month.

Sales Per Square Foot

$$= \frac{\text{Net Sales}}{\text{Square Feet of Selling Space}}$$

Stock Per Square Foot

$$= \frac{\text{Net Stock}}{\text{Square Feet of Selling Space}}$$

Expressed in either quantity or value, this measure can be used to compare alternative uses of space involving different product lines, or to compare the performance of different departments or stores using a common standard. This ratio will vary according to the type of merchandise and merchandising methods used.

Percentage of Selling Space

$$= \frac{\text{Selling Space in Square Feet}}{\text{Total Space in Square Feet}} \times 100$$

Retailers use this measure to calculate the percentage of total space used for sales. This ratio varies according to the type of merchandise and merchandising methods. For example, catalogue showrooms have little selling space, while shoe stores have little non-selling area. Changes over time, or in relation to competitors, can help track the efficiency with which space is being used.

Employees

Employee productivity is usually measured in terms of sales. Measurement parameters include total sales per day per salesperson, total number of cash memos/customers handled by a salesperson per day, or how much floor space is covered by a salesperson in the case of free-access retailing (the criteria applied for over-the-counter retailing is different). It is again the gross margin return on labour employed (GMROL) that matters.

Net Sales Per Full-Time Employee

$$= \frac{\text{Net Sales}}{\text{Total Full-time Employees}}$$

Expressed either in quantity or rupee value terms, this measure represents the average sales generated by each full-time employee. It is used to set performance targets for sales personnel.

Space Covered / Customers Served Per Full-Time Employee

$$= \frac{\text{Total Retailing Space/Number of Customers Served}}{\text{Total Full-Time Employees}}$$

Expressed in square feet, this measurement represents the space covered/ number of customers served by each full-time employee. This is extensively used by large free-access format retailers like department stores.

Labour Productivity

$$= \frac{\text{Total Labour Costs}}{\text{Net Sales}} \times 100$$

This percentage measures labour productivity by tracking the labour costs incurred to achieve a given sales volume. This measure can also be applied solely to sales employees.

Gross Margin Per Full-Time Employee

$$= \frac{\text{Gross Margin}}{\text{Total Full-Time Employees}}$$

Expressed in rupee value, this ratio indicates the gross profit generated per employee, and can be used to gauge a sales employee's performance. Though this shouldn't be the only measure of an employee's performance, it can provide a starting point for closer examination. This measure can be adapted to apply to all employees or solely to buyers.

Suppliers/Quantity or Value Purchased Per Buyer

$$= \frac{\text{Total Suppliers/Quantity or Value Purchased}}{\text{Total Buyers}}$$

This measure gives an average of the number of suppliers or the quantity or rupee value for each buyer in a store. There is no ideal number, but by comparing the workload of individual buyers through this measure, management can see how well the buying load is being distributed among purchasing staff.

Research indicates that an average buyer's ability to make appropriate decisions about buying declines as the number of suppliers increase. This measure should be looked at in conjunction with the number of SKUs the average buyer handles, as well as with the replenishment cycles involved.

Financial

Designing an operational financial parameter is critical to know beforehand the plan of operating income and expenses, so that at the end of the period one can assess the actual operating profits/losses against the planned figures. Furnished below is a pragmatic cost sheet towards profitability:

1.	Sales and Other Income	100
2.	COGS	70
3.	Shrinkage	1
4.	Occupation Cost	7
5.	Employment Cost	5
6.	Advertising & Promotion	2
7.	Energy Cost	2
8.	Operations & Administration	5
9.	PBDIT	8
10.	Interest	1
11.	PBDT	7
12.	Depreciation	2
13.	PBT	**5**

Table 7: *Pragmatic Cost Sheet towards Profitability**

USING THE STRATEGIC RESOURCE MODEL IN RETAILING

A Strategic Resource Model (SRM) gauges the performance of a retail store according to its productivity. The SRM measures the performance of the three resources in retailing — inventory, labour and space (footage), also referred to as 'Trinity Resources'. The evaluative measures in the SRM are gross margin return on inventory (GMROI), gross margin return on selling area (GMROF) and gross margin return on labour (GMROL). These measures indicate to what extent the utilisation of each of the input factors have been converted into gross profit for covering costs.

If overall **retail** performance is to remain unaffected, the model states that — other things being equal — a price cut (which eventually means a

---

* As presented by B.S Nagesh (Customer Care Associate & MD, Shoppers' Stop) at the KSA Retail Summit in Mumbai on 11th February 2003.

reduction in gross margin) requires an increase in merchandise productivity (through an increased conversion into buying), and space and labour productivity. The SRM provides tools to find out what will happen to various components of performance if any or several other components in the model are changed. Further, the model serves as an identification tool for performance while highlighting areas within the store that need management focus.

Margins	Inventory	Space	People
• Gross margin is the spread between buying and selling prices. Readjustment of markdowns and shrinkage may make all the difference.	• High cost of holding • Extremely high cost if holding the 'wrong' kind!	• Costs 20-40 percent of operating expenses. • Could be a major fixed cost.	• Typically 15-40 percent of operating expenses.
• Optimised technology investments improve net margins.	• 50-80 percent of working capital. • 40-60 percent of all assets	• 25-50 percent of all assets. • Costs Rs. 4,000 to Rs. 10,000 per square foot to build.	• Costly to get and retain. • Not enough people with the right skills and attitudes.
Favourably bought	*Wisely chosen*	*Wisely chosen and utilised*	*Intelligently selected & trained*

Table 8: *Significance of Retail Resources*

SRM Sensitivity Analysis

The SRM model suggests that retailers can develop strategies that vary on the following factors:
(a) Level of gross margin.
(b) Level of inventory productivity.
(c) Degree of merchandise intensity.
(d) Degree of service (by people) intensity.

Merchandise intensity is defined as 'inventory per square foot'; its multiplication with the margin on inventory produces the space productivity result.

If sales increase and eventually stocks turn more number of times, the other factors of space and staff remaining constant, the GMROI increases. If the gross margin is increased while the other components are held constant, GMROF will increase. Further, SRM recognises an increase in GMROF if merchandise intensity is increased within the given area of space, while gross margin percent and turnover in inventory is held constant. The SRM shows that gross margin return on labour, GMROL, is determined by the multiplicative impact of gross margin percent per full-time employee (FTE). So, if sales and gross margins per employee increase then GMROL too goes up.

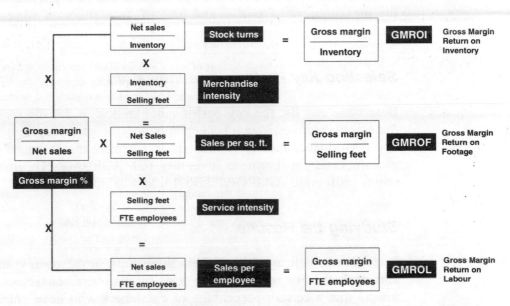

Fig. 17: *Strategic Resource Management Model**

DESIGNING A PERFORMANCE PROGRAMME

If a retailer has a definite performance measurement programme, then he knows what he needs to achieve within a particular frame of time. Many retail operations have failed for want of a clearly defined performance programme. A store may have reports and information, but if they are not defined, analysed closely with specified standards or desired goals, and acted upon promptly, the store will find it difficult to survive and prosper.

We now take a look at the steps to define or design a performance programme for a retail store.

---

* Model propounded by Prof. (Dr.) Douglas Tigert

Collating and Sieving Information

Retailers have to analyse what is relevant in the available information for meaningful performance measurement. Depending on the objective of each area of operation, the retailer will have to select information that is critical. For instance, if the objective is to examine the financial performance of the store, he will have to sieve through the data and pick information that allows the measurement of profits and growth. In a situation where the relevant information is not available, a retailer may have to gather it too.

Selecting Key Performance Indicators

Determine and list the key performance indicators for the store. Following the same objective (financial performance) as an example, one may select key performance indicators relevant to financial measurement such as, say, gross/net margin return on inventory (GMROI/NMROI), gross/net margin return on footage (GMROF/NMROF), and so on.

Studying the Results

Performance indicators acquire meaning only in the context of comparison and analysis. For instance, take a daily customer conversion figure. This means that a certain percentage of customers who have entered the store (footfalls) have done some buying. This has meaning only when it is compared with the store's average daily conversion rate during the previous month, with the same day during the previous year and so on. Comparing this conversion rate with the average cash memo size for the same day, for instance, puts one's performance into perspective. The number of customers who have made purchases multiplied by the average cash memo value gives total sales for the day.

What does a decline in sales per square foot imply? It need not necessarily be a bad thing if, say, the gross margin per square foot has increased because of changes in the merchandise assortment or if there's an alteration in pricing procedures.

Setting Goals for Action

By setting performance goals after studying results, a retailer can develop an action plan for the future. It is advisable to proceed in steps methodically while selecting a set of goals, dealing with critical problems first and setting up a measurement function as part of regular store management to get effective feedback consistently. As operations grow, it is necessary to widen the scope of the analysis of the results. This will pave the way to increased sales and profitability.

Uniformity in dealing with the identified performance measures in front-end retail operations is essential to achieve success. Besides, any successful performance requires the involvement of everyone, right through the stages of collating information, analysis, studying the results, setting goals, and reviewing. This is critical, and everyone at each operating level should be totally involved. A performance plan made properly, measured well and acted upon promptly always leads to an excellent showing by a store even during testing times.

SUMMARY

- The function of retail store operations is to ensure that the store runs smoothly and efficiently through thoroughly defined processes in every area.
- Retail operations must ensure that every process in the store is both customer-friendly and cost-effective.
- Setting performance standards is critical to the efficient functioning of a retail organization. Such standards have to be clearly defined.
- Measuring performance through defined reports provides an indication about the health of the retail store in every area of its operations. The reports enable necessary action to be taken for improvement. A process audit done periodically enhances the opportunities for achieving store operating efficiency.

Questions:

1. Elaborate on the store operating parameters in the areas of:

   — Customer Transactions
   — Merchandise and Stock Management
   — Space Management
   — Staff Management

2. What are the key factors you would consider while designing a performance programme for a retail store?

3. Design a template that describes the operating financial parameters for retail store operations.

CASELET: OPERATING CHALLENGES OF A DEPARTMENT STORE IN A MALL

Fosterfields, a department store retailing men's, ladies' and kids' apparel, casuals and related accessories, operated in an area about 35,000 sft in a mall that was around 200,000 sft. The mall had good customer entry, with an average of 20,000 visitors a day and Fosterfields was the anchor store of the mall.

Founded in 1999, Fosterfields had the advantage of riding piggy-back on the reputation of the mall (which too was founded at the same time) that it had earned because of its state-of-the-art architecture. The company, since it could attract customers who came to the mall, spent very little on building its store brand and creating an identity for itself. A few promotions were done for the brands it was retailing through a cooperative effort with the companies owning the brands, mainly through newspaper inserts. This happened only sporadically, as getting the brands to do promotions exclusively for the store was difficult because they were present in other competitive retail outlets too and could not support such exclusivity often.

In the beginning of the second year of operations, the mall management thought that they were not getting the right profile of customers and that conversions from browsing to buying in the entire mall was low. So they introduced entry conditions for customers such as the possession of mobile phones, credit cards, ID cards, etc. Alternatively, an entry fee of Rs. 50 would be charged on weekends (the amount could be redeemed on purchases). This was to prevent 'superfluous' footfalls in the mall. This had an absolute negative impact on customers and the number of people visiting the mall dipped to an average of 4,000 per day. This reduced the number of consumers coming into Fosterfields as well. Its business dipped by around 30% from the previous year, and the store found it difficult to pay the rent to the mall every month. Its payments to suppliers too were delayed.

The store management then came up with the following steps to help turn it around:

(a) In order to get high 'conversions', it introduced a loyalty programme with big benefits for customers — to the extent of 8% of the 30% average gross margins for gold card holders, 5% for silver card holders and 3% for ordinary card holders. This, however, did not lead to any significant business increase, and raised expenditure considerably.

(b) To optimize space (as the store had to clear a lot of overdue payments), the store started leasing some of it out to various brands from the store as a mall would do, adopting the 'landlord' strategy rather than retailing merchandise and earning margins. Consequently, employees who were afraid of losing their jobs — by now rumours were afloat that the store format would change and hence resources may be outsourced — started leaving for other competing companies.

(c) Despites its financial troubles, the company opened another Fosterfields departmental store of the same kind in a neighbouring town, investing a good amount of money. This was done in order to uphold the original plans of expansion and with the hope that scaled-up operations would give the company more bargaining power.

Employees were now fleeing at a fast rate as the management could not initiate timely performance appraisals. As the second financial year came to an end, the frontline manpower turnover rose to 45%. Since the store was now buying less from suppliers it was not able to bargain for large discounts from brands or avail of benefits on the agreed purchase quantities. As payments were delayed, suppliers were reluctant to deliver the goods and as a result open-to-buys (OTBs) were not followed. Markdowns too increased on slow-moving items because there was no OTB in place and because the store couldn't afford dead inventories now.

The ERP package that it had planned could not be bought and its plans to discipline its MIS and effect auto replenishments also did not happen. As a consequence, the entire inventory management process and the supply chain were rendered dysfunctional. Managers who were heading various functions then left the organization. The store was now left with a few junior- and middle-level executives — a few department managers, category merchandisers and buyers, a marketing executive, a technology executive, a warehouse in-charge, a store accounting executive, etc. And they now reported directly to the CEO.

The organization is part of a financially strong business group and its desire to make a success of its diversification into retailing is steadfast. The plus factor is that organized retailing is poised for huge growth in India, as many research agencies have reported.

Questions for Discussion

1. Should Fosterfields continue to partner the mall? Discuss.

2. Comment on the store positioning strategy that Fosterfields should follow.

3. Discuss critically the three steps the management took to turn Fosterfields around.

4. What measures would you recommend to motivate and reassure employees so that the attrition rate at Fosterfields comes down?

5. What in your opinion should be the plan of action to ensure the turnaround of Fosterfields?

CHAPTER 14

Managing Retail Personnel

CHAPTER OBJECTIVES

1. To underline the people-oriented nature of the retail business
2. To define the manpower planning process in a retail organization
3. To impart knowledge on setting retail manpower standards
4. To list the typical tasks in retailing and retailing conditions in India
5. To explain the recruitment process and the types of recruitment done in Indian retail organizations
6. To explain in detail the relevance and methods of motivation and retention in retailing
7. To enable the reader to study the reward system in retailing for a thorough performance orientation

The product or deliverable that the customer carries home from a retail store is a combination of merchandise and service. The service is delivered through the human interface between the store employee and the customer. All service organizations define the product in terms of the employee or human resources that represent them.

In retailing, employee costs form a significant part of total costs, and is often its largest or second-largest component. Since profit margins are thin in this business how well a retailer manages employee numbers, productivity and costs makes the difference between a red bottom-line and a healthy black one.

Recent studies indicate that there is a close relationship between employee satisfaction and customer satisfaction. Hence retailers whose business model depends on the USP of excellent service are now looking carefully at methods to motivate and retain employees. They regularly measure employee satisfaction levels, understanding that this would have an impact on the customer as well.

HUMAN RESOURCES ISSUES AND CONCERNS IN RETAILING

Like any other service organization, the HR function in retailing (as practised by both HR functionaries as well as managers in operations/retail) is extremely important. However, as the industry evolves, some special issues have emerged. In fact HR managers may find themselves focusing on just a few activities almost 90% of the time. These constitute:

(a) Manpower planning.
(b) Recruitment.
(c) Motivation and retention and building reward systems that ensure performance orientation.

This chapter covers the above three issues, emphasizing on aspects that are of special concern to the retailer, rather than a general coverage of manpower planning or motivation.

Manpower Planning

Since manpower costs form a major part of costs for the retailer, the decision on how many people it should have is crucial, and has a bearing on standards of performance and productivity. Most important, it affects the kind of service that a retailer may like to offer. Very often, retailers are so busy managing operations that the key issue of manpower planning is relegated to the background. What they don't realize is that a proper plan can perhaps improve performance on many fronts: the smoothness of operations, customer service levels and profitability.

How does a retailer go about deciding how many people he should employ? The following factors should be taken into consideration:

- ### *Business Planning*
  The starting point in retailing, as in all businesses, is the annual plan. With this plan, the retailer puts a fix on the volume and value of business that he intends to accomplish. This of course has a direct effect on the number of people the retailer needs to recruit in the future. For example, a retail organization needs to plan and recruit for new store openings. This may start with an arithmetic calculation using current store manning levels as a basis. However, after this, the number has to be revisited looking at other aspects that are mentioned below.

- ### *Manning Standards and Utilization*
  Developing manning standards helps optimize the number of staff. As each season passes, the retailer finds that the standards get more refined and applicable for the purposes of performance development. Factors that influence manning standards are:

- ### *Work-task Organization*
  Assuming that one is opening a new store, or is re-examining jobs with a view to redesign them more effectively, the retailer has to decide which tasks to group together to form a particular function. This will mean a work-task analysis with reference to functions that characterize retailing: buying, selling, storing, transporting, financing, information gathering and risk-taking. The retailer needs to identify tasks and map them into jobs depending on the chosen method of organization. Examples of tasks that characterize retail are given below:

Some Typical Tasks in Retail

- Forecasting Sales
- Purchasing Supplies
- Purchasing Merchandise
- Building Merchandise Assortments
- Pricing Merchandise
- Selling
- Training Employees

- Displaying Merchandise
- Billing Customers
- Packing and Gift Wrapping
- Searching for Merchandise
- Advertising
- Handling Customer Complaints
- Controlling Inventory
- Transporting Merchandise
- Supervising Employees
- Hiring and Firing Employees
- Cleaning the Store
- Handling Cash
- Paying Bills
- Customer Research
- Altering/Repairing Merchandise
- Storing Merchandise
- Preparing Merchandise Statistics
- Maintaining the Store
- Providing Store Security

The retailer needs to decide how tasks have to be grouped to provide the highest level of efficiency. For example, in a store where customer walk-ins are few, and the merchandise stocked are high-fashion garments, the same salesperson may be asked to assist the customer in selection, bill the customer, collect payment and pack the item. However, in a supermarket where a cash-and-carry system exists, the jobs may be separate, with different people stacking items on shelves, cashiering etc. In a store selling specialty products — like branded cosmetics — there is no product development effort required from the retailer since the brands are presenting developed and advertised lines. Hence the salesperson may be asked to indent for re-orders as well do selling, since he would know which items are slow and which are fast movers. However, in a fashion garments store which has its own label, a specialist merchandiser may be required to take decisions on re-orders, deciding whether continuing the product line would benefit the store image or not.

- ### *Store Positioning or Image*
The number of staff hired is often dictated by the positioning of the store. For example, a high-fashion boutique store promising exclusive service will need to ensure that every customer who walks in is attended to personally. On the other hand, a warehouse store can afford to have no staff to help the customer.

• *Store Strategy*

Sometimes the store strategy for the year might dictate a change in staffing patterns. For example, a store that is experiencing a new business scenario such as a competitor setting up store in its vicinity may want to increase staffing and provide better service as an immediate strategy to retain the customer. Another example could be an internal strategy of using employee creativity — one may need to plan time off for employees to think creatively, and therefore employ more staff.

• *Productivity Requirements*

For the retailer it is imperative that he evolves his own tangible standards of productivity and as a corollary, manning standards. The standard could be per square foot coverage per employee, per square foot sales per employee, or gross margin return on labour (GMROL). Often retailers look at several of these standards in conjunction with one another, the ultimate aim being to optimize (and not maximize) GMROL (see box).

Retailers often use GMROL as a good indicator/standard. However GMROL should be taken into account in conjunction with gross margin return on space and gross margin return on inventory (GMROI). GMROI should be calculated as per product categories at each location (and not only at a store or product category level) and standards should be evolved over a period of time. The purpose is to optimize and not maximize

Section	Store 1			Store 2			Remarks
	Cover Psf	Amt/ person	Value/ person	Cover Psf	Amt/ person	Value/ person	
Watches	1150sqft	5.4	7960	203sqft	7.2	11995	Store 2 performs better in terms of psf cover & value/person
Cosmetics	106	25.1	2790	171	39.6	4053	— do —
Trousers	420	12.9	9760	32	8.1	7027	Store 1 performs better in terms of psf cover & value/person
Shirts	325	16.6	10215	206	11.4	6684	Store 1 performs better in terms of amount and value/person
Formals	371	2.6	8530	212	4.2	10195	Store 1 may need to increase staffing to perform
Infants	165	59.8	9700	239	28.9	4300	— do —

Table 9: *Productivity Comparison*

GMROL, failing which a situation may arise when staff numbers are cut to increase GMROL and thus lead to a deterioration in customer service. Hence, ideally GMROL should always be studied in tandem with gross margin return on footage (GMROF) and GMROI.

- ## *Type of Sale*
  While arriving at manpower numbers, it is important to examine the product and the type of sale involved. For example, routine products such as toothpaste or soap can be sold in a dispenser with minimum employee interface. A specialty product such as a branded shirt (whose sizes are standardized across brands) also does not require a great deal of interface. A customer can buy a white shirt, size 42, by merely locating it (with the help of the signage and shelf talkers) and putting it into a shopping basket. A salwar kameez on the other hand is a 'shopping product' that requires assistance (for explaining the cut, fabric, sizing and assistance for trials) when the selection is being made.

- ## *Ratio of Manpower Costs to Volume of Sales*
  At a macro level, this is a good method of planning manpower. Retailers can fix a percentage of sales turnover to be utilized on manpower costs. Micro planning can then be made within this limit.

- ## *Shifts, Opening Days/Hours, Holidays, Leave Entitlement*
  The total number of staff depends on the shifts planned, and ideally should coincide with the flow of customer traffic. This is a complicated process, with the quantum of leave allowed, weekly offs, holidays etc. to be taken into account when planning.

- ## *Issue of Availability*
  A customer-focused method of looking at staffing numbers is to decide on the level of service to be offered. For example, on a particular floor, the retailer needs to decide how many service personnel should be present at a given time (like peak customer traffic time). Then staff strength should be decided after making allowances for leaves, weekly offs, staff breaks, back office work etc. that take them away from the customer. It is important to then devise a method to track availability of staff for the customer, to ensure that the targeted numbers are available.

- *Importance of Manpower Information Systems and Audits & Control in Manpower Planning*

A good manpower information system, integrated into the sales reporting system, is a must for retailers to ensure efficient manpower planning. For example, staff availability and its effect on performance can be measured by finding out the staff allocation for each product category and location, tracking attendance (using an electronic attendance recording system), and then comparing these with sales figures and fluctuations in them. The study of GMROL can be made more meaningful if section-wise sales and staffing costs are captured.

Recruitment

Retailers across the world face a scarcity of trained manpower. And because of the high employee turnover rates, they are saddled with constant recruitment activity.

Recruitment and selection has two objectives: (a) to recruit the right person for the job, and (b) to ensure that the right person is not rejected. This activity is crucial for retailers for the following reasons since proper recruitment and selection would ensure that time is not wasted on activities that do not directly add value to the bottom line, reduces recruitment costs, and, most important, reduces employee attrition rates.

Retail Employment Options

The retailer has several options in terms of types of employees, with a view to maximize productivity and minimize costs.

- Core Employees: These include full-time employees and critical resources that take time and training to build up. They are on the rolls of the company and could also include frontline sales staff.
- Short-term Contract Employees: These are on the rolls of the company for a specified duration, following a mutual agreement between them and the retailer. This is a useful option in the peak season — Divali to December — when many retailers may chalk up more than 50% of their sales, and need as many staff as they can get.
- Apprentices: These are trainees who could be working and learning on the job, usually for a specified duration.
- Part-timers: This is an arrangement commonly used in countries where retailing is a developed phenomenon. These employees are on the rolls of the company, but work for a specified short duration every day (for

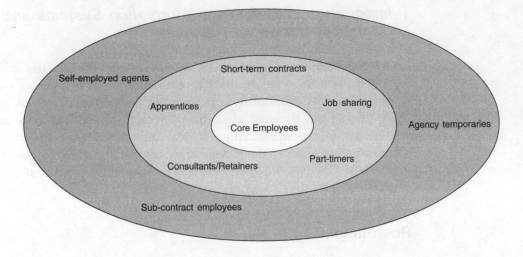

Fig. 18: *Types of Employees in Retail*

example, four hours) and get paid on an hourly basis. Popular choices for part-timers are college students and housewives. Using part-timers helps adjust employee availability with customer in-flow.

- **Consultants/Retainers:** This option is used to avail of the services of specialists who may otherwise be too expensive to employ, and whose expertise may not be needed on a regular basis, like legal experts, fashion design consultants or beauty consultants.
- **Sub-contracted Employees:** Sub-contractors are awarded jobs within the company, but are not part of its core competence. Outsourcing is gaining popularity since it works out to be more cost-effective. In retailing, these areas typically are housekeeping, security, transaction processing in accounts etc.
- **Self-employed Agents:** These include commission agents not on the rolls of the retailer, who operate outside the store and are instrumental in bringing in customers. These agents get a percentage of the business they bring in, like taxi drivers bringing in tourists, tour operators who bring in their own customers to the store.
- **Agency Temporaries:** These are staff from agencies normally used for very short durations for, say, promotions or events within the store.

Special Features of Retail Recruitment

- **Sources of recruitment:**
  In retailing, staff sources are varied and the recruiter normally has to employ unconventional methods to hire them. Since the jobs involve odd working hours, front-line staff are recruited from those living in the vicinity of the store. This helps contain employee turnover. Also, references are often a cost-effective source of recruitment, and it also has a high hit ratio.

- **Issues in the retail selection process:**
  While setting up selection policies, an important issue is defining the selection process to ensure that the right person comes on board — that is, what is the process, is it correctly defined, who is the authority making the final decision? In retail companies, where the emphasis is on service, recruitment, selection processes and job criteria are well-defined. Recruitment is viewed as an important activity, and conducted by a senior person.
  Another issue in retail selection is that of integrity. Almost all jobs in retail, especially front-line sales, are open to the possibility of theft/fraud/misappropriation. Hence the need to define a selection process that identifies the trait of integrity. Many retailers insist on careful preliminary screening of candidates, reference checks, detailed checks with previous employers and so on.

- **Scarcity of trained manpower:**
  The world over, the retail industry faces a shortage of trained personnel. And while there is no dearth of people who want the jobs, there is an acute shortage of institutes to train people in retail skills/knowledge. Several retailers have established large training teams and even institutes affiliated with them where people are trained for retail jobs on a large scale. The scarce supply position means that poaching talent is rampant and frequent job changes the norm.

- **Unsocial hours:**
  Recruiting in retail is difficult as front-line jobs involve 'unsocial hours' — that is, on weekends and public holidays — which is unavoidable for the retailer. As a result, the pool of available and willing manpower shrinks.

- **Short-term manpower demands:**
  Customer-buying is seasonal and depends on festivals, the weather, state

of the economy and other factors. Hence there are peaks and troughs in sales through the year. Recruitment must be adjusted to take into account these variations. For example, in the peak season from October to December a clothing or jewellery retailer will need more staff. However, if permanent staff are hired according to the demands of the peak season, they will be underutilized for the larger part of the year. Hence retail recruitment demands greater flexibility and resourcefulness.

- **The reputation problem:**
  In India, retailers still face a peculiar stigma where retail front-end jobs are concerned. Candidates often feel that retail jobs are merely "standing in a *dukaan*", with no career prospects. This has, however, changed with the advent of large, professionally-run department stores. But there's still a long way to go before retail jobs are seen as serious career options.

- **Front-line nature of retail:**
  All retail employees have to face customers and interact with them to a certain extent. Hence, apart from technical/job knowledge the retail recruiter needs to look for additional attributes in the candidate such as communication skills, personality and appearance. This makes finding candidates more difficult.

- **Recruitment with reference to customer profile:**
  For all jobs that involve interaction with customers, the impact on them has to be taken into account. For example, store personnel may need to know an additional language if a large proportion of customers speak a specific language. Similarly, when the customers are children, a salesman may need skills like storytelling, juggling or performing a few magic tricks apart from selling.

- **Need for mobility:**
  Front-line staff, like other employees, are concerned, even at the time of recruitment, about the growth prospects in the organization. Often sales people who seek careers in retail jobs aspire to move quickly up the ladder and become supervisors, department managers, merchandisers, store heads etc. However, the positions that become vacant are few compared to the number of aspiring salespeople at a location, and competition is fierce. Retail businesses grow by increasing their sales volume by setting up new stores in new locations. And opportunities for jobs involving more responsibility often emerge there, provided the employee has geographic mobility and across functions. Hence determining mobility while recruiting is important for employee retention.

- **Women in retail:**
  In economies where the retail industry is developed, more than 50% of women are employed in the industry. The nature of jobs that exist — such as customer service personnel or buyers — make retail an attractive option for women. In India, women are still reluctant to take on jobs that involve late hours. However, recruitment decisions depend on customer expectations and comfort. Will a female customer be comfortable buying lingerie from a salesman? Will a 50-year-old male customer be comfortable if he needs to buy trousers where a saleswoman may need to take measurements for alteration?

- **Legislation:**
  In India legislation has to be taken into account while deciding staffing. The Shops & Establishments Act has fixed store opening and closing timings, the duration an employee can work, mandatory leave/holidays and breaks after a specified number of hours, and special provisions for the employment of women. Hence while deciding shifts, breaks, weekly offs and staffing patterns, the retailer needs to ensure that he is on the right side of the law.

Motivation and Rewards for Performance

WHAT MOTIVATES RETAIL SALESPEOPLE?

The following is an illustrative list of different motivators. Most managers believe that overall compensation ranks as the No.1 motivator for salespeople. For themselves, on the other hand, they say money comes second or third.

Non-monetary Factors:
- Encouragement and contact of supervisor
- Opportunity for promotion
- Advanced training
- Participative goal setting
- Sales quotas
- Challenging/creative job
- Opportunity for learning
- Information about the organization's goals
- Opportunity to show creativity
- Helpful colleagues

Monetary Factors:

- Special recognition for outstanding performance
- Individual incentive/bonus
- Commissions
- Overall compensation
- Contests — travel or merchandise prizes
- Group incentive/bonus

However, most salespeople are just like managers when it comes to motivation. Monetary motivations may rank No.2 or No.3 in importance for a retail salesperson. No.1 would be any one of the softer factors, such as respect, accomplishment/achievement, status, security and stimulation.

Tools that can be Used by a Sales Manager to Motivate Staff

Without exploring the theories of motivation, here are a few practical tips for retail managers:

- Job variety: Salespeople get bored selling the same product day in and day out, month after month. Rotation, changing products, allowing them to do other associated jobs such as visual display, cashiering and retail statistics reduce job monotony.

- Job autonomy: Studies indicate that salespeople who are given greater autonomy — like enriching the job with the responsibility of indenting, keeping statistics of stocks, giving feedback to improve product design, redressing customer complaints, participating in customer research etc. — are more responsible and have higher levels of productivity.

- Specialized training: For many individuals the opportunity for growth and knowledge acquisition are tremendous motivators. For salespeople, training could be on product knowledge, service skills, computer skills, leadership and teamwork, visual displays, merchandising basics etc.

- Public recognition of achievements, for example, contests and meetings: The retail sales floor is a dramatic arena, where the skills and achievements of participants are constantly on display for all — superiors, peers and customers — to appreciate. Hence public recognition is often a powerful tool to motivate employees.

- Goal-setting: Setting performance benchmarks and linking rewards to the same is a time-tested tool. Very often the retail manager may be remiss in fixing targets.

- Incentives like cash prizes, travel opportunities, merchandise: These could vary from a straight percentage of sales, to innovative incentive designs which tackle specific problems such as customer conversion, increasing ticket size, increasing the number of items purchased by each customer, pushing slow movers, improving customer service, mystery shopper schemes etc.

- Salary and remuneration structures: This is covered later in this chapter.

Retention: Motivating in the Long Run

High employee exit rates are the bane of retailers the world over. Large employee turnover leads to high recruitment costs, time wasted on recruitment, and high induction and training costs. It is important to remember that employees have a career life cycle. A manager needs to respond to this and use the right motivators at each stage of his career. He also needs to recognize when the employee is likely to disengage from the organization.

Career Stage	Employee behaviour	Sales force motivator
Explore	– Searches for comfortable position, unstable	Use communication to give society basic skill-building
Establish	– Seeks stabilization – Strives for professional success/ promotion	Introduce rewards/challenges Plan career
Maintain	– Concern to retain current position, stable	Reward creativity, emphasize smart work Career development plans
Disengage	– Declining performance – Psychological disengagement	Reduce working hours Re-deploy

Fig. 19: *Career Life-cycle*

Remuneration: the Structure

Remuneration for salespeople can be structured in any of the following ways:
- Salary only
- Salary + Bonus

- Salary + Bonus + Commission
- Salary + Commission
- Commission only
- Non-cash incentives (usually an additional component of rewards)

In retail, it is the customer who finally decides the structure. For example, a department store format that advertises a USP of complete privacy and space to make one's own choice would do well to ensure that it does not structure salespersons' salaries with a heavy emphasis on commissions. Such a structure would ensure that customers are mobbed at the storefront by eager salespersons!

• Salary-only Scheme

This structure is chosen when:
— Product sales cannot be related to individual effort. For example, where sales groups function in a cash-and-carry environment, where the sales effort involves a series of negotiations over a period of time involving many people.
— Where the focus is on non-selling activity also. For example, where service is the USP.
— Where it is unethical to create a strong product push. For example, feeding bottles or baby formula.
— Where setting individual targets is difficult.
— Where sales have a partial influence on profitability.
— Where representing the company is more important than mere sales.

Salary-only scheme: the Positives
— Salespersons have security of income.
— High loyalty to the company.
— Greater flexibility. For example, transferring employees from one work group to another will meet with no resistance.
— Administratively simpler, since there are no complex incentive calculations in salary.
— Internal problems of different salespersons drawing different amounts, and resulting comparisons are minimized.

Salary-only scheme: the Negatives
— Salespersons are less aggressive.
— Salary costs are fixed, regardless of sales performance.

- ## Commissions

Commissions are chosen when:
— The market is highly competitive and products are not differentiated.
— When the sales volumes are low.
— Where there are no seasonal/economic highs and lows in the year.

Types of commissions
— Fixed: this is a constant percentage of sales. For example, 2% of business brought in.
— Progressive: here commission increases as sales grow. For example, 2% for the first Rs.1 lakh, 3% for the second lakh and 4% for the third and so on.
— Regressive: here, the commission rates start falling after a point. For example 2% for the first 3 lakhs, and 1.5% for sales beyond 3 lakhs. Regressive commissions are used when sales expectations are exponentially high and it is used as a tool to motivate multi-levels of people in the hierarchy.

Commissions entail
— A clear basis for performance measures.
— Agreed rate of commission.
— Establishing a base salary to ensure that the take-home pay is adequate in a bad month.

Commissions: the Positives
— Since pay is linked to sales volume, there is performance orientation and sales aggression.
— There is scope for flexibility. Commissions can vary for different groups of people, different functions.
— The cost of living is taken care of automatically.
— Bad performers will leave the organization.

Commissions: the Negatives
— Uncertain earnings may cause insecurity amongst employees.
— There could be very high employee turnover.
— Salespersons may turn unethical and pushy.
— Excessive pushiness may jeopardize long-term relationships.
— Management has less control over earnings.
— Undermines company loyalty.
— Non-selling service suffers.
— Differences in earnings may cause conflict between employees.
— An increase in product prices leads to an automatic pay hike.

- ## Bonus

Bonus is a financial incentive provided in cases where the commission system is inappropriate or dysfunctional.

Bonus: the Positives
— Can be used to encourage specific higher order needs.
— Aids retention (if paid at regular intervals).

Bonus: the Negatives
— Link between performance and reward may be weakened.
— Is often complex to administer.

- ## Non-cash incentives

These are usually short-term — like awards, contests for travel, merchandise, stock options — and given in addition to the salary.

Sales contests in retail can be according to:
— Increased cash volumes.
— Stimulating more contacts and conversions.
— Building off-season business.
— Pushing slow movers or ageing stock.
— Stimulating balanced selling. For instance, shirts and trousers are sold together in the proportion in which they are purchased.
— Increased use of displays.
— Improved sales ability. For example, mystery shopper schemes.
— Building multiple sales.
— Service-related contests. For example, grooming, customer adoption.

Special remuneration in retail
— Employee discounts: these are provided on items sold within the store. Discount structures/percentages vary depending on the margin earned by the retailer on different products.
— Push money: incentives whose cost is borne by a supplier/brand that wants to push its own products on the retailers' shelves. This could be transparent, with the employee knowing that the supplier has offered the scheme, or it could be managed as an incentive offered by the retailer.
— Shift allowance/unsocial hours allowance.
— Clothing/turnout allowance: often given in businesses where appearance and grooming are critical to the sale, like beauty products.

SUMMARY

- Managing personnel in a retail environment demands unique, specialized skills. Soft skills are required in addition to academic qualifications.
- Retailing is a dynamic industry and makes a lot of demands on the personnel involved in the business. Therefore they need intensive training and motivation.
- Recruiting the right personnel with the right attitude will determine the success of retailing. Integrity is of paramount importance.
- It is very important to reward employees for achieving better results.

Questions:

1. What factors impact manpower planning in a retail organization?

2. Write a brief note on the employment options available for a retailer.

3. What are the special features of retail recruitment in India?

4. What motivating tools can a retail sales manager use to enhance performance?

5. Write short notes on the following remuneration structures in India, depicting their pros and cons:

   — Salary only
   — Salary + Bonus
   — Salary + Bonus + Commission
   — Salary + Commission
   — Commission only
   — Non-cash Incentives

MANPOWER PLANNING IN A DEPARTMENT STORE

Following rapid growth in business volumes, this department store recruited 150 permanent employees to cover its working hours from 10 am to 8.30 pm. The store — which had an area of 50,000 square feet — works seven days a week.

Manpower planning in a free-access department store is done according to factors like sales volumes and value planned per salesperson, floor area covered by a salesperson, number of customers attended per day, or a combination of these. The idea is to optimize business operating results.

The pattern of business in the store is such that there is a rush of customers entering the store on weekends from Friday to Sunday. Friday's sales are thus twice that of a Monday, Saturday's sales are twice that of a Thursday and Sunday's figures are two times that of Friday's. The manpower however remains the same: that is 150 salespeople report for duty on all days in their own designated shifts. And most of the day's sales — 60% — take place during the latter part of the day.

In retail, manpower planning takes into account the number of staff needed at different times of the day. It looks at the possibility of a range of shift lengths not exceeding the statutory eight hours a day rather than rigid fixed shifts which would mean employing more people.

The store's business has been growing, and at times the management feels that there are less staff to serve customers, especially during weekends and busy hours.

Efficient manpower planning in retail stores takes into account the impact of part-timers and overtime to meet short-term peaks in demand. It uses weekenders in times of dire necessity. This store has not been following this practice, as it is new both to the company and to prospective employees. And the organization fears that the commitment of such weekenders and part-timers would be very low.

Efficiently-run retail stores unfailingly conduct the following to arrive at their optimal manpower needs:

Manpower Forecasting.
Manpower Scheduling.
Manpower Budgeting.

Manpower Forecasting allows a retail organization to generate accurate and reliable business level forecasts hours, days and weeks in advance. This is used as a basis for staffing. A unique combination of algorithms and statistical forecasting techniques — EPOS records, customers served, queue lengths, footfalls, ticket size or unit sales — are applied to both historical and current data. This allows business level forecasts to be produced. Accurate forecasts reflect the real needs of the business, where each floor or department is different as is every hour of each day. A balance between customer service levels and staff costs can be attained only when there's an accurate picture of the store's operations.

Manpower Scheduling combines business level forecasts with a user-defined model in order to provide an accurate and detailed staff requirement throughout the working day. Scheduling takes into account company policy, staff performance, multi-skilling, working time regulations, the product category needs, breaks and minimum staffing levels. It produces the best possible combination of schedules/rosters for each member of staff for the forthcoming weeks. It should detail breaks, start and finish times for each member of the staff.

Manpower Budgeting allows accurate medium and long-term budgets to be made for staff costs. These are one of the largest overheads for any retail business and are often thought too complex for accurate budgeting. Budgets are created for each floor or department or store taking into account the individual trading conditions and workloads. This ensures an efficient gross margin return on labour (GMROL).

Manpower outsourcing is an option the organization is now trying to meet its needs after following the above methods of professional manpower planning. Outsourcing a part of its manpower requirement, the management feels, would alleviate its problems, providing flexibility in to meet the dynamic staff needs. Outsourcing the right skills may even be less time-consuming for the company, since the trained talent and skill will be readily available for deployment. Further, statutory obligations such as workmen's compensation, provident fund, gratuity, bonus, maternity benefits, professional tax, etc. are not the organization's responsibility but the service provider's.

Questions for Discussion

1. Weighing all the options available, as it is now an opportune time for the organization to decide on its manpower planning and deployment strategy, what recommendations would you make?

2. Is a variable manpower fitment model during peak hours and peak days a practical strategy?

3. Will manpower forecasting, scheduling and budgeting help a retail organization arrive at the right manpower size? Discuss.

4. What in your opinion are the pros and cons of manpower outsourcing in retailing in India?

CHAPTER 15

Customer Service Management in Retail

CHAPTER OBJECTIVES

1. To define the dimensions of customer service management in retailing
2. To define the customer service management model and map the processes and steps involved for efficient delivery
3. To enable the reader to understand how to monitor, measure and fill gaps in customer service management
4. To explain how customer service feedback is sought to take action
5. To define the process of service management ownership and to help the reader understand the need to prepare store personnel by training them

Customer service in retailing focuses on customer expectations. The ability of the retail organization to identify these expectations and fulfill them will determine whether consumers enter the shop again and again. Service management thus aims to first measure customer expectations and then find ways of meeting them.

Customer service has two dimensions: the services and the service. While 'services' are the facilities, concessions or infrastructure offerings extended to customers; 'service' is how well they are offered by the store. For instance, in a garment store an alteration facility is part of the basket of services. If it is done well and the garment is delivered within the promised

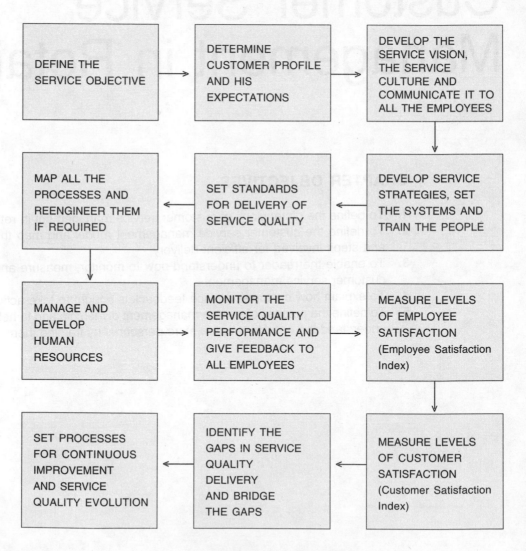

Fig. 20: *Service Management Model*

time frame, then the service is said to be good. A retailer then needs to spell his service vision and create a service culture within the organization. He has to set service standards with the right strategy, systems and people and manage processes and people to deliver them.

Defining the Service Objective

The first step to improving the quality of service is defining the objective for service performance in the organization. A retailer needs to clearly decide upon service goals, and come up with the relevant strategies and systems. He has to understand the importance of service management to attain differentiated leadership in the industry, and thus firm up his organization's service objective. He also needs to give due importance to determining the profile of the store's customers, their expectations and the means to fulfill them.

Defining the Customer Profile and Expectations

Customer expectations often depend on the profile of the buyers catered to by the retail organization. Good service means offering customers a little more than what they expect. For example, after eating in the restaurant of a five-star hotel, the customer expects the bill given to him to be placed in a leather folder. But in a non-graded restaurant, the bill can just be placed on the table. Hence, studying the profile of the customer and his expectations will enable retailers to design a complete service process.

Customer expectations can be broken up into:
Basic: Absolutely essential attributes of the experience.
Expected: Associated attributes of the experience that the customer takes for granted.
Desired: Attributes the customer doesn't expect, but knows about them and appreciates it if the experience includes them.
Unanticipated: 'Surprise' attributes that add value for the customer beyond his or her desires or expectations.

Developing the Service Vision

The organization's service vision emanates from its intent to serve its customers. The vision statement reflects what the management wants the store to become and be known for in terms of customer service. It can be called the 'defined future state of the business' in relation to the customer and the value he receives or would receive. The vision needs to be shared and communicated for uniform understanding and to enable the right delivery so that maximum customer satisfaction can be achieved.

Mapping all the Processes

The customer service process starts with the customer expressing his need, and ends when it is fulfilled. To begin, the retailer has to decide on all the elements of the process to be implemented. He then has to compare them with the current processes and map them according to the desired status. The process ends with an operational plan after a careful review.

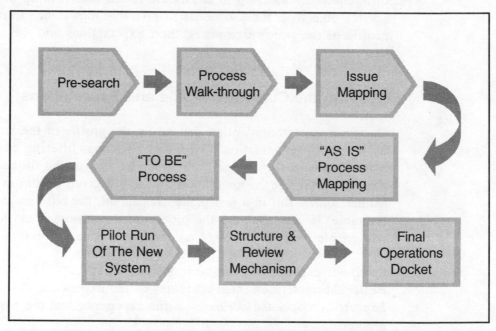

Fig. 21: *Customer Service Process Flow*

The following are the goals of the process:

- **Dependability:** Does the service provider do what is promised?
- **Responsiveness:** Is the service being provided in a timely manner?
- **Authority:** Does the service provider create a feeling of confidence in the customer during the service delivery process?
- **Empathy:** Is the service provider taking into account the customer's point of view?
- **Tangible Evidence:** Is there evidence of the service being performed?

Setting Standards and Developing a Service Strategy

After identifying areas of improvement and redesigning processes, it is necessary to now set new standards and design methods to make each department or function progressive, resulting in total customer focus. Take the example of a garment store that, after process mapping, has found that it can increase customer satisfaction by reducing the delivery time of the altered garment from the current 24 hours to half-an-hour. It has to design its methods of functioning in such a way that each garment being altered is attended to on time, concentrating its resources on it and setting up the required infrastructure. The strategy is to use customer service to differentiate the retail organization in the minds of the customers.

Managing and Developing Human Resources

Efficient customer service is all about putting people behind products and services. Human resources need to be trained at all levels to deliver the most efficient customer service as it is they who make the moments 'magical' for the customers. Further it is the store personnel who are the 'face' of the organization to the customers. Communicating the organization's vision, values, plans and strategies to the employees work wonders. They can then deliver excellent customer service to achieve the organization's service vision. Developing an effective training and development plan for the whole organization also helps people to operate a lot more efficiently. Human resources in retailing has been dealt with in more detail in *Managing Retail Personnel* (Chapter 14).

Monitoring, Measuring and Filling Gaps in Service Quality

The retailer needs to monitor quality of service to ensure that service goals are being met, that service strategies are successful, and to find out how well the systems are supporting the process. Monitoring service quality also means the continuous measurement of service quality parameters and evaluating them.

Why measure? The reason for measuring something is to understand it so that it can be done better or differently. From the angle of service quality, this means either identifying an opportunity for improvement, establishing a baseline for improvement, or verifying that the task has been accomplished.

Retailers who really believe that service quality is an important ingredient in their success recipe appreciate the need for continuous measurement of all service parameters.

Monitoring and measurement can be considered a way to close the loop around the service quality improvement effort, to lead and guide rather than drive it. The measurements help everybody know how well they are accomplishing what they have to do. Service quality measurement being a continuous process, the retailer needs to clearly state the value he would like to deliver to his customers; all the aspects of service quality need to be understood by every employee. They should be well-trained on how to deliver value to the customer. Every employee must be made to understand the organization's service vision and objectives.

Some retailers use 'mystery shoppers' to evaluate the service quality performance. Since quality of service is a subjective assessment, each person values it based on his own expectations and perceptions. If not clearly briefed on the parameters on which they need to evaluate service, the findings of the mystery shoppers may not be too accurate.

Service Qualities to be Measured

The objective of every service quality monitoring and measuring exercise is to primarily evaluate customer satisfaction levels. But before a retailer actually starts measuring it based on customer feedback he needs to do an organizational assessment of the service and culture of the organization by considering the following:

- Value delivered to the customer.
- The internal effectiveness of the organization, and areas in need of improvement.
- Quality of work life, as it has a bearing on how efficiently they work.
- The need for a service quality initiative to achieve the desired quality standards.
- The chances of the service quality initiative succeeding in the organization.
- Top management's commitment to the effort and its capability to ensure that it does succeed.

These should help determine the following:

- Adequacy of the service strategy.
- Customer-friendliness of the systems and policies.
- Competence and customer focus of the service people.
- Commitment and support provided by managers across the organization.
- Degree to which the culture is customer-centred.
- Extent of staff empowerment.

Most retailers measure service quality performance only at the store level. To be a truly service-oriented organization, the retailer needs to monitor and measure service quality of all departments/functions, both at the front and back ends. The entire organization should be one big customer service department, where everybody is responsible for service quality. Every department and employee should be accountable to the other and all departments/functions need to be given the same level of importance.

Once service quality performance has been monitored and measured internally, the results need to be carefully studied and analysed. Based on this analysis, appropriate feedback has to be given to the employees and corrective actions taken in right earnest. After measuring the culture and service quality performance internally, the retailer can consider soliciting customer feedback.

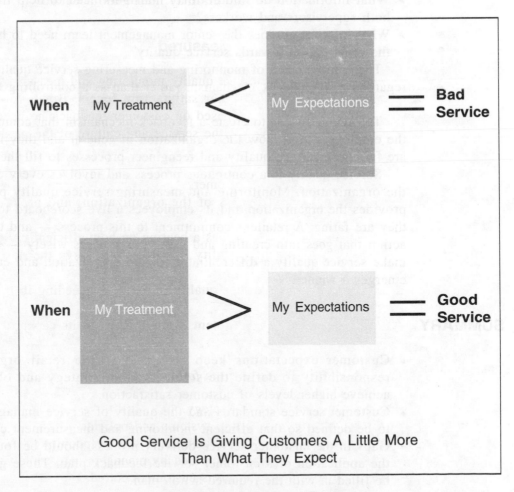

Fig. 22: *Managing Customer Expectations*

Implementation after Monitoring and Measuring Service Quality

The key factor in closing the loop is not measurement but the information itself, in the hands of those who best respond and act on it. The right dissemination of the information and results of the measurement is critical to enhance service quality performance.

The management of a retail organization needs to ask the following questions while implementing a customer service action plan:

> What information do employees need to find out how well they are succeeding in delivering quality service?
> What information do supervisors need to enable them to support frontline employees who interact directly with customers?
> What information do middle-level managers need to help them support both supervisors and workers?
> What information does the senior management team need to help it guide the organization towards service quality?

The entire process of monitoring and measuring service quality has to be regarded as a feedback mechanism rather than as a controlling tool.

The retailer needs to create a feedback mechanism that communicates to the employees as to how the organization in general and they in particular are faring on service quality and reengineer processes to fill the gaps.

Service quality is a continuous process and involves every employee in the organization. Monitoring and measuring service quality performance provides the organization and its employees a live scoreboard to know how they are faring. A retailer's commitment to this process — and the resulting action that goes into creating and using this process wisely — will help to make service quality a differentiator for the organization and ensure that it emerges a winner.

SUMMARY

- Customer expectations keep rising. It is the retail organization's responsibility to define the service vision, strategy and objectives to achieve higher levels of customer satisfaction.
- Customer service standards and the quality of service management need to be defined so that efficient monitoring and measurement can be done.
- Gaps in the customer service delivery process should be found through the application of a customer service feedback plan. These gaps need to be filled in with the required action plan.

- Empowerment of people is critical in a retail organization to ensure the fulfillment of an efficient customer service delivery process.
- It is essential to keep retail personnel in readiness to serve customers by efficiently providing customer service training. 'Service' that is provided by people is more relevant than the 'services' that are available in a retail organization.

Questions:

1. Define the customer service management model and explain the customer service process flow to be followed in a retail organization.

2. What aspects need to be measured while monitoring service quality?

3. What factors does a retail organization need to consider while implementing a service action plan?

4. Explain the relevance of human resources and their preparedness for an efficient customer service delivery.

Customer Service: The Nordstrom & Shoppers' Stop way

The Nordstrom store is known for its exceptional customer service. It is customer service that makes Nordstrom so special. The Nordstrom store differentiates and distinguishes itself from competition through excellent customer service. Customer service is said to be the culture at Nordstrom and the organization has emerged as a world wide example for customer service at retail.

The Nordstrom store targets middle to upper income women and men offering merchandise categories like shoes, apparel, accessories, cosmetics etc at competitive prices. The chain can boast of a highly motivated, "self-empowered people who have an entrepreneurial spirit, who feel that they are in this to better themselves and to feel good about themselves, to make more money and to be successful."

To cite an example of customer service at Nordstrom: There was a customer who fell in love with a pair of burgundy, pleated, Donna Karan slacks that had just gone on sale at a Nordstrom store, but the store was out of her size and the sales associate was not able to locate a pair at any other Nordstrom store in the area. Knowing that the same slacks were available with a competitor across the street, the associate secured some petty cash from the department manager, walked across to the competing department store where she bought the slacks at full price, returned to

Nordstrom and then sold them to the customer at the marked-down Nordstrom price. The culture of Nordstrom is to delight every customer. Though Nordstrom did not make money on that sale it was an investment in promoting the loyalty of an appreciative customer, who would definitely make a repeat purchase from the store. *(Source: The Nordstrom Way by Robert Spector and Patrick D McCarthy)*

Customer Service at Shoppers' Stop: Customer service in retail is all about going that extra mile which will bring a smile on the faces of customers. Here is an instance of an Associate exhibiting sincere responsibility in responding to the need of a customer at Shoppers' Stop, Mumbai and a letter the customer has written to the store bears testimony to the service culture at Shoppers' Stop:

Quote

Dear Sir,

I would like to inform you of an incident that took place in your store at Malad on 5ᵗʰ September 2004 and of the response thereafter from your Executive Ms. Darshana.

I by this letter would like to express my thanks and gratitude to the steps she took in retrieving my lost articles and returning them to me promptly.

On 5ᵗʰ September 2004, I visited your store for shopping with my family and had purchased a wallet for myself. After having made the payment as I was transferring my things from my old wallet to my new one, my wife objected to the color of the new wallet. I went to the counter and to find out whether I could exchange the wallet. The Sales Executive instantly agreed. Without realizing that I had already transferred some money from my old wallet by then to the new one, I handed over the new wallet to the sales executive and in exchange took another wallet for which a difference of payment was to be made by me.

At this juncture, firstly Ms. Darshana assisted me in making the payment instantly and then to make the balance payment. I then left the store. It was only after I reached my residence that I realized that the money had remained in the wallet I had purchased first. As by that time the store had closed down. I was given the telephone number of Ms. Darshana by your office. I called her up the next day in the morning and informed her about the matter. She agreed to look into the matter and revert, which she did.

It is really appreciable that the one wallet I had purchased was located out of those hundreds of wallets on the sales counter and the money was handed over to me on my visiting your store.

The total amount left in the wallet was Rs. 1200/-. The quantum of money is not important. What was important that the said wallet contained a very old 100 rupee note, which I have not used, for several years now. It has been my lucky one, which was returned to me.

I want to thank Ms. Darshana for her efforts and you all for your efficient and prompt action.

Thanking You,

Yours faithfully,

Sd/-
Sanjeev Ahooja
Membership No. 2210 9910 1083 5066

Unquote

This letter was written by Mr. Sanjeev Ahooja, one of Shoppers' Stop's customers overwhelmed by the excellent standard of service rendered to him by a Department Manager at their Malad Store.

It is excellent Customer Service that brings back every customer to the store and the lifetime value of a customer to the store makes the store's coffers ringing always.

Questions for Discussion

1. Why is customer service important to a retail store?

2. How can a retail store make service its culture?

3. What are the lessons of customer service we can learn from Nordstrom?

4. How can we go that extra mile to bring smiles to customers?

CHAPTER 16

Retail Research

CHAPTER OBJECTIVES

1. To provide the reader with an understanding of the areas and scope of retail research
2. To explain the various research methods followed in retailing
3. To create an awareness of the different kinds of process audits that are common in the retailing industry

Research is carried out at the retail level for concept testing, business feasibility analysis, identification of the right product mix, studying the target group profile, analysing consumer behaviour, etc. Retail audits help to ascertain the effectiveness of retail operating and back-end processes, advertising, promotions, performance of sales personnel, etc. Research and retail audits help retailers create footfalls and achieve maximum conversions.

For instance, while commissioning a new retail project, the process starts with the identification of the basic theme, arriving at the right retail format, identifying the right customer profile and getting the right product mix if a proposition has to be created in an area of choice that has not been firmed up. There are also times when the organization has firmed up the basic proposition, but the details of the elements are researched and tested.

Quantitative Survey: This studies target demographic groups by mapping target segments. By mapping the current market according to behavioural and need-based segments, the survey helps ascertain the right profile to target. This means understanding:

- Current shopping patterns. That is, which demographic group shows higher frequency of shopping as well as spend, which feels the need for a retail experience etc.
- The size of the segment.
- The means used currently to satisfy this need.
- The core/peripheral targets and their respective sizes.

A quantitative survey is also done to assess the viability of a retail business by determining the concept's appeal and measuring how that translates into potential. This involves understanding the motivators and barriers and profiling the core target group where its appeal is the maximum, which gives an indicator of likely frequency of visits/spends, etc.

Qualitative Research: While developing a product mix, the focus groups among the target segments identified are treated as lead segments for studying product preferences. This is done by:

— Identifying the most promising positioning/product proposition in the core target.
— Getting cues on ambience, shopping needs, styling, must-haves, don'ts and so on.
— Conducting a negative check (a check for possible deterrents) on the preferred initiative among the secondary target/areas to strengthen, in order to attract the peripheral target.

Qualitative research is also done while redefining an existing proposition by involving focus groups among the target audience.

Research Design: This comprises the clear objectives of the study: the nature and sources of data, sample quota size, questionnaire design, analysis methodology, etc.

DEVELOPING A METHODOLOGY

Research techniques are based on 'customer decision paths', the processes through which the customer goes — leaving home, shopping and returning home. The shopping experience begins as soon as the shopper plans the trip. While some prepare a shopping list, others work from memory. Many thoughts go through the consumer's mind before he even reaches his destination, influencing where he chooses to shop. These include:

— Proximity to the store, whether it is easy to get there or not.
— Availability of goods at the store.
— Cost/pricing of goods.
— How to carry the goods when at the store.
— Parking space.

It is important to find out what products generally go on a shopping list, whether the brand names are jotted down. Also, it pays to know if shoppers rely on in-store prompting to remind them what they need/want or think they need/want. Understanding the shopping experience and in-store influences is vital.

We now take a look at the clear objectives of the research.

Data Collection: The broad areas in which data is to be collected is defined and specified in the following examples:

• Out-of-home shopping/buying habits: frequency, occasions, type of places, type of items, average spends, frequency of shopping alone versus in a group.
• Attitudes toward shopping and eating out: motivators/drivers, how do these differ according to occasion, time of day, accompanying people, individual's demographic profile etc.
• Concerns: what are the hygiene factors (must-haves) when looking at shopping places.
• Places generally frequented: reasons why, dissatisfaction with current shopping places, etc.
• Frequency of socialising with friends while shopping, etc.

• Attitudes toward socialising: typical places for hanging out, shopping and so on.

Sample Size: This has to be fixed according to the nature and size of the research from the stratified segments.

Questionnaire Method: In the case of research covering demographic groups, most questionnaires include queries on the respondent's characteristics and circumstances. These include questions about sex, age group, occupation, education, household type, income, religion, socio-economic classification (SEC), etc.

In-depth Interview Method: In-depth interviewing involves asking questions, listening to and recording the answers, and then posing additional questions to clarify or expand on a particular issue. Questions are open-ended and respondents are encouraged to express their own views. In-depth interviews are of different kinds, such as informal conversational, semi-structured, focus group and standardized open-ended interviews. The mini-depth interviews and accompanied shopping routes enable an understanding of the feelings underlying the responses. The objective of this element is to define and gain a deeper understanding of the underlying reasons behind in-store behaviour.

Observational Method (Shopper Observation): Observational methods involve the systematic noting and recording of activities, behaviour and physical objects as an unobtrusive observer. It is often a rapid and economical way of obtaining basic socio-economic information on households or target segments. The main advantage of this method is that if respondents are not aware that they are being observed, then they are less likely to change their behaviour and compromise the validity of the evaluation.

Observation of shoppers in-store allows the researcher and the retailer to identify and measure consumer behaviour at the point of sale. How much time do shoppers spend at any given fixture? Where do they normally stop at the fixture? How do they react to promotional displays and gondola ends? Which brands do they handle and which ones do they select?

Observation of consumers can be done in several ways: trained observers discreetly positioned by the fixture can observe shoppers, or a pre-recruited shopper can be shadowed through the complete shopping cycle from home to store and back home again. Hidden cameras operated by remote control can help marketers and sales promotion companies to understand consumer behaviour. In most cases, the camera element is not complete until one approaches the shopper to find out more about his behaviour and classification details. In camera recording, shopping behaviour is studied at key points in and around the store. The following key attributes are normally studied:

Traffic flow: How many consumers pass the fixture? How many stop and look/handle/select a brand?

Price: When do consumers examine the price tag? Do certain consumers search by price alone?

Packaging: Do customers study the detail and content of the packaging? What elements are studied?

Second choice: If customers cannot find the brand they want, why is this the case? If it is there, did they locate it from a distance or did they have to go right up to the display? What influenced the choice of the second brand?

Ease of purchase: How easy did the customer find the selection process? How does this compare with the search strategy?

Trade up: What other products did the customer look at? Do some displays demonstrate trading up or trading down?

Own label: How are own-label products perceived within the two displays? Do they require preferential attention in one mode of display? If so, which products and brands lose attention?

Product view: The effects on products that are missed are also examined, coupled with the side of gondola selected. As the customer moves down the aisle, potentially 50% of the range is missed as the merchandise is on both sides of the aisle. Very few customers shop up and down both sides of the aisles.

Trolley/basket: Use of trolley/basket: how often is a trolley left? How far do customers stray from their trolley/basket?

Other consumers: Interaction with, and influence of, other shoppers.

Daily/hourly: Analysing the different sorts of behaviour and volume of customers on a daily and weekly basis allows retailers to fix staff levels, in particular the degree to which specific areas of the shop are covered. It also allows the retailer a degree of flexibility in the merchandising to reflect changes in shopping patterns.

RETAIL AUDITS

Retail audits are useful to ascertain the sales personnel's efficiency at the point of sale, for example, the operating process. An audit makes it possible to find out the average time taken on a normal day or on a weekend to check out a customer from the cash till in a supermarket.

Retail Process Audit: Retail process audits examine a store's operating processes for efficiency. Such audits are done to reengineer processes so that better efficiencies are achieved or process or cycle time reduced. For instance, if the average time taken for a customer check-out is five minutes in a supermarket, process reengineering can reduce it to three minutes, removing bottlenecks and eliminating unnecessary steps.

Mystery Customer Audit: Mystery customer audits are common in retailing and are used to enhance the skills of sales personnel through feedback and training. In mystery customer audits, auditors disguise themselves as customers and assess the performance of the salespeople on predefined parameters. The following are the audit areas identified through a questionnaire used for a 'mystery customer audit':

Mystery Customer Audit Areas for Assessing Sales Personnel
(To be rated on a scale of 1 to 5)

(1) **Greetings and Courtesy:**
Did the salesperson "Connect With Me" through greetings? Did he/she greet me in the right manner when I entered the store?
Did he/she smile at me readily?
Was his/her body language positive? (Leaving abruptly, turning the face away, etc. fall under the category of negative body language).
Was the salesperson sitting at the sales counter when I was trying to buy?
Was the salesperson talking to his/her colleague when I was attempting to buy?

(2) **Grooming:**
Was the salesperson dressed in proper uniform? Was he/she wearing the name badge?
Was he/she neat and presentable? (Clean-shaven boys, hair groomed, clean footwear, etc.).

(3) **Communication:**
Did he/she speak clearly?
Did he/she proactively communicate with me in a likeable manner?

(4) **Awareness:**
Was he/she aware of the products sold?
Was he/she aware of all the product details?

(5) **Sales Presentation:**
Did he/she try to understand my needs?
Did he/she lead me to the merchandise? Or did he/she invite me to see some new products?
Did he/she speak to me of the benefits of the merchandise?
Did he/she present the merchandise properly?
Did he/she suggest a few things as add-ons that I could buy in relation to what I was looking for?
Did he/she recommend anything with offers or any benefits that I could get?
Did he/she help me choose?

Research provides direction to retailing; audits show areas that could do with improvement. Research needs to be meticulous and it pays to study, say, consumer behaviour, before the retail store puts together its product mix. Organizations like ORG-MARG, AC Nielsen, KSA Technopak, etc. specialize in retail research in India.

SUMMARY

- Research in retail is very important. As customer preferences and choices are dynamic and change frequently, the retail organization needs to understand these before redesigning its processes for improvement.
- Since customer interaction takes place at the retail store, there's a big opportunity to gather first-hand information and feedback from customers through research. Understanding customers and their expectations leads to better performance, and research provides the way forward for the organization to grow.
- Frequent process audits ought to be undertaken by retail organizations to reduce cycle times, improve customer service deliveries and improve performance.

Questions:

1. What are the different kinds of research undertaken in retail? Explain.

2. Write notes on the following methods of data collection in retail research:

- — Questionnaire Method
- — In-depth Interview Method
- — Observational Method

3. Explain the key attributes studied by observation in retail research.

4. Write short notes on retail process audit and mystery customer audit.

Key Global Research Studies

Internationalization is the buzz word in global retailing and retailers who have grown in their home countries have set their foot on various other countries as part of their expansion plans. India is the country where all multinational retailers eagerly await the government to open up the market by allowing higher degrees of Foreign Direct Investment (FDI). Wal-Mart aims for market entry with a cash & carry type of format soon. Metro Group, the German retailer opened its first Indian cash & carry store in 2003 in the city of Bangalore and has since added a few more stores to its operations, the latest one being in Mulund, Mumbai. Several CEOs of leading retailers travelled to India in person to lobby with the Government of India to open the retail sector to FDI. John Menzer, International President & CEO, of Wal-Mart, visited India in May 2005. He has been quoted in the media as having observed the Indian retail market thus: "It is amazing that India, which has huge retail potential, is under-retailed. We are looking forward to the government relaxing FDI norms in retail. As and when this happens, we will invest significantly here. India is a huge organic growth opportunity for Wal-Mart." Retailers like Tesco and Carrefour too are waiting in the wings to venture into India if given the go-ahead by the government policy. Such global retailers rely on research rather than going into new markets based on a gut feel. As global retailers intend to set up shop in new territories outside their home countries, they are said to largely depend upon research studies like Goldman Sachs' BRICs Report or the Global Retail Development Index (GRDI) developed by AT Kearney every year, in addition to falling back upon information generated by their own studies.

Global Retail Development Index

According to AT Kearney, "Global retail is experiencing an explosive modernization as investment rushes into developing markets. From small proprietors with a mainly local focus, retail's ambitions now stretch worldwide, embracing the latest trends in marketing, distribution and supply. Modern retail grew between 25 and 30 percent in India and 13 percent in both China and Russia. As the wealthiest markets mature, more retailers are pursuing new growth opportunities. They are eyeing countries new to modern retailing, smaller cities (as larger cities become saturated), and customer segments hungry for specialty products. Retailers that can identify the most promising markets will become fierce global competitors—able to saturate the obvious markets and gain first-mover advantage in new ones. Retailers understand these new realities. Modern retail has been expanding to new markets for a few years now. The trouble is, it is difficult to determine which new market is the most promising one. As one market becomes saturated, is it enough simply to follow the crowd into the next one? With this in mind, AT Kearney developed the Global Retail Development Index. Now in its sixth year, the GRDI identifies windows of opportunity to help retailers make strategic investments in exciting new markets."

India has been topping the Global Retail Development Index in 2006 and 2007 in succession as the most attractive retail destination from among the 30 emerging countries studied by AT Kearney. The annual AT Kearney Global Retail Development Index ranks 30 emerging countries on a 100- point scale—the higher the ranking, the more urgency there is to enter a country.

On the research parameters adopted for GRDI 2007, AT Kearney says that the countries were selected from a list of 185 based on the following three criteria:

- **Country risk:** more than 35 in Euromoney's country-risk score
- **Population size:** more than two million
- **Wealth:** GDP per capita more than $3,000 (GDP per capita for countries with populations of more than 35 million is more flexible due to the market opportunity.

The GRDI top ten markets are the markets that are always on the radar screen of international retailers.

BRICs Report

Another frequently discussed research report in the retailing circles in India is the BRICs Report. Goldman Sachs came up with the BRICs Report in the year 2004. The report on Brazil, Russia, India and China (BRIC) states that India will be the third largest economy, after the US and China by 2050. The BRIC study assumes strong and stable macro economic policies, stable political institutions, and high levels of education and openness as the fundamentals to the model used. The Goldman Sachs global economics team released a follow-up report also to its initial BRIC study in 2004. The report states that in BRIC nations, the number of people with an annual income over a threshold of $3,000, will double in number within three years and reach 800 million people within a decade. This predicts a massive rise in the size of the middle class in these nations. In 2025, it is calculated that the number of people in BRIC nations earning over $15,000 may reach over 200 million. This indicates that a huge pickup in demand will not be restricted to basic goods but impact higher-priced goods as well. According to the report, first China and then a decade later India will begin to dominate the world economy.

The Goldman Sachs Global Economics Department has recently released *BRICs and Beyond*. This book compiles their recent research on the BRICs—Brazil, Russia, India and China—and the changing nature of the global economy. Goldman Sachs Economics Department observes, "It is now six years since we coined the term 'BRIC' in our Global Economics Paper, 'Building Better Global Economic BRICs', published on November 30, 2001. Since then, these countries' equity markets have seen a remarkable increase in their value: Brazil has risen by 369%, India by 499%, Russia by 630%, and China by 201%, using the A-share market, or by a stunning 817% based on the HSCEI (Hang Seng China Enterprises Index)."

The BRICs report is now constantly quoted as a validation of India's emerging economic prowess.

Information Sources: www.atkearney.com & www2.goldmansachs.com

Questions for Discussion

1. Discuss the significance of global research for multinational retailers.

2. How does AT Kearney's Global Retail Development Index (GRDI) help retailers understand emerging markets?

3. What are the major findings of the BRICs research studies made by Goldman Sachs?

CHAPTER 17

Visual Merchandising and Displays

CHAPTER OBJECTIVES

1. To explain the role of visual merchandising and displays in enhancing atmospherics and the customer shopping experience
2. To provide the reader with inputs on the applications/influence of visual merchandising and displays in the customer's buying process
3. To discuss displays as a tool in effective functional retailing
4. To elaborate on the role of the retail visual merchandiser

"You never get a second chance to make a first impression."

In modern retailing, attaining leadership and building an image in the customer's mind requires a great deal of skill and planning. Al Ries and Jack Trout long ago talked about positioning as being a 'battle of the mind'. Even today this holds true: a store brand has to break through the clutter and make an impression on the customer's mind to eventually convert the coordinated entity of the store that's in the customer's mind into a particular image.

Image can be described as the overall look of a store and the series of mental pictures and feelings it evokes in the beholder. For the retailer, developing a powerful image provides the opportunity to embody a single message, stand out from the competition and be remembered. Image is the foundation of all retailing efforts. While store layout, presentation, signage, displays and events can all change to reflect newness and excitement from one season to the next, they must always remain true to the underlying store image.

Studies indicate that a retailer has roughly seven seconds to capture the attention of a passing customer. The following elements combine to form a distinctive image that not only reaches out and grabs the customer's attention, but also makes a positive impression in those precious few seconds.

VISUAL MERCHANDISING

Visual merchandising, also known as the 'silent salesman', is the science and art of suggestive selling by display and presentation. Visual merchandising focal points are located strategically to circulate the customer in the store, and communicate the features and benefits of the merchandise besides the in-store promotion in vogue. This is done by converting a passerby to a browser with an effective window display, a browser to a spender through the process of 'conversion', a spender to a big spender by increasing the 'ticket size' assisted by the process of cross-merchandising.

Retailers also use the space in the non-trading common areas in addition to the merchandise presentation space for brand promotions paid for by companies owning the brands. In the FMCG category, dealer signboards, windows and in-store space of outlets like chemists and grocers are used as point of purchase promotional areas. In the fashion retailing category, space in common areas like the building façade, staircase landings and columns are given to brands on hire at a price. These add to the revenue generated from the space and also adds value to the store ambience.

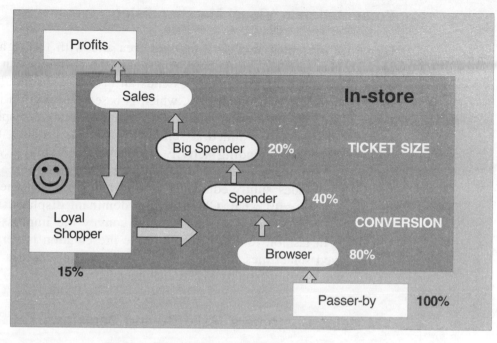

Fig. 23: *The Customer Stickiness Progression Model*

Visual Merchandising Enhances the Shopping Experience

Visual merchandising enhances the shopping experience by providing the right ambience, besides creating an image of the store in the minds of the customers. Such an enjoyable ambience is created through a combination of colours, display presentations, graphics, lighting, forms and fixtures. If done by the store in an exciting and dynamic fashion, the shopping experience would be pleasurable for the consumer and make him come repeatedly.

Visual Merchandising as a Communication Tool

Visual merchandising communicates to customers the right message about the merchandise by projecting the latest trends, colours and fashion in apparel retailing. In retailing other merchandise, such effective visual merchandising often communicates the latest arrivals in the store. Visual merchandising, by creating basic forms, mannequins and fixtures around the merchandise, often tells the story to the customers. Visual displays are the perfect communication vehicle, and provides an opportunity for retailers to sell a variety of merchandise.

Presentation in Visual Merchandising

Elegantly presented in a well-defined area and with the right fixtures, an open display provides an environment where the customer can be around an array of merchandise. It silently extends an invitation to him/her to see and touch the goods. A theme display, which is based on a season or an event, is used to promote an appropriate product range. Lifestyle displays are more subtle, not necessarily aimed at selling a particular product, but an image, which has a corresponding activity. Coordinated displays, which contain items that are normally used together, are a way of increasing multiple purchases, besides subtly educating or informing the customer of what can be coordinated with what. Classification dominant displays, which contain all varieties of one product, are used to convey the impression of a wide selection. In fashion retailing, merchandise presentation is very creative and is displayed sometimes in non-standard fixtures that express the mood and its relevant psychographics to the customer.

VM Helps Customers Make Buying Decisions

Visual merchandising helps influence buying decisions a great deal. Sometimes, mere presentation creates an impact on the customer, who then decides to buy the product. For instance, in apparel retailing, customers often ask for the whole set of outfits shown on display. The buying process initiated by visual merchandising starts with the act of grabbing the *attention* of the customer. Then the presentation creates in them the *interest* to buy. The story-telling in visual merchandising generates the *desire* in the customers. The final *action* of buying is triggered by the visual merchandising and displays communicating one message — the merchandise is 'for you'.

Store Atmospherics

Store atmospherics include the exteriors and interiors of the store and the manner in which they are designed to create the ambience for a fashion boutique or a store.

Exteriors: A store's exterior look is often referred to as the architecture, and comprises aspects such as building materials, architectural style and detail, colours and textures. Harrods in London has a unique architectural façade, thus creating a distinct identity for itself.

Signage: The store signage is a vital element of the storefront, attracting the customer's attention. Realizing the value of a strong storefront sign, many retailers like Shoppers' Stop have employed unique designs combining its black and white identity. The Planet M music store has a distinctive 3D signage. The Barista café's signage is brightly configured and, along with its brightly-lit façade, beckons the customer from afar.

Interiors or Store Layout: Fashion retailers often lay out the store in a free-flow format with a great deal of aisle space to enable the free movement of customers within the store and also to create a more specific atmosphere and image. Such a layout creates an image in the shopper's mind, because of the functional qualities and psychological appeal. Layout is just one part of store image, other factors being colour, music (aural), scent (olfactory), types of promotion used, service and store cleanliness.

In fashion retailing, developing the image of the store is considered more important than the optimum use of space. Therefore it is the image of a fashion retailer that is ultimately more profitable. However, since image is easily damaged the positioning and overall look of the store is vital. The vast majority of women see shopping for clothes as a leisure activity and hence want the experience to be a pleasant one. An overcrowded store tends to annoy shoppers, who then move on to more inviting premises.

VM and Displays in Fashion Retailing: Visual merchandising is part of the language the store speaks with its customers. Fashion retailers use a variety of visual merchandising and display techniques. Visual merchandising begins as a theme that runs all through the store, giving people an idea of what the theme is all about. This is coordinated more often with the merchandise offerings, the presentation underlining the relevance of the theme, its applicability to the offerings and thus the reasons for consumers to buy. Retailers try to carry the theme from the window to the interior. Therefore the window display is vital in attracting customers to the store.

The retail visual merchandising theme is usually lifestyle-based, in accordance with the research done on the target market. Lifestyle coordination is not just about the actual lifestyle of customers; it focuses on the ambitions and aspirations of the group. Therefore the products consumers buy are for who they see themselves as being or aspire to be — this is normally different from who they actually are.

The types of lifestyle images presented to customers depend on the type of merchandise offerings. They create a more modern image than the traditional use of mannequins, and save on valuable sales space, without an overcrowded look.

In the fashion retailing industry, thematic visual merchandising involves placing garments along with the relevant accessories (cross-merchandising) so that shoppers treat them as an entire outfit, thus increasing multiple purchases. Classification-dominant displays are sometimes used in large, low-priced retailers as it enables them to present vast amounts of stock. However, this can lead to a rather cluttered image and may not be suitable for many types of fashion retailers.

A store's exterior or glass storefront provides an additional opportunity to reach out and grab the passing customer. Windows are integral in creating a positive impression before the customer enters the store, and many retailers use them effectively.

THE ROLE OF VISUAL MERCHANDISERS IN RETAILING

Visual merchandisers play a major role in enhancing sales and the customer experience. Depending on where they work, visual merchandisers' duties include:

- Planning the VM theme and creating displays.
- Arranging props for displays.
- Arranging display fixtures and lighting.
- Setting up stores before openings.
- Working with floor plans and store requirements.
- Training personnel on the sales floor to create displays.
- Organizing merchandising units such as racks and shelves.

SHOP DISPLAYS

Displaying merchandise in the store allows customers to make quick decisions on purchases. Shop displays — done both in the exterior and in the interior of the store — are of different types. A few significant ones are listed below:

Window Displays: Store window displays attract the attention of passers-by. The design of display windows plays a major role in organizing the display in the store. They are of two types:

Exclusive Windows: Windows are exclusive when they have an absolutely closed backdrop. The store's show window is a separate area and displays are organized in the windows following the theme and seasonal motif.

Open Windows: Open windows do not have any backdrop, and the passing customer can see the interior of the store through the displays. This is often done in large stores, especially those that sell apparel and related accessories. A wide façade with a glazed frontage automatically serves as an open window to entice eyeballs.

Live Displays: Live models are used sometimes for product displays at the entrance of the store. They may also demonstrate the use of products. Children's stores often use people dressed as cartoon characters to attract kids' attention. Kids' Kemp in Bangalore is one example where live characters are used.

Marquee Displays: These are done under a marquee panel erected in the front of the store or in the forecourt. Marquee panels have a canopied or an extended roof, which are sometimes used in spacious stores. Marquee panels are often used in large supermarkets too, and form an ideal platform for category indicators and related signage.

Freestanding or Island Displays: These are displays of merchandise found generally at the entrance of stores (inside) to announce new arrivals, special offers, etc. A display podium is erected and decorated suitably to highlight the merchandise. The use of nested tables is currently in vogue to enhance visibility of freestanding displays.

Counter Displays: Merchandise is displayed in counters that have glazed display shelves. Categories like jewellery and watches have counter displays lit from within to highlight the merchandise.

Brand Corners: Brand corners are displays of exclusive brands and are common in supermarkets and convenience stores. A devoted space in shelves or gondolas carry the exclusive displays of the brand. This happens during a paid promotion campaign or when the brand has an offer or a scheme to benefit the consumer.

End Cap Displays: These are done at the terminal sides of the gondolas on both sides, and are commonly found in the gondola fixtures used in supermarkets, convenience stores and book stores.

Cascade/Waterfall Displays: Found commonly in garment stores, these displays are done on the linear walls with the help of stooping rods. Such cascade/waterfall displays are used for blazers, jackets etc.

Displays are organized and coordinated with appropriate props for an immediate eye appeal. It is the displays that show customers what is in store for them, converting them into purchasers.

SUMMARY

- Visual merchandising is both a science and an art; it requires conceptual, aesthetic and analytical skills to create footfalls into the store, guide buyers, influence buying decisions and motivate customers to come to the store again. It is the essence of retailing and can induce the prospective customer to stop, look and buy.

- Through their visual merchandising efforts, successful retailers try to create an exclusive tangible visual identity that is synonymous with the store brand so that customers can identify with it easily.
- Visual merchandising and displays help the store cross-merchandise to create a lifestyle or to suggest complementary items, thus serving as silent salesmen.
- A store that is well-presented, with its visual merchandising and displays speaking for it, creates the right impact on the customer keeping the cash registers ringing all the time.

Questions:

1. Discuss the role of visual merchandising in the process of sales conversions.

2. Write short notes on visual merchandising as:

    — An enhancer of the shopping experience for the customer.
    — A communication tool.
    — An enabler of purchase decisions.

3. Describe the elements of store atmospherics and their role in creating the right environment for the customer.

4. How does the mechanics of display work in fashion retailing?

5. Briefly explain the role of a visual merchandiser in retailing.

6. Briefly describe the types of displays in retail stores.

Guidelines for Good Visual Merchandising

Today's world of visual merchandising is as varied as the retailers who use these display techniques to sell their merchandise. Good visual merchandising today runs the gamut from boldly hued, avant-garde displays to tasteful monochromatic vignettes.

No matter what their themes, good visual merchandising displays have one thing in common: They do the jobs of selling merchandise, educating customers and reinforcing their stores' images.

Too many displays fall down on the job because they're poorly planned and executed. For instance, the displays may contain too much or too little merchandise or props. They may lack a theme or may ignore good design and display principles. Sometimes displays may be poorly lit or they may not be regularly maintained.. Displays may not be changed at the required intervals and this may allow them to become obsolete and not current with the times. Where would the customer prefer to shop - at a store that has vibrant, frequently changing displays appearing in crystal-clean windows or at a store where the sun-faded display hasn't been changed in 3 years and can barely be seen through the dirty window littered with a plethora of outdated fliers?

VM Themes

All effective visual merchandising displays have themes that pull the items on display together. The store's VM team may have a plethora of themes at their disposal:

    Holidays

    Seasons

    Back-to-school

    Festivals

    Sports

    National "months" or "weeks"

    Gift-giving occasions, such as birthdays or Mother's Day

    The store's merchandise mix may also provide valuable theme inspiration. If your shop stocks a selection of, say, rabbit-adorned items, then one may come up with a bunny theme for visual displays. The store can either develop a display that features an ample supply of identical items to create visual impact or one that includes a selection of complementary items, which gives consumers clues about how they can incorporate your merchandise into their own homes.

Principles of Good Design

No matter what the theme and type of product being sold, good visual displays embody 5 design principles: balance, harmony, proportion, emphasis and rhythm. Here's a brief look at each principle:

1.   **Balance**—displaying merchandise in a way that results in a pleasing distribution of visual weight within the display.

2.   **Emphasis**—having a dominant point of interest in the display area, similar to a floral arrangement's focal point.

3.   **Harmony**—arranging the various elements of a display, including the merchandise, props, signage and lighting, as well as color and texture, to produce a pleasing effect.

4. **Proportion**—keeping the ratio of one aspect of a display in relationship to the others. For example, one item shouldn't seem to be too large or small in portion to other items in the display.
5. **Rhythm**—creating a path the eyes will follow once they've made initial contact with the item of emphasis. A display with good rhythm leads consumers' eyes throughout the entire display.

The Use of Colour

Good visual merchandising also uses color to maximum effect to attract passersby's attention. As the florist is a master at using color harmonies, the same are the principles for visual merchandising. For example, visual displays will use a monochromatic, analogous, triadic, complementary, split complementary, double complementary or tone-on-tone color scheme. As regards the display's components, the visual merchandiser shall keep in mind the merchandise and the shop's image along with the customers' likes and dislikes when working with color schemes.

The Significance of Appropriate Lighting

Many retailers may forget to plan adequate lighting when they create their displays. Generally, there are two basic types of lighting that one can employ when creating displays:

General lighting—illuminates both merchandise and the store's general traffic paths. General lighting is usually not movable.

Accent lighting—accentuates particular pieces of merchandise. Accent lighting fixtures are designed to be moved and adjusted, depending on the need.

There are dozens of fixture and bulb choices available for both general and accent lighting. Many lighting supply stores offer free advice, so the VM personnel can check with the local supplier for expert tips.

Graphics and Signage

When a visual merchandiser advises a store to get graphic with a customer, he or she isn't being rude. Instead, the visual merchandiser is suggesting that the store should use graphics and signage to convey information that will educate customers and motivate them to buy.

Signage gives customers important information they'll need - the price of an item, the location of coordinating products, product information and more. One must make sure that the shop's graphics and signage are professional-looking and in tune with the shop's image. For example, customers may find bold, contemporary graphics jarring if they were used in a store that carries mostly traditional merchandise.

Many stores have found success using oversized in-store or window graphics to add visual impact to displays. The graphics can be repeated on a smaller scale throughout the store to earmark featured merchandise or sale items.

The Use of Props in VM

Other critical components that can either make or break the store's display's effectiveness are its props, which are defined as the items that go into a display but aren't being sold. The key to using props in displays is to avoid having the props overshadow the items the store is trying to sell. One must also use props that enhance the merchandise, rather than detract from it.

Props can be anything from simple, colorful foam-board cut-outs, to antique furniture to children's toys. The VM team needn't spend thousands of dollars on props. They can go to garage sales (or the *chor bazaar* in Mumbai!), antique shops and flea markets for interesting items. Retail organizations may even work with non-competing retailers in the area to share props, which can rotate among the cooperating stores. One must remember, almost anything can be a prop - a rock, a tree branch, a child's red wagon, a lacy tablecloth or even a bale of hay.

The team can visit fabric stores to seek out inexpensive material to drape tables, create swags or staple on backdrops. The VM team of the store can even stock up inexpensive fabrics, such as tulle and burlap, both of which add instant texture and visual interest to displays.

Questions for Discussion

1. What are the principles of Good Design in Visual Merchandising?

2. Discuss the significance of the use of colour and lighting in Visual Merchandising.

3. Explain the use of graphics and signage in VM.

4. Discuss the importance of props to VM.

CHAPTER 18

Role of Personal Selling in Retailing

CHAPTER OBJECTIVES

1. To underline the importance of personal selling in retailing
2. To define the salesperson as a true representative of the retail store, projecting its philosophy and principles
3. To provide an overview of the qualities required for an effective retail salesperson
4. To elaborate on the retail sales process with details of the selling steps to be followed

Sales personnel play an important role in retailing. They are the ambassadors of the store brand and form part of the imagery of the store. Personal selling essentially involves developing relationships to enable both customers and retailers achieve mutually satisfying results, to sustain and enhance future interactions.

THE ROLE OF RETAIL SALES PERSONNEL

The behaviour of the salesperson towards the customer is an important aspect in retailing. Retail sales people always look for opportunities to serve customers. A personal greeting when he enters the store gives the customer a feeling of belonging there. Guiding the customer through the store, assisting him/her in locating the products required, presenting features and models of various products as well as demonstrating their use are all part of a salesperson's job. Salespersons, especially those selling expensive items, need special product knowledge and selling skills. They also need to be dependable, with high levels of integrity.

A salesperson should do the following in order to serve customers:

- Be a resource for information as he or she is knowledgeable about the store's merchandise, services and policies.
- Be a value counsellor, assisting the customer with value comparisons with items in the store or competing brands.
- Be a public relations representative for the store.
- Be a custodian of the merchandise and service, ensuring effective stock turns for the store and selling the inventory, which is the primary objective of the business.
- Be able to advise customers with good selling suggestions that will improve customer satisfaction and build sales.
- Be able to explain the benefits of the merchandise and services that he or she sells and not just its features.
- Ensure that the customer's needs are met so that complaints are kept to the minimum.
- Develop by virtue of his or her attitude knowledge and skills, and ensure that the store's merchandise has a loyal customer following.

The Mindset of an Ideal Salesperson

A salesperson has to undergo the following tests before initiating the sales process in a retail environment:

Test of Attitude: The question that the salesperson has to ask himself/herself is: "Do I have a positive attitude towards what I do?" A positive attitude or disposition is a must for a salesperson.

Test of Skills: There is a set of skills that the salesperson needs to have, like customer service skills, selling skills and communication skills. The salesperson has to ask himself/herself: "Am I thorough in all the skills required to succeed in my selling efforts?"

Test of Knowledge: The salesperson should check his knowledge levels in every area of the sales process — product knowledge, knowledge of prices, benefits, competition, etc. — so that he can answer customers' questions confidently. The question he should ask himself/herself is: "Do I know what I need to close a sale satisfactorily?"

Test of Integrity: The salesperson needs to do a thorough introspection of his/her integrity levels. Integrity does not just refer to refraining from stealing or pilfering but also includes having the right ethical standards in every area of the job, from arriving to work on time to being attentive on the floor. The salesperson should ask himself/herself: "Are my integrity levels high?" High integrity levels enable one to have a great deal of confidence and be ready to face any sales situation.

THE PROCESS IN PERSONAL SELLING

The process in retail selling begins from the moment the customer enters the store. The first step involves connecting with the customer and then sailing through different steps until the sale is successfully closed. Conservative processes have predefined greeting methods but an innovative and result oriented-method would be to naturally connect with the customer, gauge his/her needs, present merchandise properly, handle objections, look for buying signals, conduct a trial close, suggest add-ons and then close the sale.

1. **Connect with the customer:**
   Go beyond the technique of smiling, making eye contact and small talk. The salesperson can't connect with the consumer if he or she has a premeditated opening. A salesperson with a smooth automatic opening that has had a positive response in the past will have a hard time doing this. But to bring passion into the sale later on, even the most successful salespeople need to learn how to connect on a different level, and with a few more customers. To achieve this, one must bring a bit of his/her personality to the sales floor. There's no substitute for

this genuine approach. The salesperson has to be humorous, sweet, shy or confident while interacting with customers. He/she should help the customer open up and be able to look for signs that would trigger the desire to buy.

2. **Probe needs subtly:**
By communicating freely with the customer and striking a harmonious note, the needs of the customers can be understood even if they are not spelt out clearly.

3. **Presenting merchandise:**
The merchandise has to be presented properly without loss of time. The salesperson should initiate the trial of the product by the customer and give truthful opinions. As far as personal products are concerned, salespersons need to be subtle and allow for the kind of personal space that the customer needs while trying out such products.

4. **Handling objections and indecision:**
The customer's doubts ought to be clarified by the salesperson to his/her satisfaction. Sometimes the price of a product may be compared with those of competitors; a clear rationale for the price needs to be given in such cases. Trade journals, product hangtags, information booklets can be referred to while handling objections, if the merchandise involves high involvement.

5. **Recognize buying signals:**
The salesperson must respond quickly to buying signals, which may come in the form of certain positive statements by the customer. This is the opportune time to 'ask' for the sale. Most of the time, salespeople fail to 'ask' for the sale and hence run the risk of losing it.

6. **Trial close and add-ons:**
The trial close follows the process of 'asking' for the sale and add-ons (complementary) for the merchandise selected by the customer. The objectives of selling add-ons are as follows:
— *Up-selling:* Up-selling is the process of increasing the ticket size by offering a larger-value item, or an item of a larger size in the case of merchandise in a supermarket, say upgrading from 250ml to a 500ml.
— *Cross-selling:* Cross-selling involves offering related merchandise. For instance, if one buys a cutting board, cross-selling would mean offering knives. Or if one buys a shirt, an accessory like cuff-links.

— *Suggestive selling:* This involves salespersons making suggestions to customers on, say, the best offers in the store or the latest arrivals. It is the responsibility of the salesperson to suggest something, leaving the decision making to the customer.

7. **Closing the sale:**

   The salesperson initiates the process of preparation of the cash memo for the customer and leads him or her to the cash counter for making payment. Closing the sale would also mean thanking the customer for the sale and for the opportunity to serve while extending an invitation to come again to the store.

Customer service is key in the entire sales process and salespersons must be trained thoroughly. If required, re-training should be done so that the role the salesperson plays in a retail organization is fruitful.

SUMMARY

- The salesperson is a significant part of retailing as personal selling plays a key role in India. Customers are dependent on expert opinion for making purchase decisions.
- Personal selling is also the key to bridging customer service gaps in retailing. Through this retailers can gain a competitive advantage.
- In a nutshell, personal selling in retailing is matching the customer's needs with the store's products and services. This is achieved by having well-trained staff.
- It is the sales people who make a difference to the customer. They enable the store to develop 'stickiness' as far as customers are concerned.

Questions:

1. What are the functions of a retail salesperson?
2. What introspective tests should a salesperson undergo in order to be successful?
3. Elaborate each step of the recommended selling process in retailing.

Building customer relationships through personal selling: The Titan Way

Personal selling is a matter of creating one-on-one relationships with the customer by the retail store's sales personnel. Building relationship with customers through personal selling ensures that customers come back to one's retail store in future. A few simple practices would invariably go a long way in making a customer feel important and happy for buying from one's retail store.

While the customer is browsing in the retail store the sales person should open up the conversation by offering to help the customer. Such personal conversation with the customer can make him/her feel important and the customer would want to return to the store to buy more. In many successful retail stores, the sales associates unfailingly recognize their regular customers by name. In the Titan showrooms in India, as part of the personal selling efforts the sales associates always adhere to the following steps:

- They ask the customer whether he/she would like the watch he/she is wearing (may not be Titan), to be cleaned or buffed. This gesture is greatly appreciated by the customer and this goes a long way to establish a personal rapport with the customer.
- While selling the watch, the sales associates mention some technical details about the watch. Customers appreciate the information that they receive regarding the purchase.
- The sales associates always appreciate a customer's choice. They ask customers for constructive suggestions and this gives the customers a feeling that their opinions and suggestions are important.
- While handing over the purchased watch to the customer, the sales associates always thank customers for visiting and buying from the Titan showroom.
- The sales personnel ask customers visiting the showroom to leave their visiting cards and use those for adding to the database of customers. To ensure that they have an exhaustive data base they also organize a lucky draw from the visiting cards collected from time to time and give away prizes.

In Titan, personal selling does not end with the conclusion of each sales transaction with the customer. Since the store has the database of customers with details such as their names, addresses and telephone number, the sales associates utilize the database to make follow up phone calls inquiring about their purchased watch, especially high value products. Customers are said to appreciate such follow up actions from the store personnel, which often result in repeat customer visits to the store. The store personnel even use the database to wish the regular customers on occasions like birthdays and wedding anniversaries.

Questions for Discussion

1. Why is personal selling important to a retail store?

2. How can a store build relationships with customers?

3. What are the steps followed in a Titan store to build personal relationships with customers?

4. Write notes on the Titan store personnel's after-sales follow up with customers.

CHAPTER 19

Online Retailing
or e-Tailing

CHAPTER OBJECTIVES

1. To elaborate on the current status of online retailing in India while providing a glimpse of its future
2. To discuss the factors that impact online retailing
3. To compare online retailing with brick-and-mortar retailing
4. To discuss the pitfalls of online retailing and the strategies of a few survivors in India

Online retailing is going through a negative phase since the crash of most of the dot-com companies recently. However, it is not the end of online retailing in India, simply because net access and PC use is growing by leaps and bounds. According to a recent report by the Internet and Mobile Association of India, internet users in India will be 54 million by the turn of 2008.

The rate of growth of online retailing in the USA has been encouraging: it went up from $27.3 billion in 2000 to $33.3 billion in 2001, $50.3 billion in 2002 and expected to reach $316 billion by 2010. In India though the current turnover in e-Tailing is yet small, the opportunities are immense given the current rate of growth in Internet usage. As Metcalfe's Law of Networks says: "The value of a network increases exponentially as the size of the network grows arithmetically."

As in brick-and-mortar retailing, online retailing too has its twin challenges:
  (i) Getting clicks which is equivalent to footfalls in physical store retailing.
 (ii) Conversions into buying from among the clicks, which is equivalent to conversion from footfalls.

The advantages of online retailing are as follows:

— An opportunity to move from physical space to cyber space.
— No location boundaries.
— Wider spectrum of customers.
— Non-geocentric buying habits of customers.

Online Store Front — Creating a Look and Feel: Every e-Tailing site has a store front with an identity, image and positioning. The online store front has its signature identity with features that trigger off browsing and persuade customers to buy its product offerings. The navigation triggers the browser buttons and the "cookies" lead the customers completely through the site's offerings.

Visual Density: Visual density is all about virtual space utilization like shelf space management in retail. Online retailers use visual density very effectively to promote offerings and sell merchandise. A site's visual appeal ensures that the browser stays with the site for a long time.

Online Merchandising: One of the major advantages of online merchandising is that the site can have an unlimited number of SKUs on display. This is because virtual space is almost unlimited. The offering mix can be made to appeal to a wide customer base. Back-end merchandise analysis can be made for the click stream analysis and conversions thereof. One can also measure the number of non-buyers who visit the site. Offers linked to purchase act as buying triggers. In online retailing, there is no obsolescence due to the fact that merchandise is not exposed at all nor is there an inventory carrying cost on the web. Expenses being low, there is potential for high margins in e-Tailing. The following table shows, gender wise, the most shopped categories across the world online.

Product/Service	Gender Ratio	
	Male	*Female*
Groceries	25%	75%
Flowers	31%	69%
Travel (Preview)	50%	50%
Books	57%	43%
Computers	75%	25%
CDs	50%	50%

Table 10: *Most Shopped Categories Online*

Online Pricing: Prices of merchandise online are competitive compared to brick-and-mortar stores. This is because operating expenses saved by working through the Internet are generally passed on to the consumer.

TIRED (brick and mortar)	WIRED (online)
Demographics	Technographics
PC	E-mail Address
User	Participant
Marketplace	Marketspace
Location, location, location	Mindshare
Store	Point Of Sale
Geocentric Shopping Habits	Online Freedom
Facade	Electronic Store-Front

Table 11: *E-Tailing Phrases*

THE NEW ONLINE RETAIL CATEGORIES

The recent development of sending e-greetings has helped customers get into the habit of using the Internet. Another area of development is bill presentment. Retail banking and related services through the Internet is also being promoted and a good deal of transactions takes place through the net. Shopping robots on the net help instant price comparisons to enable customers make purchase decisions.

Logistics and supply chain in online retailing: The key success factor for online retailing is efficient logistics to ensure that the right product is delivered to the right customer at the right time. The supply chain network is triggered in an automatic fashion, meeting promised delivery dates. Alliances are critical in the areas of sourcing and vendor management, warehousing, transportation and couriering (effective order deliveries). Storing merchandise in satellite warehouses enables timely deliveries in operations that are spread over a wide area.

Promotions online: There is good scope for promoting on site products merchandised and sold online. The site itself can host links of products/ services offered by other companies for a fee. Banners, crawlers, browser buttons, URL links, etc. can be put on other non-competing sites. There is a lot of opportunity to create customer stickiness by constantly communicating with them through e-mail. Personalised offerings can be made to individual customers based on individual's shopping characteristics.

Pitfalls of e-Tailing

No Theatrical Ambience: The online retailing site does not have a theatrical ambience which can be felt by the customer.
No Emotional Experience: There is no emotional shopping experience that the customer can get in e-Tailing as he would in a brick-and-mortar environment.
Intangible Merchandise: The customer cannot hold, smell, feel or try the product.
Security Issues: Customers online are reluctant to part with their credit card details on the net, fearing they may be misused. Customers are not yet convinced that these methods are foolproof.
Impersonal Customer Service: Indian customers are used to tangible personalised customer service which online retailing cannot provide.

Some instances of Indian companies doing business on the net:

— Rediff.com does a good deal of merchandising on its site with innovative product offerings and prices.
Indiatimes.com is a popular internet selling site with multi-faceted merchandise offerings.
— Bazee.com is a site very widely known in India for its "bidding sale".
— Fabmart.com does food retailing.
— PlayWin is an online lottery that is catching on with the masses.

Some organizations have tried to use the Internet along with their brick-and-mortar operations. It is just a matter of time before online retailing picks up in India. If there is consistency in quality and delivery on time, certain convenience categories like books and music will undoubtedly perform well.

SUMMARY

- The e-commerce scenario has not been too bad in India. In retail banking, Indian banks have been pretty successful in adapting the technology to provide customers with facilities like real-time account status, transfer of funds, bill payment and so on.
- The future does look bright for online retailing in India and the areas expected to grow include financial services, travel, entertainment and groceries. For those considering opening a virtual storefront, the forthcoming technology and agreements on standards will not only make setting up web-sites easier; they will also safeguard them against payment fraud.
- On the downside, some experts feel that it will be increasingly difficult for smaller sites and the online version of mom-and-pop shops to attract customers. On the other hand, big stores and large organizations with established brand names and deep pockets may do well.

Questions:

1. What are the factors that impact online retailing in India?
2. Briefly describe the online categories frequently shopped and why?
3. Discuss the pitfalls of e-Tailing.
4. Can e-Tailing be a successful independent format of retailing? Discuss.

Retail Banking in India

Retail banking in India has assumed great importance recently with a number of retail banking products available to the consumer. Off-the-shelf finance solutions and options too are available today. Retail banking has been aided significantly by:

— The emergence of new-age banking companies.
— The development of advanced technology-based solutions to connect with the customer in a jiffy and to enable facilities like multi-location, multi-branch banking based on the 'martini' principle of 'anytime, anywhere, anyhow'.

The Internet has been a successful enabler of retail banking in India. Payments are made through the net, and demand drafts prepared and sent to customers online. Phone banking too has become part of the retail banking scene. Gone are the days when rule-bound conventional banks used to dictate terms to customers!

Retail banking is the new mantra in the banking sector and retail customers are displacing corporate clients from the spotlight. For instance, home loans alone account for nearly two-thirds of the total retail portfolio of the banks. The total number of bank customers in India currently stands at 334 million and it is expected to swell by nearly 8 million more in the next four years and bring in additional annual business worth an estimated Rs.150 billion. And according to one estimate, the retail banking segment is expected to grow at CAGR 28-30% in the coming years. No wonder then that banks are coming up with novel instruments like net banking, phone banking, mobile banking, ATMs and bill payments.

HDFC Bank is the first bank in India to offer real-time online transactions. The bank has deployed three Internet banking solutions that gives retail customers the convenience of accessing their accounts over the Internet, getting real-time information such as account details, checkbook balances, and account histories. Net banking also offers the facility to conduct core financial transactions such as cheque stop payment, bill payment and fund transfers between accounts. HDFC Bank's Mobile Banking service gives retail customers real-time transaction capabilities from their cellphones, a true convenience. And its corporate Internet banking provides core account and real-time transaction services to commercial customers, including a link to the bank's business-to-consumer Internet gateway for bill presentment and payment.

ICICI Bank is one of the leading private sector banks in India, and combines financial strength with a reputation for innovation and a universal culture that embraces change. On 31 March 2002 ICICI Ltd. (parent company of ICICI Bank) formally merged with ICICI Bank and emerged as India's first Universal Bank. ICICI Bank's retail distribution network continues to expand. Its strategy after the merger with ICICI Ltd. is that of building a diversified portfolio. The merged entity will continue to be into project finance, but the focus will be to tap the potential in retail financing (*Business Line*, 1 April 2002).

ICICI Bank has been quick to realize that e-banking has changed from a somewhat experimental delivery vehicle into an increasingly mainstream one to deliver a broad spectrum of banking products and services. Basic e-banking services are rapidly changing from being a competitive differentiator to a necessity. The bank has been offering phone banking free of charge and was the first — in the year 2000 — to launch an Internet banking service, called Infinity, in the country. Infinity now provides a host of online banking solutions to retail as well as corporate customers.

India's largest commercial bank, the State Bank of India (SBI), proposes to focus on retail- and fee-based income as part of its broad-business strategy. SBI has invested a lot of money to interconnect about 5,100 branches and it has, set up a Disaster Recovery Management Centre. The bank has even attempted to bridge the digital divide and take technology banking to rural India. Retail banking is critical to SBI, considering the spread factor. Housing finance will form a key component of the bank's retail strategy. Besides Internet banking, SBI has launched services like quick-decision banking, 24-hour banking, etc.

Boston Consulting Group experts Michael Silverstein, David Rhodes and Carlos Trascasa recently observed the following while comparing retail banking to world-class retail organizations: "Bankers rarely think of their branches as retail stores. They tend to view them as secure and convenient locations for financial transactions. In contrast, the best retailers use their stores to woo customers with tailored products, promotions and services that are offered with flair and style; they also use them to experiment relentlessly to find new ways of keeping their customers engaged. This drive to build loyalty allows world-class retailers to earn trust, word-of-mouth referrals, and an increasing share of purchases. We believe that banks can learn important lessons from successful retailers. Many of the things that McDonald's, Victoria's Secret, Carrefour, Best Buy, Starbucks, and Tesco do so well in retailing can be adopted by financial institutions.

"The banks' lacklustre record in retailing is understandable. Their historical priorities weren't customers and retailing, but credit and risk. Moreover, their interactions with customers have generally been transactional (and indeed, many customers prefer to transact remotely, avoiding branches altogether). Consequently, banks have tended to focus on transactional efficiency rather than service and sales. Worse, many banks struggle just to convince consumers that their products differ from those of the competition.

"Let's imagine how a bank might use a retailer's approach to transform its business. To behave like a world-class retailer, a bank must gain a deep understanding of its customers, use it to build relationships by developing solutions that customers value, and constantly test those solutions to ensure that they remain relevant. Moreover, a great retail bank would use customers to win referrals and drive sales leads.

"The good news for banks is that customers are eager to get the dialogue going. Research by The Boston Consulting Group shows that consumers across the world seek trusted advice to navigate the ocean of available information and to compensate for their lack of financial sophistication. They also desire much greater transparency in their dealings with banks and often feel underserved. Many fear the responsibilities that come with money and are suspicious of the untailored approach often used by financial institutions. In short, there is a large, dissatisfied market that would welcome more of a retailing approach from financial institutions: targeted, relevant promotions; solicitous and helpful salespeople; timely and effective service driven by more than a desire to cut costs; and a pleasing ambience.

"To date, few financial-services companies have tried such a retailing approach. Commerce Bank in New Jersey is one exception. It tries to deliver a vibrant experience and has grown rapidly with a "fast food" approach that seeks to provide speedy and reliable banking service. It builds out its branches as if they were McDonald's stores — making them uniform, bright, and clearly signed. It caters to customers' needs by being open on evenings and weekends. It stresses service training for employees. And, to complement its cheerful, well-lit environment, it uses such child-related promotions as coloring books and toy money-boxes to attract the family. The result is growth and high returns. Taking notice of successes like this, a handful of other banks — including Washington Mutual in the United States, HBOS in Britain, and Barclays and Citibank in Europe — are slowly adopting more of a retailing approach.

Five Focus Areas:

"Great retailers can boast of many advantages, including recognized value, brand consistency, high consumer awareness and proximity, and enduring and rewarding relationships. Consumers appreciate the quality and consistency of their merchandise and service. Customer loyalty translates into superior volumes per store, higher sales and margin per square foot, and growing comparable-store sales.

"For their part, banks often lack energy and excitement in customer management. As a consequence, they generally do not sell to hopes and wish lists. But world-class retailers do just that, by focusing on five areas.

Imagination. Starbucks doesn't just sell coffee. With its Lattes and Frappuccinos and advice on exotic blends, it offers a sense of the romance of Italy and the lure of travel to exotic places. Successful retailers sell dreams, not pure reality. They offer a vision of where the customer can go. Using such an approach, a bank could, for example, sell the dream of a comfortable and secure retirement as it markets reverse mortgages to wealthy aging customers.

Emotional connection. Retailers seek to pair the customer to a sales associate and to develop a bond based on expertise, exclusive customer information, and appropriate selling cues. At Neiman Marcus, associates match outfits and accessories to earlier purchases. Although banks encourage their sales associates to sell to valuable customers, they generally do not provide those associates with key information and suitable products as life events loom and new needs develop. To be sure, the general banking style is to close the sale instead of to serve and bond.

Functional and technical advantages. Leading retailers sell products that have functional and technical advantages. Some of the best stores also feature daycare centres and restrooms for busy shoppers. It is no excuse to argue that financial services products are commodities. Starbucks, Nike, and Gillette have all shown that it is possible to bring new technical and functional benefits to mature products. Retail bankers can also learn from "monoline" specialists in financial services, such as mortgage or credit-card providers, many of which take great care to differentiate the technical advantages of their products or services. After all, functional and technical advantages lie at the heart of Charles Schwab's success story.

Personalized contact. The retailer's voice is personified by the sale's associate. It is not an anonymous face. Retail banks have enormous amounts of information so consistently gathered that their staff can even use to 'personalize' contacts. If they see unattended financial needs — such as the lack of a savings plan, for example — they can offer advice to the customer to improve his or her money management.

Testing and improvement. Leading retailers view each store as a chance to test. They know how to carry out experiments, assess the results, design improvements, and roll out new programs. A world-class retailer like Tesco can turn data into a series of offerings based on the needs of household members. Bank branches are ideally suited for such test-and-learn exercises.

The Five Commandments

"Once the aspiring banking retailer understands the critical importance of these five concerns, it must then observe the five commandments to achieve retail success.

- Keep the mass-market offering simple and clear. Understand what the customer really needs. Don't offer three accounts when one is sufficient. Wal-Mart, for example, uses "Every Day Low Prices," or EDLP, to assure its customers that the lowest sale price is always available to them. Make branch environments and formats appealing. Use attractive in-store merchandising and promotions to inform the customer and to enhance the experience of the brand and the branch office. The consumer should be able to recognize good value at first glance. For this reason, HBOS has positioned itself as the consumer champion in Britain. It is perhaps no accident that its head of retail is a former supermarket executive.
- Be consistent and respectful in all dealings with customers. Never allow the customer to feel alienated. The service provider needs to show customers that it is mindful of their needs and doing its best to meet them. The best retailers religiously track, measure, and correct errors and misperceptions among their customers, offering toll-free numbers to make it easy to provide feedback. Banks can do the same.
- Know and outdo the competition. Best-practice retailers constantly survey their competitors, monitoring their offerings, responding to their initiatives, understanding their strategies, and beating their promotions. For example, Target, the U.S. retail chain, has built a successful market in part by positioning its offerings and designing its shopping

experience to outperform both Wal-Mart and Kmart.

- Listen to customers carefully and continually. Conduct — and respond to — customer surveys. Develop in-store capabilities to measure speed of service, to provide responses to commonly asked questions, and to generate sales leads.
- Tie compensation to performance measures. Track satisfaction and intent to repurchase, and tie them to branch-staff compensation. This applies to sales and frontline staff as well as to back-office personnel and top management. The Accor hotel group successfully energized its sales staff and increased productivity dramatically by revamping its incentives.

Customer Discovery

"The challenge is to forge a strategy from the five concerns and commandments. This means starting with customer needs and targeting those needs relentlessly to discover what drives the customer. A world-class retailer like Victoria's Secret, for example, conducts in-depth interviews with young female customers in their homes to understand their needs.

"For banks, connecting with customers is particularly important as key life events loom, such as college, marriage, the birth of children, and the need for estate planning. Banks must use such events not only to sell products but also to bond with valuable customers in order to understand their lifetime financial needs and to craft an approach to them.

"Once the financial retailer has built a truly differentiated experience, it must let people know by showcasing its brand. Brands that have become successful in financial services — such as Charles Schwab in the United States and Egg in the United Kingdom — grew up with strong, new, focused, and differentiated value propositions. To develop a strong brand, a bank must take a number of important steps.

Develop segmented offerings to serve the mass-affluent customer. These offerings should centre on life stages and levels of financial need. If the offerings are good ones, a skillful and well-supported relationship manager, working remotely with telephone and online channels, can serve many hundreds of customers.

Use language that customers understand. Consumers don't speak financial jargon. Simplify marketing and merchandising materials so that customers can quickly understand the value that the product or service offers. It's better still to tie those messages to the customers' aspirations.

Steer the customer to the next logical purchase. In the apparel business, if the customer is buying a suit, the salesperson is sure to try to sell a matching shirt — not to mention a tie, a scarf, and other accessories. In financial services, the whole offering means not just the checking and savings accounts but also the retirement plan, life insurance, the mortgage, and an educational savings plan. The financial institution should sell a complementary product to the target customer, offering life insurance with a mortgage, for example, and health insurance with financing for a small-business start-up.

Reward loyalty. When the bank gets the lion's share of a household's financial business, it should celebrate and reward the customer explicitly. Consumers are often wary of giving all, or even most, of their business to one financial institution. Loyalty prizes and bonuses help to overcome their reluctance and show them that the institution values their business.

Organize information so that it is easily accessible. The bank's technology is the servant, not the master. Banks should be able to collect data quickly, even overnight, from a pilot marketing program. The data need to be available to the frontline sales force.

Execute the first-generation offering while planning version 2.0. A world-class retailer of couture finalizes arrangements for its fall and winter fashions even as it rolls out summer suits. Offerings are not static.

"If banks and other retail financial businesses don't implement such changes, they will probably lose many of their most promising customers. Already, in some countries, banks control a diminishing share of the deposit market. Other financial companies, and even the best retailers, are well positioned to steal the growth in retail banking.

"Unless established retail banks respond, they are likely to fall behind their more agile competitors in financial services, particularly the focused monoline players as well as newcomers like Wal-Mart and Tesco. Unchecked, those companies will provide more categories of service. And they will do it at lower cost, with better customer insight and a broad range of products that will allow them to expand rapidly in consumer credit, mortgages, and insurance. Many retail banks, meanwhile, will be left to wither like the old, now-defunct Main Street grocer and corner butcher."

Questions for Discussion

1. Discuss the retail banking strategies adopted by a few new-age banking organizations in India.

2. What are the steps taken towards transforming retail banking by banks like SBI?

3. Should retail banking be treated like retail stores in terms of its operations to meet with success in India as suggested by the experts of The Boston Consulting Group? Discuss.

Automated Retailing (VENDING)

Automated retailing through vending machines is a concept that has been exploited by entrepreneurs around the world for over four decades. India, however, is a relatively virgin market though with huge potential.

A vending machine is essentially "a coin-operated machine for selling certain kinds of merchandise and refreshments". It is an automated retail solution that, at one stroke, eliminates the need to browse through messy outlets, ensures exclusivity, extends reach, provides round-the-clock convenience and triggers impulse purchases.

Retailing includes all the activities involved in selling goods or services directly to final consumers for their personal, non-business use. Vending is classified under non-store retailing and can be defined as "providing service at an alternative point of sale through the use of monetarily-driven equipment". These are sometimes used by retailers as part of their non-store-based strategy to reach additional consumers. Non-store retailing in India is set to grow, and will compete with brick-and-mortar stores for all consumer goods, just like in other parts of the world.

Today, vending machines are operated by thousands of companies worldwide. These machines range from relatively simple to highly sophisticated ones, offering a diverse array of products, including impulse and convenience products like cigarettes, soft/cold drinks, chocolates and confectionery, newspapers and hot beverages. Other products include hosiery, cosmetics, food snacks, hot soups, paperbacks, records, T-shirts, insurance policies, fishing worms, etc. In Japan, vending machines dispense even jewellery, spectacles, frozen beef, fresh flowers and whisky.

These machines are found in factories, offices, large retail stores, petrol pumps, hotels, restaurants, and many other locations. They offer customers the advantage of quick, 24-hour service and no handling by people. More and more consumers are spending a lot of time commuting to and from work. Hence, they don't have the time or the inclination to shop at retail stores. The convenience and ease of such non-store retail outlets make them very attractive.

Manufacturers also have been using vending machines to promote their products, increase distribution and sales and enhance their brand recognition and reputation.

Brief History of Vending Machines

Vending may be considered a new concept in India, but it has been in existence for thousands of years (see table below):

Vending Timeline	Details
215 B.C.	Device to dispense holy water used in the temples of Egypt, described by the mathematician Hero, who lived in Alexandria.
1076 A.D.	The Chinese produce a coin-operated pencil vendor.
1700s	Coin-operated tobacco boxes appear in English taverns.
1886	U.S. grants several patents for coin-operated dispensers.
1888	Thomas Adams company installs Tutti-Frutti gum machines on New York elevated train platforms.
1902	Horn and Hardart Baking Company opens Automat restaurant in Philadelphia.
1905	U.S. Post Office begins to use stamp vendors.
1920s	First commercial cigarette vending machines enters the market.
1930s	Bottled soft-drink machines, cooled with ice, appear on the market.
1936	National Automatic Merchandising Association is founded.
1946	Invention of the first coffee vendors leads to the use of vending machines for coffee breaks.
1950	First refrigerated sandwich vendors expand lunch menu.
1957	U.S. Public Health Service approves Model Vending Sanitation Code, and NAMA establishes industry's first evaluation programme to certify vending equipment.
1960	Dollar bill changers are added to vending banks.
1980	Electronic components applied to vending machines.
1985	Credit card/debit card devices for vending machines introduced.

Vending Timeline	Details
1986	Hundredth anniversary of vending machines in the U.S.
1991	Flavored coffees, espresso, and cappuccino introduced in machines.
1993	First remote wireless transmission of data from machines to warehouses.
1999	New dollar coin introduced by U.S. Mint.

Emerging Trends in Vending in India

Vending is a retailing format that dispenses goods — such as beverages, chocolates and snacks — and services (such as ATMs) through coin, note or card-operated machines. It does away with the need for a salesperson and enables round-the-clock sales of products.

Machines can be placed wherever they are most convenient for consumers — inside or outside stores, in office/hotel corridors, at railway platforms/bus stations or even on high-traffic street corners.

Vending machines are used for foods ranging from sandwiches to simple chocolates/wafers as also for hot and cold beverages. In India, local snacks like samosas, idlis, wadas, etc. have proved to be very popular.

The greatest sales volume can be achieved in offices, school/college lunchrooms, refreshment areas, hospitals, high traffic public places and any other highly visible/popular sites.

To improve productivity and customer relations, a lot of new innovations are being incorporated into vending machines. For instance, machine malfunctions have been reduced by applying electronic mechanisms to coin-handling and dispensing controls. Microprocessors built into the machine track consumer preferences, trace malfunctions, and record receipts.

Internationally, note and coin-operated vending machines have proved to be far more popular than those using cards. Innovations in technology could even see vending machines operated through mobile phones by simply sending SMS messages.

Who's Doing What in India

Vending per se is not new to Indians. Starting off in a simple and very basic way, the use of such machines has seen tremendous growth.

- The first popular vending machines probably were the colourfully-lit weighing-machines installed at many railway and bus stations. They can be seen even today.
- The tea/coffee vending machines of Brooke Bond Lipton and Nestle are there practically in all offices/canteens and railway stations in India. These however are not automatic and therefore serve more as dispensers than automatic vending machines. Tata Tea has also entered the fray in a limited way.
- Both Nestle and Hindustan Lever have gotten into 'cold vending' of beverages. Their iced tea and cold coffee dispensers are small steps in a much larger plan.
- The Ministry of Health along with NGOs and other social organizations regularly install mechanical — coin operated — condom vending machines.
- Pepsi and Coke came up with the idea of dispensing cold drinks from 'fountain cold drink machines'.
- Foreign banks and credit card companies introduced ATMs that dispense cash all over India.
- Mumbai-based Chevend Technologies Pvt. Ltd. introduced truly automatic vending machines to sell snacks, cold drinks, etc. The company is still the market leader in the field.
- The first vending machine with Cadbury's products was installed at Wankhede stadium in Mumbai by Chevend. Since then Cadbury has gone on to install Chevend machines at a variety of locations such as airports, railway stations, embassies, recreational centres, etc.
- A Coca-Cola can vending machine was first installed at an Irani restaurant in Bandra, Mumbai.
- Snack vending machines have been installed at the corporate offices of Jindal, ICICI, Morgan Stanley, etc. Offices all over the country are finding it very convenient to offer vending services for their employees.
- Nagpur-based Haldiram has become the first Indian savouries/ namkeens & sweets brand to install a vending machine at Churchgate railway station in Mumbai.
- Chevend is driving the vending business in India. Its innovations include vending small oil sachets of Parachute oil, or prasad tokens at

the Sidhivinayak temple in Mumbai.

- Britannia has also installed machines at various locations. The vending machines at airports with stills from Aamir Khan's movie *Lagaan* on them were quite popular.
- The Malayala Manorama group launched India's first automatic magazine/newspaper vending machine branded 'The Week'. Specially customized by Chevend, these machines were installed at major airports around India.
- The major players in the paint industry have set up paint boutiques where a computerized machine dispenses paints of customized colours. Customers can mix and match to come up with the shade of their choice. For example, Asian Paints' Colourworld, Jenson & Nicholson's Instacolour or ICI's Colour Solutions.
- Thermax Culligan of Pune was the first company in India to install water vending machines. The seven-feet high machines offered consumers 300ml of instantly purified water for Rs.2.
- Probably the most unique project was one jointly implemented by the Ministry of Health, Hindustan Latex Ltd., Chevend Technologies and Threshold RMC Pvt. Ltd. In an attempt to save people the embarrassment of purchasing contraceptives, condoms were introduced in automatic vending machines that offered wafers, biscuits, confectioneries, etc. Not surprisingly, 26% of the machine's overall sales were accounted for by condoms.

Now several companies and entrepreneurs have entered the vending arena. In fact, some companies have set up separate divisions for vending. This provides an indicator of the importance being attached to this new field.

In every country, one or more companies have been in the forefront when it came to automatic vending. In most markets, it has been either Coke or Pepsi. The rest have followed their lead. Thus, on an average, for every snack-dispensing machine there are four to five cold-drink machines. In India, however, it has been quite different. The cold-drink companies have not concentrated on promoting cans, the thrust being on fountain dispensers and visi-coolers.

The organization that has played a key role in establishing automated retailing in India has been Chevend Technologies. "The first five years of the business were primarily spent on getting customers to accept the concept. A lot of handholding had to be done," says Chevend's Managing Director Ammaar Huseini. "We couldn't limit ourselves to just being vending equipment suppliers but had to offer the entire service — from finding a suitable location, negotiating with the location authorities for permission to install a machine, assisting the interested customer to install the machine at the location, tying up and training people to refill the machines, monitoring and promoting sales. We had to sell a complete opportunity."

Chevend initiated India's first vending operations to sell snacks. Says Huseini: "It was very important to experience first-hand the benefits and intricacies of operations, product choice, placement in the machine, machine placement at the location etc. before recommending it to our customers. The past decade has been a continuous learning process."

THE USAGE TREND

For any given location there is a typical pattern of usage. Automatic vending, being relatively new, still has novelty value. Thus, whenever a machine is installed at a location customers want to use it and satisfy their curiosity. Gradually as the novelty begins to ebb, there is a small dip in usage, but people continue to use the machine for its convenience. As is typical in all countries, convenience gradually becomes a habit. Even though there is growth at this point, it is gradual. For any marketer promoting products through vending machines, the aim is always to reach the final stage as soon as possible.

The speed of movement from phase to phase depends on the location and the product offered by the machine. For example, the transition from novelty to habit is much faster in an office where the same users come back to the machine. At locations like railway stations, there will be people using the machine for the first time even after five years of installation.

Like in any other form of retailing, a proven method of moving the habit plateau to a higher level is effective and continuous promotion.

Automated Vending Machines as Marketing Tools

There are several compelling reasons for marketing organizations to concentrate on this avenue of retailing.

➢ **Unbeatable Product Visibility:** The machines not only display the products but also sell them. Nowadays, customers are bombarded with a huge number of brands and options when they enter an average retail outlet. However, as far as vending machines go, brand visibility is completely exclusive. In companies across the world, the budget for purchasing vending machines is shared by the advertising department and distribution/sales.

➤ **Impulse Purchases:** Due to their striking visibility, automatic vending machines generate impulse purchases. The common marketing principle is at work here: the more they see, the more they buy.

➤ **Wider Distribution:** By placing machines at locations where its products are not normally available, manufacturers instantly create a new distribution outlet. For example, in an office.

➤ **Hygienic & Protected Storage:** A closed environment ensures that the product sold to a customer is always clean and undamaged.

➤ **Vehicle for Unbiased Customer Response:** A retailer typically promotes products that offer larger returns by influencing the customers' buying decisions and choices. Unmanned automatic vending machines are the ideal vehicle to test the customer's response to new products and new packaging.

➤ **Silent Salesman:** These machines work quietly to generate sales round the clock, 365 days a year, taking no holidays, never going on strike or leave. All this with minimal supervision and attention.

➤ **Eradication of Duplication & Adulteration:** Many leading FMCG companies face the problem of duplicates, copies and adulteration of their products. This is not only bad for their brand image, it also leads to a big loss of potential revenue. Now, for the first time customers can be absolutely sure that the product they are purchasing is genuine and not an inferior duplicate.

➤ **Enhanced Brand Image:** Using this sophisticated method of merchandising automatically positions the company and its brands as sophisticated and forward-minded.

➤ **Incremental Sales:** Vending machines have been used as an effective tool to enlarge the distribution network and increase sales.

➤ **Deeper Market Penetration:** This method allows companies to tap newer locations and move one step closer to the customer.

➤ **Advertising & Promotions:** The side panels and the top and bottom of the machine can be used for valuable point-of-sale advertising and promotions. The latest cold-drink machine designs also incorporate LCDs in the vending machines to continuously play advertisements.

Internationally, product manufacturers use a variety of methods to install automatic vending machines:

Method 1: Purchase the equipment and place them in the market directly. Either the location personnel or designated operators operating for a commission on sales can replenish merchandise in the machines.

Method 2: Subsidise the cost of purchase for their franchisee. This involves more of a joint effort in not only finding lucrative installation sites but also conducting promotions. The franchisee receives better margins on sales as opposed to the previous arrangement.

Method 3: Product manufacturers offer the machines on rent to vending operators.

So far methods 1 and 2 are being used in India. The third method will become popular as the concept of automated retailing matures.

The following factors ensure successful vending operations:
➢ Identifying the vending need, choosing reliable equipment suppliers, and ensuring that service support is very strong. A few hours of down-time in the field means loss of revenue.
➢ Making sure that the machine is placed strategically. It's not just the location but the placement of the machine there that determines the optimum quantity sold.
➢ Getting the right product mix. The machines should address the tastes and needs of the consumers in that location.
➢ Strategic placement of brands in the machine. Product placement in the machines should be carefully thought out. In multi-brand vending, the strongest brands should be prominently displayed to attract customers. New product introductions should be given more visible space, etc.
➢ An efficient vending operator, especially in India, is required near the vending machine to help customers operate the machines. This is a very important link in running vending machines smoothly. From refilling the machines efficiently to keeping them clean or interacting with the customer, a good vending operator plays a very important role. Efforts to develop vending operators through training and incentives always pays dividends.

Questions for Discussion

1. Discuss the applications of automated retail vending in the global scenario.

2. What trends do we see in retailing through vending machines in India?

3. Can vending machines complement brick and mortar retailing in India? Discuss.

4. How are vending machines used as a marketing tool by Indian organizations? Discuss with a few examples.

Glossary

ABC Analysis: Ranks SKUs (see Stock Keeping Unit) according to profitability to determine which items should never be out of stock.

Accessibility: The degree of ease with which customers can get into and out of a shopping centre.

Accordion Theory: A cyclical theory of retailer evolution that says changes in retail institutions can be explained in terms of depth versus breadth of assortment. The cycle of retail institutions start from high-depth/low-breadth to low-depth/high-breadth and back again.

Accounts Receivable (AR): Money due for merchandise or service sold but not yet collected.

Addition to Retail Percentage: Measures price rise as a percentage of the original price.

Additional Markup: An increase in retail price above the original markup. It's used when demand is unexpectedly high or when costs are rising.

Additional Markup Percentage: Looks at total rupee additional markups as a percentage of net sales.

Advertising: Any paid, non-personal communication transmitted through out-of-store mass media by an identified sponsor.

Affinity: Exists when various stores at a given location complement, blend, and cooperate with one another, each benefiting from the others' presence.

All-You-Can-Afford Method: A promotional budgeting technique in which a retailer first allots funds for each element of the retail strategy mix except promotion. Whatever funds are left over are placed in a promotional budget.

Analog Model: A computerized site-selection tool in which potential sales are estimated on the basis of existing store revenues in similar areas, the competition at a prospective location, the new store's expected market shares at that location, and the size and density of the location's primary trading area.

279

Anti-competitive Leasing Arrangement: A lease that limits the type and amount of competition a particular retailer faces within a trading area (for example, a lease that won't allow two supermarkets in one shopping centre or area).

Asset Turnover: A performance measure based on a retailer's net sales and total assets. It is equal to net sales divided by total assets.

Assets: Any items a retailer owns with a monetary value.

Assortment Display: An interior display in which a retailer exhibits a wide range of merchandise for the customer. It may be open or closed.

Assortment Management: A computerized method that breaks down barriers in merchandising by allowing retailers to offer the right amount of products at the right time. Retailers accomplish this through comprehensive computer analyses which forecasts consumer preferences, buying patterns and buying trends.

Atmospherics: The architecture, layout, signs and displays, colour, lighting, music and odours which together create an image in the customer's mind. In short, the extra elements that enhance a retail strategy mix.

Automatic Markdown Plan: Controls the amount and timing of markdowns on the basis of the length of time merchandise remains in stock.

Automatic Reordering System: Orders merchandise when stock-on-hand reaches a predetermined reorder point. An automatic reorder can be generated by a computer on the basis of a perpetual inventory system and reorder point calculations.

B-to-B (Business-to-Business): A rapidly growing category of Internet sites aimed at selling products, services or data to commercial customers rather than individual consumers.

B-to-C: Business-to-Consumer sites.

B-to-G: Business-to-Government sites.

Bait Advertising: An illegal practice in which a retailer lures a customer by advertising goods and services at exceptionally low prices; then, once the customer contacts the retailer, he or she is told that the particular product/service is out of stock or of inferior quality. A salesperson tries to convince the customer to purchase a better, more expensive substitute that is available. The retailer has no intention of selling the advertised item. Also called bait-and-switch advertising.

Balanced Tenancy: Occurs when stores in a planned shopping centre complement each other in the quality and variety of their product offerings. The kind and number of stores are linked to the overall needs of the surrounding population.

Balance Sheet: Itemizes a retailer's assets, liabilities and net worth at a specific point in time; it is based on the principle that assets equal liabilities plus net worth.

Bania **Shop:** Small stores run by Banias (a popular Indian community) and which have convenience merchandise *(see also Kirana Store).*

Barcode Label: A printed label containing black and white coded images meeting industry standards to route packages or retrieve information about the box or merchandise to which the label is attached.

Basic Stock List: Specifies the inventory level, colour, brand, style category, size, package, and so on for every staple item carried by the retailer.

Battle of the Brands: When retailers and manufacturers compete for shelf space allocated to various brands and for control of display locations.

Benchmarking: Occurs when the retailer sets standards of performance based on those of competitors, high-performance firms, and/or the prior actions of the company itself.

Bifurcated Retailing: Denotes the decline of middle-of-the-market retailing due to the popularity of both mass merchandising and positioned retailing.

Book Inventory System: Used to keep a running total of the value of all inventory on hand at cost at a given time. This is done by regularly recording purchases and adding them to existing inventory value; sales transactions are then subtracted to arrive at the new current inventory value (all at cost).

Bottom-Up Space Management Approach: Exists when planning starts at the individual product level and then proceeds to the category, total store, and overall company levels.

Boutique Layout: A store design that places all departments on the main aisle by drawing customers through the store in a series of major and minor loops. Also known as a loop.

Box (Limited-Line) Store: A food-based discounter that focuses on a small selection of items, moderate hours of operation (compared to supermarkets), few services, and limited national brands.

Budgeting: Outlines a retailer's planned expenditures for a given time period based on its expected performance.

Bundled Pricing: Involves a retailer providing a combination of products/ services for one basic price.

Business Format Franchising: An arrangement in which the franchisee receives assistance on site location, quality control, accounting systems, startup practices, management training, and responding to problems — besides the right to sell goods and services.

Canned Sales Presentation: A memorized, repetitive speech given to all customers interested in a particular item.

Capital Expenditure: Retail expenditure that is a long-term investment in fixed assets.

Case Display: Used to exhibit heavier, bulkier items than what racks hold.

Cash Flow: Relates the amount and timing of revenue received to the amount and timing of expenditure made during a specific time period.

Category: A related assortment of items (e.g. ladies, men's clothes).

Category Killer: Discount retailer that offers a complete assortment in a *category* and thus dominates it from the customer's perspective. Also known as a category specialist.

Category Management: A relationship-oriented technique that some firms, especially supermarkets, are beginning to use to improve shelf-space productivity.

Central Business District (CBD): The hub of retailing in a city. It is the largest shopping area in that city and is synonymous with the term 'downtown'. It has the greatest concentration of retail stores.

Census of Population: Supplies a wide range of demographic data for all Indian cities, towns and surrounding vicinities. Data are organized on a geographic basis.

Centralized Buying: A situation in which a retailer makes all purchase decisions at one location, typically the headquarters.

Centralized Buying Organization: Occurs when all purchase decisions of a retailer emanate from one office.

Chain Store Format: Multiple retail units under common ownership that engage in some centralized (or coordinated) purchasing and decision-making.

Channel Control: Occurs when one member of a distribution channel dominates decisions made in that channel.

Channel of Distribution: Comprises all the businesses and people involved in the physical movement and transfer of ownership of goods and services from producer to consumer.

Class Consciousness: Extent to which a person desires and pursues social status.

Classification Dominance: A situation where a retailer has an assortment so broad that customers are able to satisfy all their consumption needs for a particular *category* by visiting it (e.g., Toys 'R' Us).

Classification Merchandising: A group of similar items or *SKUs*, such as pants (as opposed to jackets or suits), supplied by different *vendors*.

Close-out Store: A retailer offering low-priced merchandise obtained through liquidations.

COD (Collect on Delivery): Lets customers pay for products after they are delivered.

Cognitive Dissonance: Doubts that occur after a purchase, which can be alleviated by customer after-care, money-back guarantees, and realistic sales presentations and advertising campaigns.

Community Shopping Centre: A moderate-sized, planned shopping facility with a branch department store, a variety store, and/or a category killer store, in addition to several smaller outlets. Usually serves 20,000 to 100,000 people, who live or work within 10 to 20 minutes' distance.

Comparative Advertising: Messages comparing a retailer's offerings with those of competitors.

Compensation: Includes direct monetary payments (such as salaries, commissions, and bonuses) and indirect payments (such as paid vacations, health and life insurance benefits, and retirement plans).

Competition-Oriented Pricing: An approach in which a retailer sets its prices according to those of competitors.

Competitive Advantages: The distinct competencies of a retailer relative to competitors.

Competitive Parity Method: A promotional budgeting technique by which a retailer's budget is raised or lowered based on the actions of competitors.

Competitive Pricing: A marketing-oriented strategy whereby a service retailer sets its prices on the basis of prices charged by competitors.

Computerized Checkout: Enables retailers to efficiently process transactions and ensure strict inventory control. In a UPC-based system, cashiers manually ring up sales or pass items over or past optical scanners. Computerized registers instantly record and display sales, customers get detailed receipts, and all inventory data are stored in a computer memory bank.

Concentrated Marketing: Selling goods and services to one specific group.

Consignment Goods: Items not paid for by retailer until they are sold. The retailer can return unsold merchandise, and does not take title until the final sale is completed.

Consignee: The individual or organization to which a package is delivered.

Constrained Decision Making: Excludes franchisees from or limits their involvement in the strategic planning process.

Consumer Behaviour: The way people buy goods and services — what, when, where, how, from whom, and how often.

Consumer Cooperative: A retail firm owned by its customer members. A group of consumers invests in the company, receives stock certificates, elects officers, manages operations, and shares the profits or savings that accrue.

Consumer Decision Process: The stages a consumer goes through while buying goods or services: stimulus, problem awareness, information search, evaluation of alternatives, purchase, and post-purchase behaviour. Demographics and lifestyle affect this process.

Consumerism: Involves the activities of government, business, and independent organizations designed to protect consumers from practices infringing upon their rights.

Contingency Pricing: An arrangement whereby the retailer does not get paid until after the service is performed and payment is contingent upon satisfactory service.

Controllable Variables: Aspects of a business that the retailer can directly control (such as hours of operation and sales personnel).

Control Units: Merchandise categories for which data are gathered.

Convenience Store: A food-oriented retailer that is small, well-located, is open for long hours, and carries a moderate number of items. It has average to above-average prices, and an average atmosphere and customer services.

Conventional *Kirana* Store: Concentrates on a wide range of food and related products. Sales of general merchandise are very limited.

Convenience Centre: A shopping centre that typically includes such outlets as a convenience store and a dry cleaner.

Convenience Stores: Stores that are between 3,000 and 8,000 square feet in size providing a limited assortment of merchandise at a convenient location and time (e.g., 7-Eleven).

Cooperative (co-op) Advertising: A programme in which the vendor agrees to pay all or part of a retailer's ads for the *vendor*'s products.

Cooperative Buying: The procedure used when a group of independent retailers gets together to make quantity purchases from a supplier.

Core Customers: Consumers with whom retailers should seek to nurture long relationships. They should be singled out in a firm's database.

Cost Complement: The average relationship of cost to retail value for all merchandise available for sale during a given period.

Cost Method of Accounting: Requires the retailer to record the cost of every item on an accounting sheet and/or coded on a price tag or merchandise container. When a physical inventory is conducted, every item's cost must be ascertained, the quantity of every item in stock counted, and the total inventory value at cost calculated.

Cost of Goods Sold: The amount a retailer has paid to acquire the merchandise sold during a given time period. It equals the cost of merchandise available for sale minus the cost value of ending inventory.

Cost-oriented Pricing: An approach through which a retailer sets a price floor which is the minimum price acceptable to the firm to reach a specified profit goal. A retailer usually computes merchandise and retail operating costs and adds a profit margin to these figures.

Cost-plus Pricing: Occurs when a retailer adds its costs to desired profit margins to derive selling prices.

Cross-docking: A process by which finished goods from the manufacturing source are taken and delivered directly to the retail store with little or no handling involved in between. Cross-docking involves receiving merchandise from multiple suppliers and consolidating by way of sorting them to out-bound shipments to different stores. This process results in the reduction of handling and storage of inventory.

Cross-Merchandising: Carrying complementary range of products and services in a retail store which can trigger impulse purchases resulting in the shopper buying more at the store is known as cross-merchandising.

Cross-training: Enables personnel to learn tasks associated with more than one job.

Customary Pricing: A pricing strategy whereby a retailer sets prices for goods and services and seeks to maintain them for an extended period.

Customer Loyalty (Frequent Shopper) Programmes: Intended to reward a retailer's best customers, with whom it wants to form long-lasting relationships.

Customer Relationship Management (CRM): The automation of integrated business processes involving customers — sales (contact management, product configuration), marketing (campaign management, telemarketing) and customer service (call centre, field service).

Customer Service: Refers to the identifiable, but sometimes intangible, activities undertaken by a retailer in conjunction with the basic goods and services it sells.

Customer Space: The area required by shoppers that contributes greatly to a store's atmosphere. It can include a lounge, benches and/or chairs, dressing rooms, rest rooms, a restaurant, vertical transportation, a nursery, parking, and wide aisles.

Cut Case: An inexpensive display, in which merchandise is left in the original carton.

Data Analysis: The stage in the research process where secondary and/or primary data are assessed and related to the defined issue or problem.

Database Management: The procedure used to gather, integrate, apply, and store information related to specific subject areas. It is a key element in a retail information system.

Database Retailing: A way of collecting, storing, and using relevant information on customers.

Data Warehousing: A new development in database management whereby all the databases of a company are maintained at one location and can be accessed by employees at any locale.

Debit-card System: A computerized system whereby the price of a product or service purchased is immediately deducted from a consumer's bank account and entered into a retailer's account.

Decentralized Buying Organization: It lets purchase decisions be made locally or regionally.

Deferred Billing: Enables customers to make purchases and not pay for them for several months, without interest.

Demand-oriented Pricing: An approach by which a retailer sets prices based on consumer desires. It determines the range of prices acceptable to the target market.

Demographics: The breakdown of the population into statistical categories such as age, education, sex, etc.

Department Stores: Very large stores carrying a wide variety and deep assortment of products while offering considerable customer services. Stores are organized into separate departments (e.g., Shoppers' Stop, Lifestyle). However, the majority of them tend to focus on apparel.

Depth of Assortment: Refers to the variety of goods/service categories offered by a retailer.

Destination Retailer: A retailer to whom consumers will make a special shopping trip. May be a store, a catalogue or a web-site.

Destination Store: A retail outlet with a trading area much larger than that of a competitor that has less unique appeal among customers. It offers a better merchandise assortment, promotes more extensively, and enables customers to plan and visit the store.

Differentiated Marketing: Aims at two or more distinct consumer groups, with different retailing approaches for each group.

Direct Marketing: A form of retailing in which a customer gets information about a product or service through a non-personal medium like mail, phone or even computer and can then order it if needed.

Direct Product Profitability (DPP): This involves finding the profitability of each category or unit of merchandise by computing adjusted per-unit gross margins and its direct product costs (in expense categories such as warehousing, transportation, handling, and selling). It equals an item's gross profit less its direct retailing costs.

Direct Selling: Includes both personal contact with consumers in their homes (and other non-store locations such as offices) and soliciting over the phone initiated by a retailer.

Direct Store Distribution: Exists when retailers have at least some goods shipped directly from suppliers to individual stores. It works best with retailers that also utilize EDI.

Direct Mail Catalogue Retailer: A retailer offering merchandise and/or services through catalogues mailed directly to customers.

Discount Store: A general merchandise retailer offering a wide variety of merchandise, limited service and low prices (e.g., Target or Kmart).

Disguised Survey: A technique in which the respondent is not told the real purpose of a research study.

Distressed Goods: Items that have been damaged or soiled.

Diversionary Pricing: A practice used by deceptive service firms. A low price is stated for one or a few services (emphasized in promotion) to give the illusion that all prices are low.

Downsizing: Exists when unprofitable stores are closed or divisions are sold off by retailers dissatisfied with their performance.

Dump Bin: A case display that houses piles of sale clothing, marked-down books, or other products.

E-commerce: Conducting business through the Internet. It includes both *business-to-consumer* and *business-to-business* websites.

Economic Order Quantity (EOQ): The quantity per order (in units) that minimizes the total costs of processing orders and holding inventory.

Effective Buying Income (EBI): Personal income (wages, salaries, interest, dividends, profits, rental income, and pension income) minus taxes, statutory deductions, savings and insurance. It is commonly known as disposable personal income.

Efficient Consumer Response (ECR): A form of logistics management through which supermarkets incorporate aspects of quick response inventory planning, electronic data interchange, and logistics planning.

Electronic Article Surveillance (EAS): A proven loss prevention technique that protects assets and merchandise by utilizing security tags and labels and detection equipment. EAS systems provide security for buildings, entrances, exits and enclosed areas by sounding alarms when items protected with an active tag or label pass through the detection equipment.

Electronic Banking: Involves both the use of automated teller machines (ATMs) and the instant processing of retail purchases.

Electronic Data Interchange (EDI): Involves retailers and suppliers regularly exchanging information through their computers on inventory levels, delivery times, unit sales, and so on, of particular items.

Electronic Point-of-Sale System: Performs all tasks of a computerized checkout and also verifies cheque and charge transactions, provides instantaneous sales reports, monitors and changes prices, sends intra- and inter-store messages, evaluates personnel and profitability, and stores data.

Employee Empowerment: A method of improving customer service in which workers can use their discretion to do what they believe is necessary — within reasonable limits — to satisfy the customer, even if this means bending some company rules.

End Caps: Display fixtures located at the end of an aisle. Also, in real estate, the end unit or corner unit in a strip shopping centre.

Ensemble Display: An interior display where coordinated merchandise is grouped and displayed together.

Enterprise Resource Planning (ERP): Packages that enable the creation of a single corporate entity from disparate, decentralized divisions, enabling users to keep track of underlying business processes, reshape them and renovate their businesses.

Everyday Low Pricing (EDLP): A version of customary pricing, whereby a retailer strives to sell its goods and services at consistently low prices throughout the selling season.

Everyday-Low-Price Strategy: A pricing strategy that attempts to have, on average, low prices on all items every day rather than periodically advertising price promotions on a few items. These retailers will often match competitors' prices.

Factory Outlet Stores: Off-price retail stores owned by manufacturers.

Factory Outlet: A manufacturer-owned store selling that firm's closeouts, discontinued merchandise, irregulars, cancelled orders, and, sometimes, in-season, first-quality merchandise.

Family Life Cycle: Describes how a traditional family evolves from bachelorhood to children to solitary retirement.

FIFO Method: Assumes old goods are sold first, while newer items remain in inventory. It matches inventory value with the current cost structure.

Financial Merchandise Management: Occurs when a retailer specifies exactly which, when and how many products are purchased.

Fixed Pricing: Situations where the government decrees that retailers must conform to a stated price structure.

Flat Organization: A firm with many subordinates reporting to one supervisor.

Flea Market: Many small vendors offering a range of products at discount prices in plain surroundings. Many are located in non-traditional sites not normally associated with retailing. They may be indoor or outdoor.

Flexible Pricing: A situation that allows consumers to bargain. Consumers good at bargaining obtain lower prices than those who are not.

Floor-Ready Merchandise: Items that are received at the store that can be put directly on display without any preparation by retail workers.

FOB (Freight-On-Board) Destination: A term of sale where the shipper owns the merchandise until it is delivered to the retailer. The shipper is therefore responsible for transportation and any damage claims.

Food-Based Superstore: A retailer that is larger and more diversified than a conventional supermarket but usually smaller and less diversified than a combination store. It caters to consumers' complete grocery needs and offers them the ability to buy fill-in general merchandise.

Footfalls: A measure of the total number of customers entering a store or a mall.

Franchising: Involves a contractual arrangement between a franchisor (a manufacturer, a wholesaler, or a service sponsor) and a retail franchisee, which allows the latter to conduct a given form of business under an established name and according to a given pattern of business.

Free-standing Retailer: A location for a retailer that is a building by itself, frequently on a site near or in front of a shopping centre.

Frequency of Reach: The average number of times each person who is reached is exposed to a retailer's ads in a specific period.

Frequent Shopper Programmes: See Customer Loyalty Programmes.

Full-Line Discount Store: A type of department store characterized by (1) a broad merchandise assortment; (2) centralized checkout service; (3) merchandise normally sold through self-service with minimal assistance; (4) private-brand non-durable goods and well-known manufacturer-brand durable goods; (5) hard goods accounting for a much greater percentage of sales than at traditional department stores; and (6) a relatively inexpensive building, equipment and fixtures.

Functional Product Groupings: A store's merchandise displayed according to categories and common end uses.

Gap Analysis: Enables a company to compare its actual performance against its potential performance, and then determine the areas in which it must improve.

Generic Brands: No-frills goods stocked by some retailers. These items usually receive secondary shelf locations, have little or no promotion support, are sometimes of lower quality than other brands, are stocked in limited assortments, and have plain packages.

Geographic Mapping: A technique used by retailers to evaluate the location of a store. With it, a firm learns the distances people are apt to travel to get to a store, the population density of the geographic area surrounding the store, the travel patterns and time taken.

GMROI: See Gross Margin Return on Investment.

Gondola: A four-sided shelving cum display cum selling unit, often movable, used on the retail floor as part of the merchandise fixture.

Goods Retailing: Focuses on the sale of tangible (physical) products.

Goods/Service Category: A retail firm's line of business.

Graduated Lease: Involves precise rent increases over a specified time.

Grey Market Goods: Brand-name products purchased in foreign markets — or goods trans-shipped from other retailers — and often sold at low prices by unauthorized dealers.

Gross Margin: The difference between the maximum retail price the customer pays for merchandise and its cost (wholesale price). Also known as the gross profit.

Gross Margin Return on Investment (GMROI): Shows the relationship between total operating profits and the average inventory investment (at cost) by combining profitability and sales-to-stock measures.

Gross Profit: The difference between net sales and the cost of goods sold. Also known as gross margin.

Haat: A weekly village fair in India with temporarily set up stores normally spread on the ground, with each seller retailing diverse product offerings.

Hard-lines: Durable, non-apparel items, such as furniture, appliances and houseware.

Hierarchy-of-Effects Model: The sequence of steps a consumer goes through in reacting to a retailer's communication — from awareness to knowledge to liking to preference to conviction to a purchase.

Horizontal Cooperative-Advertising Agreement: Enables two or more retailers (usually small, situated together, or franchisees of the same company) to share an ad.

Horizontal Price Fixing: Involves agreements among manufacturers, wholesalers, or retailers to set prices. This is without considering how 'reasonable' the resulting prices may be.

Horizontal Retail Audit: Involves analysing a retail firm's overall performance — from its organizational mission to goals to customer satisfaction to basic retail strategy mix and its implementation in an integrated, consistent way.

Household Life Cycle: Involves the life stages of both family and households.

Hypermarket: A very large retail organization that offers low prices and is a combination of a discount store and a superstore food retailer in one warehouse-like building. These stores may be as large as 200,000 square feet.

Image: Represents the perception of a retailer by consumers and others.

Impulse Purchases: Occur when consumers purchase products and/or brands they had not planned on buying before entering a store, by reading a mail-order catalogue, seeing a TV shopping show, surfing on the Internet, and so on.

Independent Retailer: A retailer who owns only one or two retail stores.

Informal Buying Organization: Does not view merchandising as a distinct retail function; the same personnel handle both merchandising and other retail tasks.

Initial Markup (at Retail): Based on the original retail value assigned to merchandise less its cost, expressed as a percentage of the original retail price.

Inventory Management: The process of acquiring and maintaining a proper assortment of merchandise while keeping ordering, shipping, handling and other related costs in check. Since it is expensive to own and stock inventory, proper management is vital. Dillard's and Wal-Mart are famous for advanced inventory management.

Inventory Shrinkage: Involves employee theft, customer shoplifting, and vendor fraud.

Inventory Turnover: Net sales divided by average retail inventory; used to evaluate how effectively managers utilize their investment in inventory.

Isolated Store: A freestanding retail outlet located on either a highway or a street. There are no adjacent retailers with which it shares traffic.

Just-In-Time-Inventory: A computerized method of tracking inventory needs and writing purchase orders, timed so that inventory arrives only on the day it is needed.

Keystone Method: A method of setting retail prices in which retailers simply double the cost of the merchandise to determine original retail price.

***Kirana* Store:** A small Indian neighbourhood mom-and-pop store dealing with basic grocery and top-up convenience products, offering personalized service.

Layaway Plan: Allows customers to give a retailer deposits to hold products. When customers complete payments, they take the items.

Leader Pricing: Occurs when a retailer advertises and sells selected items in its goods/service assortment at less than usual profit margins. The goal is to increase customer traffic in the hope of selling regularly priced goods and services in addition to the low-priced items.

Leased Department: A department in a retail store operated by an outside party. The outside party either pays fixed rent or a percentage of sales to the retailer for the space.

Licensed Brands: Brands for which the licensor (owner of a well-known name) enters into a contract with a licensee (a retailer or a third party). The licensee either manufactures or contracts with a manufacturer to produce the licensed product and pays a royalty to the licensor.

Lifestyle Merchandising: Merchandise lines based on certain consumer living patterns.

Logistics: The total process of moving goods from a manufacturer to a customer in the most timely and cost-efficient manner.

Loss Leader: Merchandise sold at or below cost to lure more customer traffic.

Maintained Markup (at Retail): Based on the actual prices received for merchandise sold during a time period less merchandise cost, expressed as a percentage.

Markdown: A reduction of the selling price (MRP) to match the lower prices of another retailer, to adapt to inventory overstocking, clear out shopworn merchandise, reduce assortments of odds and ends, and increase customer traffic.

Markdown Percentage: Total markdown as a percentage of net sales (in value).

Market Penetration: A pricing strategy in which a retailer seeks to achieve large revenues by setting low prices and selling a high unit volume.

Market Skimming: A pricing strategy wherein a firm charges premium prices and attracts customers less concerned with price than service, assortment, and status.

Markup: The difference between merchandise costs and maximum retail price.

Markup Percentage (at Cost): Difference between maximum retail price and merchandise cost expressed as a percentage of merchandise cost.

Markup Percentage (at Retail): The difference between maximum retail price and merchandise cost expressed as a percentage of retail price.

Markup Pricing: Where a retailer sets prices by adding per-unit merchandise costs, operating expenses and desired profit.

Marquee: A tent or canopy used to display a store's name and/or logo, sometimes big enough to even sell merchandise or services additionally from.

Mass Merchandising: A positioning approach whereby retailers offer a discount or value-oriented image, a wide and/or deep merchandise assortment, and large store facilities.

Mass Marketing: Selling goods and services to a broad spectrum of consumers.

Maximum Retail Price (MRP): The maximum price at which a firm can sell its goods is known as the Maximum Retail Price. This price which includes all taxes is printed on the packaging to actually stop the consumer from being cheated by any retailer.

Mega Mall: An enormous planned shopping centre with one million-plus square feet of retail space, multiple anchor stores, up to several hundred specialty stores, food courts, and entertainment facilities planned to achieve synergy with merchandising.

Megaplex: If a movie theatre complex is large, having more than 10 multiple screens, it is usually referred to as a Megaplex.

Membership Club: Aims at price-conscious consumers, who must be members to shop.

Memorandum Purchase: This occurs when the retailer does not pay for the merchandise until it is sold. The retailer can return unsold merchandise. However, it takes title on delivery and is responsible for damages.

Merchandise Available for Sale: Equals beginning inventory, purchases, and transportation charges.

Merchandise Buying and Handling Process: Comprises an integrated and systematic sequence of steps from establishing a buying organization through regular re-evaluation.

Merchandise Space: The area where non-displayed items are kept in stock or inventory.

Merchandising: Consists of the activities involved in acquiring particular goods and/or services and making them available at the places, times, and prices and in the quantity to enable a retailer to reach its goals.

Micro-Merchandising: A strategy whereby a firm adjusts shelf-space allocations to respond to customer and other differences among local markets.

Model Stock Approach: A method of determining the amount of floor space to carry and display a proper merchandise assortment.

Model Stock Plan: The planned composition of fashion goods, which reflects the mix of merchandise available based on expected sales. The model stock plan indicates product lines, colors, and size distributions.

Multiplex: A type of movie theatre complex with multiple screens, usually three or more, where movies can be screened according to the number of screens available.

Mystery Shoppers: People hired by retailers to pose as customers and observe their operations, from sales presentations to how well displays are maintained to in-home service calls.

Net Sales: The revenues received by a retailer during a given time period after deducting customer returns, markdowns, and employee discounts.

Net Worth: Computed as a retailer's assets minus its liabilities.

Never-Out List: Used when a retailer plans stock levels for bestsellers. Items accounting for high sales volume are stocked in a manner that ensures they are always available.

Niche Retailing: Enables retailers to identify customer segments and deploy unique strategies to address the desires of those segments.

Non-goods Services: The area of service retailing in which intangible personal services (rather than goods) are offered to consumers, who experience services rather than possess them.

Non-store Retailing: Utilizes strategy mixes that are not store-based to reach consumers and complete transactions. Examples: direct marketing, direct selling and vending machines.

Objective-and-Task Method: A promotional budgeting technique by which a retailer clearly defines its promotional goals and then prepares a budget to satisfy these goals.

Odd Pricing: A strategy in which retail prices are set at levels below even-rupee values, such as Re.0.49, Rs.4.99, and Rs.199.

Off-Price Chain: Sells brand-name apparel and accessories, footwear, linen, fabrics, cosmetics, and/or house wares at everyday low prices in an efficient, limited-service environment.

One-Price Policy: A strategy where a retailer charges the same price to all customers buying an item under similar conditions.

Open-to-Buy: The difference between planned purchases and the purchase commitments already made by a buyer for a given time period, often a month. It represents the amount the buyer has left to spend for that month and is reduced each time a purchase is made.

Operating Expenditures: The short-term selling and administrative costs of running a business.

Operating Expenses: The cost of running a retail business.

Operations Management: The efficient and effective implementation of the policies and tasks necessary to satisfy a firm's customers, employees, and management (and stockholders, if a publicly-owned company).

Opportunistic Buying: Negotiating special low prices for merchandise whose sales have not lived up to expectations, end-of-season goods, items consumers have returned to the manufacturer or another retailer, and closeouts.

Opportunity Costs: Benefits forgone by choosing one type of opportunity over another.

Order Lead Time: The period from the date an order is placed by a retailer to the date the merchandise is ready for sale (received, price-marked, and put on the selling floor).

Organizational Mission: A retailer's commitment to a type of business and to a distinctive role in the marketplace. It is reflected in the firm's attitudes to consumers, employees, suppliers, competitors, government, and others.

Over-stored Trading Area: A geographic area with so many stores selling a specific good or service that some retailers will be unable to earn an adequate profit.

Paan **Shop:** A small Indian shop in a temporary structure selling betel leaves, cigarettes, etc. They are in the form of concessions on the front space of small hotels or kiosks in busy high streets.

Parasite Store: An outlet that does not create its own traffic and that has no real trading area of its own.

Perceived Risk: The level of risk a consumer believes exists while purchasing a specific product or service from a specific retailer, whether or not that belief is factually correct.

Percentage Lease: Stipulates that rent is related to the retailer's sales or profits.

Percentage-of-Sales Method: A promotional budgeting technique whereby a retailer ties its promotion budget to sales revenue.

Performance Measures: The criteria used to assess retailer effectiveness. They include total sales, average sales per store, sales by goods/service category, sales per square foot, gross margins, gross margin return on investment, operating income, inventory turnover, markdown percentages, employee turnover, financial ratios, and profitability.

Perpetual-Inventory Unit-Control System: Keeps a running total of the number of units handled by a retailer by ongoing record-keeping entries that adjust for sales, returns, transfers to other departments or stores, receipt of shipments, and other transactions. It can be done manually, use tags processed by computers, or rely on point-of-sale devices.

Personal Selling: Involves oral communication with one or more prospective customers to sell products.

Personnel Space: The area required for employees for changing clothes, lunch and coffee breaks, and rest rooms.

Petty Cash: Retail stores often need small amounts of discretionary funds in the form of cash known as Petty Cash, to meet expenses at the store where it is not practical to make the disbursement by cheque. This works on the imprest system where such expenses are reimbursed to the store usually by the head office accounts department and the petty cash float is always maintained. This system does not allow anyone to spend from the sale proceeds.

Petty Shop: A very small store, often a mobile kiosk selling cigarettes, sweets etc. These items are often sold in single units and not in packs.

Physical Inventory System: Involves actual counting of merchandise. A retailer using the cost method of inventory valuation and relying on a physical inventory system can make gross profits only as often as it conducts a full physical inventory.

Planned Shopping Centre: Consists of a group of architecturally unified commercial establishments built on a site that is centrally owned or managed, designed and operated as a unit, based on balanced tenancy, and surrounded by parking facilities.

Planogram: A visual (graphical) representation of the space to be allocated to selling, merchandise, personnel, and customers — as well as to product categories.

Point of Indifference: The geographic dividing point between two cities (communities), so that the trading area of each can be determined. At this point, consumers would shop in either area.

Point-of-Purchase (POP) Display: An in-store/interior display that provides consumers with information, adds to store atmosphere, and serves a substantial promotional role.

Point-of-Sale (POS) Terminal: A cash register that has the capability to electronically scan a UPC code with a laser and electronically record a sale; also known as computerized checkout.

Positioning: The design and implementation of a merchandising mix, price structure and style of selling to create an image of the retailer, relative to its competitors, in the customer's mind.

Post-Purchase Behaviour: Further purchases or re-evaluation based on a purchase.

Poverty of Time: Occurs when greater striving for financial security leads to less rather than more free time since consumers have a large number of alternatives to choose from.

Power Centre: A shopping site with: (a) up to a half-dozen or so category killer stores and a mix of smaller stores, or (b) several complementary stores specializing in a product category.

Power Retailer: The status reached by a company that is dominant in some aspect of its strategy. Consumers view the company as distinctive enough to become loyal to it and go out of their way to shop there.

Predatory Pricing: A method of pricing merchandise at very low levels to drive competition out of the marketplace.

Premium: Merchandise offered at a lower price, or free, as an additional incentive for a customer to make a purchase.

Prestige Pricing: Assumes consumers will not buy goods and services at prices deemed too low, since they may fear it is of poor quality.

Pre-training: Indoctrination on the history and policies of the retailer and a job orientation on the hours, compensation, chain of command, and job duties. Also known as induction training.

Price Elasticity of Demand: The effect of a price change on consumer demand, that is, the quantity that they buy. Measured by percentage change in demand divided by percentage change in price.

Price Fixing: An illegal pricing activity in which several companies collude to establish a fixed retail price for a product within a market area.

Price Guarantees: Protect retailers against possible price declines. If a retailer cannot sell an item at a given price, the manufacturer pays the difference between planned retail and actual retail selling prices.

Price Line Classifications: Enable retail sales, inventories, and purchases to be analysed by retail price category. Also referred to as price point groups.

Price Lining: Selling merchandise at a limited range of price points, with each price point representing a distinct level of quality. Generally used by service retailers providing a wide selection of services. A range of prices is matched to service levels.

Price-Quality Association: The feeling among consumers that high prices connote high quality and low prices the opposite.

Primary Customer Services: Basic components of the retail strategy mix to satisfy customers; they must be provided.

Primary Trading Area: Has 50% to 80% of a store's customers. It is the geographic area closest to the store and has the highest density of customers to population and the highest per-capita sales.

Private (Dealer) Brands: Names designated by wholesalers or retailers as being more profitable for them, better controlled, not sold by competing retailers, less expensive for consumers, and loyal to them.

Private-Label Brand: A brand of products that is produced by a store. The brand carries the store's own name or one that it has created. For example, Shoppers' Stop has STOP and Pantaloons has BARE brand of clothes. This is also known as a store brand.

Product Life Cycle: Shows the expected behaviour of a product or service over its life. The traditional cycle has four stages: introduction, growth, maturity and decline.

Product/Trademark Franchising: In this arrangement, franchised dealers acquire the identities of their suppliers by agreeing to sell the latter's products and/or operate under suppliers' names.

Productivity: The efficiency with which a retail strategy is carried out.

Profit-and-Loss (Income) Statement: Summary of a retailer's revenues and expenses over a particular period of time, usually on a monthly, quarterly, and/or yearly basis.

Profit Margin: Net profit after taxes divided by net sales.

Proof of Delivery: Verification provided by a freight company that a shipment was delivered at a certain time and place and was signed for by the recipient.

Proprietary Store Credit Card System: A system in which credit cards have the store's name on them and the accounts receivable are administered by the retailer; also known as in-house credit system.

Prototype Stores: An operations strategy that requires multiple outlets in a chain to conform to relatively uniform construction, layout and operations standards.

Psychological Pricing: Refers to consumer perceptions of retail prices.

Public Relations: Communication intended to create a favourable image for a retailer among the public (consumers, investors, government, channel members, employees, etc).

Purchase-Motivation Product Groupings: Appeal to the consumer's urge to buy a product and the time he or she is willing to spend on shopping.

Quick Response (QR) Inventory Planning: Enables a retailer to reduce the amount of inventory it keeps on hand by ordering more frequently and in lower quantity.

Rack Display: An interior display that hangs or presents products neatly.

Rack Jobber: A wholesaler that is allowed by a store to install, stock and replenish selected items on display racks.

Rain check: A record of commitment made by the retailer for future fulfillment of an order/service.

Rationalized Retailing: A strategy involving a high degree of centralized management control combined with strict operating procedures for every phase of business.

Reach: The number of distinct people exposed to a retailer's ads in a specified period.

Relationship Retailing: Exists when retailers seek to establish and maintain long-term bonds with customers, rather than act as if each sales transaction is a completely new encounter with them.

Rented-Goods Services: The area of service retailing in which consumers lease and use goods for specified periods of time. Some book stores extend this service to customers.

Reorder Point: The stock level at which new orders must be placed.

Resident Buying Office: An inside or outside buying organization that is usually situated in important merchandise centres (sources of supply) and provides valuable data and contacts.

Retail Audit: The systematic examination and evaluation of a firm's total retailing effort or some specific aspect of it. Its purpose is to study what a retailer is presently doing, appraise how well the firm is performing, and make recommendations for future actions.

Retail Balance: Refers to the mix of stores within a geographic area.

Retail Chain: A firm that consists of multiple retail units under common ownership and usually has some centralization of decision-making in defining and implementing its strategy.

Retail Information System: Anticipates the information needs of retail managers; collects, organizes and stores relevant data on a continuous basis, and directs the flow of information to the decision makers.

Retail Institution: Refers to the basic format or structure of a business. Institutions can be classified according to ownership or its retail strategy mix — store-based, service versus goods, or nonstore-based.

Retail Life Cycle: A theory according to which institutions — like the goods and services they sell — pass through identifiable life-cycle stages: innovation, accelerated development, maturity and decline.

Retail Method of Accounting: A way in which the closing inventory value is determined by calculating the average relationship between the cost and retail values of merchandise available for sale during a period.

Retail Organization: How a firm structures and assigns tasks (functions), policies, resources, authority, responsibilities and rewards to efficiently satisfy the needs of its target market, employees and management.

Retail Performance Index: Includes five-year trends in revenue growth and profit growth, and a six-year average return on assets.

Retail Promotion: Any communication by a retailer that informs, persuades, and/or reminds the target market about any aspect of that firm.

Retail Reductions: Difference between beginning inventory plus purchases during the period and sales plus ending inventory. Includes anticipated markdowns, employee and other discounts, and stock shortages.

Retail Strategy: The overall plan guiding a retail firm. It has an influence on the firm's business activities and its response to market forces, such as competition and the economy.

Retailing: Consists of those business activities involved in the sale of goods and services to consumers for their personal, family, or household use.

Retailing Concept: Comprises these four elements: customer orientation, coordinated effort, value-driven, and goal orientation.

Retailing Effectiveness Checklist: Lets a firm systematically assess its preparedness for the future.

Return on Assets (ROA): A performance ratio based on a retailer's net sales, net profit and total assets.

Return on Net Worth: A performance measure based on a retailer's net profit, net sales, total assets and net worth.

Revolving Credit Account: Allows a customer to charge items and be billed monthly on the basis of the outstanding cumulative balance.

Sales Forecasting: Lets a retailer estimate future sales.

Sales Opportunity Grid: Rates the promise of new goods, services, procedures, and/or store outlets on a variety of criteria.

Sales Per Square Foot of Selling Space: Net sales divided by the square feet of selling space.

Sales-Productivity Ratio: A method for assigning floor space on the basis of sales or profit per foot.

Sales Promotion: Encompasses the paid marketing communication activities other than advertising, public relations and personal selling that stimulate consumer purchases and dealer effectiveness.

Saturated Trading Area: A geographic area having a proper amount of retail facilities to satisfy the needs of its population for a specific good or service, as well as to let retailers prosper.

Scenario Analysis: Lets a retailer project the future by examining the key factors that will affect its long-run performance and then preparing contingency plans based on alternative scenarios.

Scrambled Merchandising: Occurs when a retailer adds goods and services that are unrelated to each other and to the firm's original business.

Secondary Trading Area: A geographic area that accounts for 15% to 25% of a store's customers. It is located outside a primary trading area, and customers are more widely dispersed.

Selective Distribution: Takes place when suppliers sell through a moderate number of retailers. This allows suppliers to have higher sales than in exclusive distribution and lets retailers carry some competing brands.

Sell-Through Analysis: A comparison between actual and planned sales to determine whether early markdowns are required or whether more merchandise is needed to satisfy demand.

Selling Space: The area set aside for displays of merchandise, interactions between salespeople and customers, demonstrations, and so on.

Separate Store Organization: Treats each branch as a separate store with its own buying responsibilities. Customer needs are quickly noted, but duplication by managers in the main store and the branches is possible.

Service Blueprint: Systematically lists all the service functions to be performed and the average time expected for each one's completion.

Service Retailing: Involves transactions between companies or individuals and final consumers where the consumers do not purchase or acquire ownership of tangible products. It encompasses rented goods, owned goods, and non-goods.

Shelf-talkers: Part of the signage used to announce the offers/prices/product features etc. placed usually on fixtures near the products applicable.

Shrinkage: The difference between the recorded value of inventory (at retail) based on merchandise bought and the retail value of actual inventory in stores and distribution centres divided by retail sales during a time period. Shrinkage is caused by employee theft, customer shoplifting or by merchandise being misplaced, damaged or mispriced.

Simulation: A type of experiment whereby a computer program is used to manipulate the elements of a retail strategy mix rather than test them in a real setting.

Situation Analysis: The candid evaluation of the opportunities and potential problems facing a prospective or existing retailer.

SKU: See Stock Keeping Unit.

Soft Goods: Apparel and linens.

Sole Proprietorship: An unincorporated retail firm owned by one person.

Sorting Process: Involves the retailer collecting an assortment of goods and services from various sources, buying them in large quantities, and selling them to consumers in small quantities.

Specialty Department Store: A store with a department store format that focuses on apparel and soft home goods (e.g., Westside).

Specialty Store: A general merchandise retailer that concentrates on selling one product or service line. In other words, a store specializing in one category of merchandising, frequently fashion-related.

Stock Keeping Unit (SKU): An identification number assigned to a unique item by the retailer signifying its position in the merchandise hierarchy. The SKU may be an internal number for that retailer representing each aspect of the merchandise hierarchy or classification, or may be tied to an item's UPC (Universal Product Code).

Stock-to-Sales Ratio: The beginning-of-month (BOM) inventory divided by sales for the month. The average stock-to-sales ratio is 12 divided by planned inventory turnover. This ratio is an integral component of the merchandise budget plan.

Stock Turnover: Represents the number of times that the average inventory on hand is sold during a specific period, usually one year. Stock turnover can be computed in units or rupees (at retail or cost).

Store Brand: See Private-Label Brand.

Store Loyalty: Exists when a consumer regularly patronises a particular retailer (store or non-store) that he or she knows, likes, and trusts.

Store Maintenance: Encompasses all the activities involved in managing a retailer's physical facilities.

Storefront: The total physical exterior of a store. It includes the marquee, entrances, windows, lighting and construction materials.

Straight Lease: Requires the retailer to pay a fixed amount per month over the life of a lease. It is the simplest, most direct leasing arrangement.

Strategy Mix: A firm's particular combination of these factors: store location, operating procedures, goods/services offered, pricing tactics, store atmosphere and customer services, and promotional methods.

String: An unplanned shopping area comprising a group of retail stores, often with similar or compatible product lines, located along a street or highway (example: the ladies' footwear string along Linking Road, Mumbai).

Super Centre: A special type of combination store that blends an economy supermarket with a discount department store.

Supermarket: A self-service food store with grocery, meat and produce departments. This retail category includes conventional supermarkets, food-based superstores, combination stores, box (limited-line) stores, and warehouse stores.

Superstores: A large supermarket or specialty store, usually between 20,000 and 100,000 square feet.

Tactics: Actions that encompass a retailer's daily and short-term operations.

Tall Organization: A format with several levels of managers. It leads to close supervision and fewer employees reporting to each manager.

Target Market: The customer group that a retailer seeks to attract and satisfy.

Terms of Occupancy: Include ownership versus leasing, the type of lease, operations and maintenance costs, taxes, etc.

Theme-Setting Display: An interior display that depicts a product offering in a thematic manner and lets a retailer portray a specific atmosphere or mood.

Theory X: The traditional view of motivation that assumes employees must be closely supervised and controlled. It has been applied to lower-level retail positions.

Theory Y: A more modern view of motivation that assumes workers can be self-managers and be given authority. The motivation is social and psychological, and management is decentralized and participatory. It applies to all levels of retail personnel.

Theory Z: Advocates more employee involvement in defining their jobs and sharing decision-making with management. It adapts elements from Theory Y and Herzberg's theory.

Threats: Environmental and/or marketplace factors that can adversely affect retailers if they do not react to them (and sometimes, even if they do).

Ticket Size: Refers to the average cash memo value in a particular period for a retail store.

Top-Down Space Management Approach: Exists when a retailer starts with its total available store space (by store and for the overall firm, if a chain), divides the space into categories, and then works on in-store product layouts.

Total Retail Experience: Consists of all the elements in retail offering that encourage or inhibit consumers during their contact with a given retailer.

Trading Area: A geographic area containing the customers of a particular firm or group of firms for specific goods or services.

Unbundled Pricing: Involves a retailer's charging separate prices for each service offered.

Uncontrollable Variables: Those aspects of business to which the retailer must adapt (such as competition, the economy, and laws).

Unit Control: Relates to quantities of merchandise a retailer handles during a stated time period.

Unit Pricing: A practice required by many states, whereby retailers (mostly food stores) must show both the total price of an item and its price per unit of measure.

Universal Product Code (UPC): A system for putting machine-readable data onto products with a series of thick and thin vertical lines. It lets a retailer record data instantaneously as to the model number, size, colour etc. when an item is sold. The data is then transmited to a computer monitoring unit sales, inventory levels, and other information.

UPC: See Universal Product Code.

Value Delivery System: Comprises all the activities needed to develop, produce, deliver and sell and service particular goods and services.

Value Pricing: Occurs when prices are set on the basis of fair value for both the service provider and the consumer.

Variable Markup Policy: A strategy whereby a retailer varies markups according to merchandise category.

Variable Pricing: A pricing strategy where a retailer alters its prices to coincide with fluctuations in costs or consumer demand.

Variety Store: A retail store that handles a wide assortment of inexpensive and popularly priced goods and services, such as stationery, gift items, women's accessories, health and beauty aids, light hardware, toys, houseware, confectionery items and shoe repair.

Vending Machine: A retailing format that involves coin- or card-operated dispensing of goods and services. It eliminates the use of sales personnel and allows around-the-clock sales.

Vendor: Any firm such as a manufacturer or distributor from which a retailer obtains merchandise.

Vertical Cooperative-Advertising Agreement: Enables a manufacturer and a retailer or a wholesaler and a retailer to share an ad.

Vertical Price Fixing: Occurs when manufacturers or wholesalers are able to control the retail prices of their goods and services.

Vertical Retail Audit: Involves analysing — in depth — a retail firm's performance in one area of its strategy mix or operations.

Video Kiosk: A freestanding, interactive computer terminal that displays products and related information on a video screen; it often uses a touch screen for people to make selections.

Visual Merchandising: A process of creating visual displays by using a relevant theme with the required props to enhance the visibility of a product or merchandise assortments in a retail store to ultimately increase footfalls and sales.

Want Book (Want Slip): A notebook or slip in which store employees record consumer requests for un-stocked or out-of-stock merchandise. Also known as the raincheck.

Wheel of Retailing: A theory stating that retail innovators often first appear as low-price operators with a low-cost structure and low profit-margin requirements. Over time, these innovators upgrade the products they carry and improve their facilities and customer services. They then become vulnerable to new discounters with lower cost structures.

Wholesale Club: A retail store that sells a limited assortment of general merchandise to customers who are members of the club. Memberships are generally fee-based, margins are small and there is little customer service provided to the members.

Width of Assortment: Refers to the number of distinct goods/service categories with which a retailer is involved.

Word-of-Mouth Communication: Occurs when one consumer talks to others. Also known as 'viral communication'.

Yield Management Pricing: Used when a service firm determines the combination of prices that yield the highest level of revenues for a given time period.

Zero-Based Budgeting: The practice followed when a firm starts each new budget from scratch and outlines the expenditures needed to reach that period's goals. All costs must be justified each time a budget is done.

Index

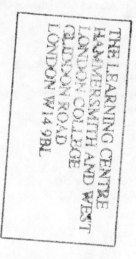